観光客・留学生・地球規模の労働者

Tourists, International Students, and Global Workforce

朝水宗彦【著】
Munehiko ASAMIZU

Saganoshoin
嵯峨野書院

観光客・
留学生・
地球規模の労働者

朝水宗彦 著

Tourists,
International Students,
and Global Workforce

Munehiko ASAMIZU

まえがき

　本書は人的な移動の歴史と現在の諸事象について手短にまとめたものである。現在では生存のために自宅を去った難民や，より良い生活を求めて移動した移民など，さまざまな種類の人的な移動がある。

　短期的な人的移動はさらに多様である。国際的な移動を伴う労働者は移民のようにより良い生活を求めるが，母国へ帰るまでの滞在期間がより短い。留学生は通常卒業まで学術機関に留まるが，いくつかの国では卒業後も滞在の延長を認めている。

　観光客は通常上記の人々よりも滞在期間が短い。しかしながら，人的移動は時代と共に変化している。産業革命以前では，旅はしばしば徒歩や船で行われ，目的地に到着するまで長い時間がかかった。しかし，航空による旅が発達したことにより，1泊の海外旅行も選択できるようになっている。他方，低価格の宿泊施設の発達により，現在では希望すれば長期間の滞在も気軽に行うことができる。

　本書は著者が山口大学の協定校であるウダヤナ大学で行った講義がベースになっている。これらの講義はインドネシア人の学生に英語で人的な移動について説明するために行われた。これらの教材を教科書として活用するため，すでに公開されている内容をいくつか加えた。

　近年山口大学では主に英語を話す留学生の数が増加している。大学院経済学研究科の公共管理コースに加え，2015年には学部生のために国際総合科学部が設立している。同僚の武本ティモシー先生や富本幾文先生のおかげで，著者は留学生に英語で日本について教える良い機会を持つことができた。

Preface

This book was written to provide a brief introduction to the history and current state of human mobility. Currently, there are many kinds of human mobility, including refugees leaving home simply in order to survive, and immigrants moving in search of a better life.

Short-term human mobility is another variable. Some international migrant workers are essentially like other immigrants in seeking a better life, though many may only stay for a shorter time before returning to their home country. International students may normally remain at an academic institution until graduation, though some countries allow extensions of residency even after graduation.

Tourists usually have shorter stays than the people above. However, human mobility is historically subject to change. Before the industrial revolution, travel was often on foot or by ship, and it took longer to reach one's destination. With the advent of air travel, however, overnight trips abroad became an option. On the other hand, the development of budget accommodations now makes it easier for people to stay longer if they wish.

This book is based on my lectures at Udayana University, which has a cooperative agreement with Yamaguchi University. These lectures were delivered in English to explain human mobility to Indonesian students. To better use these teaching materials as textbook content, I also added some content that has already been published.

Yamaguchi University recently has increasing numbers of primarily English speaking international students. Following up on the public administration course in the Graduate School of Economics, the Faculty of Global and Science Studies for undergraduate students was established in 2015. Thanks to my colleagues, Professor Timothy Takemoto and Professor Ikufumi Tomimoto, I have had the good fortune to

さらに，授業の経験のいくつかを共有する機会を書籍として与えてくれた嵯峨野書院の平山妙子氏に感謝したい。山口大学や，著者の以前の勤務先である立命館アジア太平洋大学のように，ネイティブの英語話者が少ない国々において，英語ベースのコースが増えている。本書が世界的な人的移動，特に日本に関する移動について，理解を促すためのお役に立てることに期待する。

2019 年 9 月

朝 水 宗 彦

teach international students about Japan in English.

Thanks to Ms. Taeko Hirayama (Sagano Shoin), I now also have the opportunity to share some of my teaching experiences in this book. As with Yamaguchi University and my previous employer, Ritsumeikan Asia Pacific University, English language based courses are increasing in countries that have few native English speakers. I hope this book will contribute to understanding global mobility, especially as it relates to Japan.

September 2019,

Munehiko Asamizu

目　次

まえがき　2

第 **1** 章　人的移動入門：観光客・留学生・地球規模の労働者　　12

第 1 章のはじめに　12

1-1. ツーリストと「観光客」　12

1-2. 教育による移動　14

1-3. 国際労働者　16

1-4. 複合的なケース　18

第 1 章のおわりに　20

第 **2** 章　ホモ・モビリタス：人的移動の略史　　24

第 2 章のはじめに　24

2-1. 人的移動に関する研究　24

2-2. 古代の人的移動　26

2-3. 中世の人的移動　30

2-4. 近代化と人的移動　34

第 2 章のおわりに　38

第 **3** 章　現代における国際労働力移動の諸問題　　44

第 3 章のはじめに　44

3-1. 国際的な移動の背景　44

3-2. 国際労働者の歴史的トレンド　46

Contents

Preface   3

Chapter 1   Introduction to Human Mobility: Tourists, International Students, and Global Workforce   13

Introduction of Chapter 1   13

1-1. Tourists and *Kankoukyaku*   13

1-2. Educational Mobility   15

1-3. International Workers   17

1-4. Complex Cases   19

Conclusion of Chapter 1   21

Chapter 2   Homo Mobilitas: A Brief History of Human Mobility   25

Introduction of Chapter 2   25

2-1. Studies Related to Human Mobility   25

2-2. Ancient Human Mobility   27

2-3. Medieval Human Mobility   31

2-4. Modernization and Human Mobility   35

Conclusion of Chapter 2   39

Chapter 3   Contemporary Issues in International Labor Mobility   45

Introduction of Chapter 3   45

3-1. The Background of International Mobility   45

3-2. Historical Trends of International Workers   47

3-3. ターゲットとなる移民労働者　50

第 3 章のおわりに　56

第 4 章　日本から／への労働者の移動のトレンドと社会背景　58

第 4 章のはじめに　58

4-1. 日本から／への人的移動：文献レビュー　58

4-2. 日本の入国移民と出国移民の歴史的背景　60

4-3. 移民受け入れ国としての日本　62

4-4. 近年における日本からの人的移動　72

4-5. 海外における日本国籍者のジェンダーの差異　78

第 4 章のおわりに　88

第 5 章　国際学生移動の小史　94

第 5 章のはじめに　94

5-1. 第 5 章の方法論　94

5-2. 古代と中世における学生移動　96

5-3. 近代における留学　100

5-4. 近年の国際学生移動　106

第 5 章のおわりに　110

第 6 章　日本における国際学生　116

第 6 章のはじめに　116

6-1. 日本における教育の国際化に関する小史　118

6-2. 明治維新と西洋化　122

6-3. 日本における国際的な高等教育の普及　124

8　目　次

3-3. Targeted Immigrant Workers   51

Conclusion of Chapter 3   57

Chapter 4   Migration Trends and Social Backgrounds of International Migrant Workers from and to Japan   59

Introduction of Chapter 4   59

4-1. Human mobility from and to Japan: Literature Review   59

4-2. The Historical Backgrounds of Japanese Immigrants and Emigrants   61

4-3. Japan as an Immigrant Destination Country   63

4-4. Current Issues in Human Mobility from Japan   73

4-5. Gender Differentiations of Japanese Citizens outside of Japan   79

Conclusion of Chapter 4   89

Chapter 5   A Brief History of International Student Mobility   95

Introduction of Chapter 5   95

5-1. Methodology of Chapter 5   95

5-2. Ancient and Medieval Student Mobility   97

5-3. Study Abroad in the Modern Era   101

5-4. Contemporary International Student Mobility   107

Conclusion of Chapter 5   111

Chapter 6   International Students in Japan   117

Introduction of Chapter 6   117

6-1. A Short History of Educational Internationalization in Japan   119

6-2. Meiji Restoration and Westernization   123

6-3. Popularization of International Higher Education in Japan   125

6-4. 日本におけるグローバリゼーションと英語基準プログラム　130

6-5. 日本における教育観光　134

第 6 章のおわりに　140

第 7 章　地球規模の移動と日本における国際観光　146

第 7 章のはじめに　146

7-1. 日本における人的移動小史　148

7-2. アウトバウンド観光国としての日本　150

7-3. バブル後の観光のトレンド　154

7-4. 日本におけるインバウンド観光政策　158

第 7 章のおわりに　164

第 8 章　インバウンド観光プロモーションのトレンド　170

第 8 章のはじめに　170

8-1. 研究方法と先行研究　172

8-2. 国家組織による観光開発と観光プロモーション　176

8-3. 国際観光客のための多国籍開発とプロモーション　182

8-4. 日本のインバウンド観光政策のケーススタディ　192

第 8 章のおわりに　204

あ と が き　212

索　　引　216

6-4. Globalization and English-Based Programs in Japan   131

6-5. Japan's Educational Tourism   135

Conclusion of Chapter 6   141

Chapter 7   Global Mobility and Japan's International Tourism   147

Introduction of Chapter 7   147

7-1. A Short History of Human Mobility in Japan   149

7-2. Japan as an Outbound Tourism Country   151

7-3. Post Bubble Tourism Trends   155

7-4. Japan's Inbound Tourism Policies   159

Conclusion of Chapter 7   165

Chapter 8   Trends of Inbound Tourism Promotions   171

Introduction of Chapter 8   171

8-1. Research Methods and Literature Reviews   173

8-2. Tourism Developments and Promotions by National Organizations   177

8-3. Multinational Developments and Promotions for International Tourists   183

8-4. Case Studies of Japanese Inbound Tourism Policies   193

Conclusion of Chapter 8   205

Postscript   213

Index   217

第1章

人的移動入門：観光客・留学生・地球規模の労働者

第1章のはじめに

本書ではいくつかの人的な移動について手短に紹介する。はじめに，強制的な移動と希望した移動は全く異なったものである。難民や避難民，人身売買などは強制的な移動の典型的なものである。他方，観光客は通常目的地への訪問を希望している。旅の後，通常では観光客は自宅へ戻る。

1-1. ツーリストと「観光客」

人的な移動の定義はまた国によって異なっているが，統計的な理由により，国際機関は共通の定義を有している。たとえば，日本語の「観光客」はしばしば余暇目的の訪問者を指すことが多い。日帰り訪問者で観光地を訪問する人を「日帰り観光客」と呼ぶこともある。

他方，UNWTO（国際連合世界観光機関）は1泊以上1年未満の滞在者をツーリストと定義する。日本やオーストラリアなど地理的に孤立した国々では，国際観光客の数を数えるのは容易である。しかしながら，国際観光客にはビザ免除の人々も含まれるので，シェンゲン協定の締結国であるヨーロッパの国々にとって宿泊施設における統計調査は重要である。

UNWTO によると，旅人と訪問者，観光客は図1-1のように定義づけられている。厳密な入国審査がない国々の場合，旅行の目的（娯楽，教育，ビジネス

Chapter 1

Introduction to Human Mobility: Tourists, International Students, and Global Workforce

Introduction of Chapter 1

This book aims to briefly introduce a few types of human mobility. To start with, forced mobility and desired mobility are totally different issues. Refugees, evacuees, and human trafficking are typical cases of forced mobility. On the other hand, tourists generally desire to visit their destinations. After traveling, tourists normally return home.

1-1. Tourists and *Kankoukyaku*

Definitions of human mobility also differ from country to country, though international organizations have agreed on common definitions for statistical purposes. For example, *kankoukyaku* ("tourists" in the Japanese language) is often defined to include visitors who visit for pleasure. Sometimes, single day-trip visitors to tourist destinations are called *higaeri kankoukyaku* in Japanese.

On the other hand, UNWTO (United Nations World Tourism Organization) defines a tourist as someone who stays longer than one night and less than one year. It is easy to count the number of international tourists in geographically isolated countries such as Japan and Australia. However, as people who have visa exemptions are often included as international tourists, statistical surveys in hotels and inns are important for European countries that are part of the Schengen Agreement.

According to UNWTO, travelers, visitors, and tourists are defined as shown in Figure 1-1. As the purpose of travel (pleasure, education, business, etc.) is difficult to

図 1-1 UNWTO による観光客の定義

出典：UNWTO（n. d.）"Understanding Tourism: Basic Glossary," http://media.unwto.org/en/content/understanding-tourism-basic-glossary, 2017 年 3 月 20 日閲覧

など）を調べることが難しいため，このような国々の間では訪問期間が定義のために重要である。

1-2. 教育による移動

　同様に，留学生の定義も多様である。日本では，通常「留学生」とは海外で学ぶ人のことを指す。時に，短期間の学習プログラムに参加する人を「短期留学生」と言うこともある。しかしながら，教育学の専門家の間では，これらの短期の教育訪問者を「短期研修生」と呼ぶ。日本における教育専門家によって，「留学生」とは学生ビザを有する者に限定されている。

　統計上のターゲットとなる留学生もまた国によって異なっている。たとえば，日本やオーストラリアでは 3 か月以上の修学を希望する者には学生ビザが求められている。そのため，日本とオーストラリアではこれらの学生に対する統計がある。学生ビザが必要ではない短期間の教育訪問者は，日本では「短期研修生」，オーストラリアではスタディ（または教育）・ツーリストと専門家の間で呼ばれている。

　しかしながら，いくつかの国々では短期間の外国人研修生や交換留学生に学生ビザを求めていない。このスキームにより，UNESCO（国際連合教育科学文化機関）の統計では，留学生とは学位コースに所属する外国人のことを指す（UNESCO 2014：113）。職業訓練コースや語学研修プログラムの学習者は日本やオーストラリアの留学生の統計では顕著であるが，この UNESCO のスキー

Figure 1-1 Definition of Tourists According to UNWTO

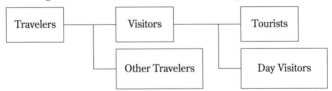

Source: UNWTO (n.d.) "Understanding Tourism: Basic Glossary," http://media.unwto.org/en/content/understanding-tourism-basic-glossary, accessed March 20, 2017

assess in countries without strict border controls, the length of stay is more important to these definitions in such countries.

1-2. Educational Mobility

In a similar manner, definitions of international students also differ. In Japan, *ryugakusei* (international students) generally describes anyone who studies abroad. Sometimes, those who attend short-term study programs are called *tanki ryugakusei*. However, for specialists in education, these short-term educational visitors are called *tanki kenshusei* (short term trainees). Only those who have student visas are referred to as *ryugakusei* by education specialists in Japan.

Statistical-target related international students also differ from country to country. For example, someone who expects to study longer than three months is required to have a student visa in Japan and Australia. So Japan and Australia have statistics related to these students. Short-term educational visitors without student visas are called *tanki kenshusei* in Japan and "study (or education) tourists" in Australia by specialists.

However, some countries do not require student visas for short-term foreign trainees and exchange students. As with this scheme, UNESCO (United Nations Educational, Scientific and Cultural Organization) statistics relating to international students apply to foreign people who are engaged in a degree course (UNESCO 2014: 113). Under this scheme, vocational and language program students are not included in

ムには含まれない。

1-3. 国際労働者

同様に，国際労働者のスキームも国によって異なっており，定義もまた異なっている。しかしながら，ILO（国際労働機関）（2016）によると，国際的な移動を行う労働者は以下のように定義されている。

1. 現在雇用されている，あるいは雇用されていないが現在在住している国での雇用を求めている者
2. 一時的な移動を行う労働者や家族再会のための移民，難民・亡命希望者は通常これらの調査に含まない

出典：ILO（2016）*Promoting fair migration*, p. 3

2番目の定義に加え，国際移動を伴う労働者にはいくつかの例外がある。典型的な例は留学生である。ILO によると，パートタイムや限定された仕事を行う留学生，入国登録にて独立したカテゴリーによる研修プログラムの学生は国際的な移住労働者の統計に含まれない（ILO 2016：41）。ワーキングホリデービザを有する者もまた，国際的な移住労働者の統計に含まれない。

移民労働者に関する需要・供給モデルは，古典的に図 1-2 のようにあらわされている。この図の中のDは需要，Sは供給を指している。労働者数が Q_0 から Q_1 に変化した時，賃金は W_0 から W_1 に変わる。これは，特に移民労働者が低いスキルの時に当てはまる。しかしながら，ビジネス（または起業家）移民の流入は新たな仕事を生み出し，ハイテク（または高度教育）移民の流入は新たな産業を拡大する。

international student statistics by UNESCO, despite their significance in Japan and Australia.

1-3. International Workers

Working schemes for international workers once again also differ by country, and the definitions are also different. However, according to ILO (International Labour Organization) (2016), international migrant workers are defined as follows:

1. Those who are currently employed, or who are unemployed but seeking employment in their current country of residence
2. Temporary migrant workers, family reunification migrants, refugees and asylum seekers are normally excluded from these estimates

Source: ILO (2016) *Promoting fair migration*, p. 3

In addition to definition No. 2, there are some exceptions for international migrant workers. Typical cases are international students. According to ILO, foreign students who are allowed part-time or limited work and trainee programs fall under separate categories in immigration legislation, and are not counted as international migrant workers (ILO 2016: 41). Those who have a working holiday visa are also excluded from the category of international migrant workers.

The supply and demand model regarding migrant workers is classically designed as in Figure 1-2. D means demand and S means supply in this figure. When the quantity of workers changes from Q_0 to Q_1, wages may change from W_0 to W_1. This is especially so when immigrant workers are less skilled. However, the influx of business (or entrepreneurial) immigrants has seen the creation of new jobs, and high-tech (or highly educated) immigrants may expand new industries.

図 1-2 移民労働者による需要・供給モデル

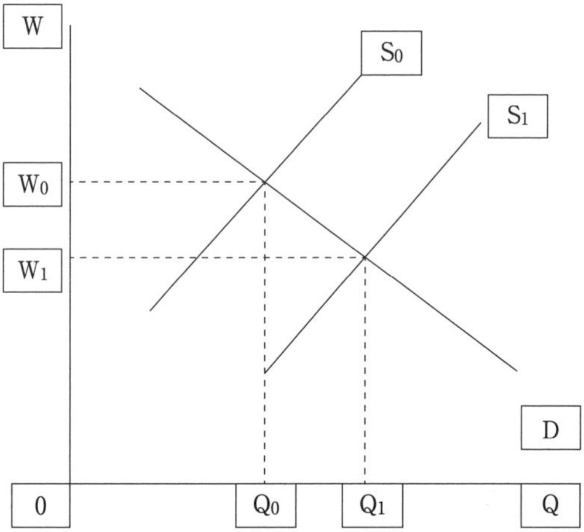

出典：リーソン ピーター，ゴチェノアー ザッカリー
（2016）「国際労働者移動の経済効果」パウエル ベン
ジャミン編『移民の経済学』（日本語版），東洋経済
新報社，p. 18

1-4. 複合的なケース

　通常，移民労働者は経済的に不利な労働者として見られてきた。旧西ドイツ
やいくつかのヨーロッパの国々では低スキルの労働者として国際的なゲスト
ワーカーを受け入れてきた。他方，オーストラリアやニュージーランドでは海
外からの企業家（またはビジネス移民）や高度技能労働者（またはハイテク移民）
のためのポイントシステムを有している。統計的には留学生と移民労働者は異
なっているが，オーストラリアやニュージーランドでは技能労働力として政治
的に緊密な関係がある。技能労働者や才能のある人々の供給源の国々にとって
は，頭脳流失が問題になっている。

　公的には，日本は高技能の外国人労働者を志向している。明治時代以降，海
外からの専門職や高度の技術者は優遇され，高い給料をもらっていた。運動選
手や芸術家もまた日本では重要である。これらの恵まれた外国人労働者は長年

Figure 1-2 Supply-demand Model for Immigrant Workers

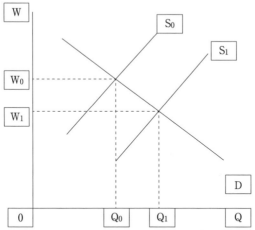

Source: Leeson, Peter and Gochenour, Zachary (2016) "The Economic Effects of International Labor Mobility" in Powell, Benjamin ed., *The Economics of Immigration*, Toyo Keizai Shinpousha, p. 18

1-4. Complex Cases

Migrant workers have most usually been seen as economically disadvantaged workers. Former West Germany and some European countries accept international guest workers for low-skilled labor. On the other hand, Australia and New Zealand have a point system for entrepreneurs (or business immigrants) and highly skilled workers (or high-tech immigrants) from abroad. Though, statistically, international students and migrant workers are quite different, international students are closely politically related to the skilled workforce in Australia and New Zealand. For source countries of these skilled workers and talents, brain drain will be a problem.

Officially, Japan leans toward highly-skilled foreign workers. Since the Meiji period, professors and skilled engineers from abroad have been treated as desirable assets, and received attractive salaries. Athletes and artists from abroad are also

「お雇い外国人」と呼ばれてきた。近年の人口減や高齢化にもかかわらず，看護や介護の国際技能研修生はいまだに日本人受験者と同じ資格の国家試験の合格が求められている。医療研修生が試験に合格しなければ，特定の期間内に日本を去らなくてはならない。

　他方，人口減と一般的な労働力不足は日本にとって大きな問題である。製造業での労働力不足を緩和するために，1990 年の出入国管理及び難民認定法の改正では日系人とその家族の入国の緩和が行われた（Kataoka 2008：52）。さらに，1993 年の外国人技能実習制度の改訂により，研修できる職種が増加した。しかしながら，このことは，日本中に低賃金の外国人労働者を広めることにもなった（外国人研修生問題ネットワーク編 2006：14）。

　オーストラリアやニュージーランドのように，日本における留学生は卒業時に高価値の労働者として期待されている。しかしながら，多くの私費留学生は工場やレストラン，スーパーマーケット，コンビニなど，日本人の労働力が不足している分野で働いている。日本における若年者の減少は深刻である。留学生なしでは留学生に依存している地方大学の多くは破たんするだろう。さらに，日本の地方における労働力もまた様々な点で留学生や研修生に依存している。これらの複雑な人的移動の諸ケースを理解するために，本書では歴史的・社会的な背景を考察する。

第 1 章のおわりに
　交通の発達は旅を容易にしてきた。しかし，時に近代化は政治的に旅を規制する。フランス革命後，パスポートとビザのシステムが発達してきた。この章で述べてきたように，ビザは観光客，留学生，外国人労働者を分類する上で重

important in Japan. These gifted foreign workers have long been called *oyatoi gaikokujin*. Despite the current depopulation and aging trends, international trainees in nursing and care working are still required to pass the national examination, which is the same test that qualified Japanese candidates take. Unless they can pass this difficult examination, these international trainees are required to leave Japan within a certain period.

On the other hand, depopulation and shortages in the general workforce are also serious problems in Japan. To mitigate the shortage of manufacturing workers, the reformed Immigration Control and Refugee Recognition Act of 1990 deregulated the immigrants of Japanese descent (*Nikkei Jin*) and their families (Kataoka 2008: 52). In addition, reformation of the international technical intern trainee system (*Ginou Jissyu Seido*) of 1993 expanded the types of work that could be taught. However, it also created what were essentially poorly paid international laborers all over Japan (Gaikokujin Kenshusei Mondai Network ed. 2006: 14).

As in Australia and New Zealand, international students in Japan are expected to be high-value workers when they graduate. However, many private international students work in factories, restaurants, supermarkets, and convenience stores, which are suffering from the shortage of Japanese workers. Depopulation of the younger generation is serious problem in Japan. Without international students, many Japanese universities in remote areas would go bankrupt. In addition, workforces in remote areas in Japan rely on international students and trainees in many regards. To understand these complex cases of human mobility, this book examines some historical and social back grounds.

Conclusion of Chapter 1

The development of transportation has made travel easy. However, in some cases modernization has led to the political regulation of travel. After the French Revolution, the passport and visa system gradually developed. As shown in this chapter, the visa is

要である。アメリカ合衆国では，仕事の種類により，ビザはさらに細分化されている（第3章を参照）。オーストラリアや日本を含むいくつかの先進国では，同じようなシステムを有している。

参考文献

外国人研修生問題ネットワーク編（2006）『外国人研修生　時給300円の労働者』明石書店

ILO（2016）*Promoting fair migration*, ILO

KATAOKA, Hiromi（2008）"Changes in the community caused by the influx of Brazilians," in Asamizu, Munehiko ed., *Human Mobility in Asia Pacific*, Office SAKUTA, pp. 52-97

リーソン ピーター，ゴチェノアー ザッカリー（2016）「国際労働者移動の経済効果」パウエル ベンジャミン編『移民の経済学』（薮下史郎他訳），東洋経済新報社，13-45頁

UNESCO（2014）*Higher Education in Asia: Expanding Out, Expanding Up*, United Nations

UNWTO（n. d.）"Understanding Tourism: Basic Glossary," http://media. unwto. org/en/content/understanding-tourism-basic-glossary，2017年3月20日閲覧

important for categorizing tourists, international students, and immigrant workers. In the United States, visas are also sub-categorized by type of employment (see chapter 3). Some developed countries, including Australia and Japan, have a similar system.

References

Gaikokujin Kenshusei Mondai Network ed. (2006) *Gaikokujin Kenshusei Jikyu 300 Yen no Roudousha*, Akashi Shoten

ILO (2016) *Promoting fair migration*, ILO

KATAOKA, Hiromi (2008) "Changes in the community caused by the influx of Brazilians," in Asamizu, Munehiko ed., *Human Mobility in Asia Pacific*, Office SAKUTA, pp. 52-97

LEESON, Peter and GOCHENOUR, Zachary (2016) "The Economic Effects of International Labor Mobility" in POWELL, Benjamin ed., *The Economics of Immigration* (Japanese Version), Toyo Keizai Shinpousha, pp. 13-45

UNESCO (2014) *Higher Education in Asia: Expanding Out, Expanding Up*, United Nations

UNWTO (n. d.) "Understanding Tourism: Basic Glossary," http://media. unwto. org/en/content/ understanding-tourism-basic-glossary, accessed March 20, 2017

第2章

ホモ・モビリタス：人的移動の略史

第2章のはじめに

本章では人的移動の歴史的背景について述べる。新たな知識が社会を変えてきたように，人的な移動も変わってきた。新たな交通システムの導入は旅を容易にしてきた。ここにおける新たな知識には技術や雇用，哲学，教育，エンターテイメントなどの発達が含まれ，旅の目的にもなり得る。

世界的な視野から歴史的な背景を分析するには，文献のレビューが必要である。地理的な比較のため，様々な種類の文献の使用が重要である。この章では異なった時代や場所を扱った文献に依拠する。

2-1. 人的移動に関する研究

人的移動に関する研究は多数ある。アーリーはランカスター大学教授で，『観光のまなざし』（Sage 1990）や『場所を消費する』（Routledge 1995），『社会を越えた社会学』（Routledge 2000）などの移動に関する研究分野の著者として知られている（Lancaster University: web）。観光人類学の分野では，『ホストとゲスト』（University of Pennsylvania Press 1989）の著者であるスミスが知られている。彼女は1998年に設立されたIUAES（国際人類学・民族学科学連合）観光コミッションの創立時の座長でもある（Smith: web）。

人的な移動は複雑である。佐藤（2013）は人的投資として，経済的なトレー

Chapter 2

Homo Mobilitas: A Brief History of Human Mobility

Introduction of Chapter 2

This chapter introduces the historical background of human mobility. As new knowledge has changed society, human mobility too has changed. The introduction of new transportation systems has made travel easier. New knowledge here includes developments in technology, employment, philosophy, education, and entertainment, which are also found as purposes of travel.

To analyze the historical background from a global perspective, a review of the literature is essential. For a geographical comparison, the use of various types of literature is important. This chapter relies on literature focusing on different eras and places.

2-1. Studies Related to Human Mobility

There has been much research on human mobility. Urry, a professor at Lancaster University and the author of *The Tourist Gaze* (Sage 1990), *Consuming Places* (Routledge 1995), *Sociology beyond Societies* (Routledge 2000), and many other publications related to mobility, is a well-known researcher in this field (Lancaster University: web). In tourism anthropology, Smith, the author of *Hosts and Guests* (University of Pennsylvania Press 1989) is also well regarded. She is the founding chair of the IUAES (International Union of Anthropological and Ethnological Sciences) Commission on Tourism, which was established in 1998 (Smith: web).

Human mobility is a complex matter. Sato (2013) surveys the cost of education as

ドとして，教育のコストを研究している（佐藤：41-43）。山田（2009）は高度技能移民における国家政策の重要性について示唆している。1978 年の改革開放政策の導入以降，中国は特にアメリカや世界各地の著名な学術機関へ行く高度技能移民の供給源として知られるようになった。しかしながら，経済成長と *haigui*（ウミガメ）政策の普及により，後述のように多くの高度技能移民は高給取りとして中国に戻るようになった（山田：471-477）。

多数の先行研究により，人的移動に関する著作は容易に挙げることができる。青木と稲村（1997）は移民に関する諸研究をレビューし，分類した。彼らは歴史的な移民のトレンド，移民のフロー，地域ベースの移民パターンなどを類型化した（Aoki and Inamura：224）。重松（1995）は特に南アジアにおける移民に関する諸研究を調査し，特に古典的なプッシュ・プル理論や近代世界システム理論などのアプローチで分類化した（重松：268-269）。高橋（2014）は冷戦後のヨーロッパにおける事例を中心に，トランスナショナリズムに関する移民文献のレビューを行った（Takahashi：49-50）。

学術研究は個人レベルから組織へと発展することがしばしばある。ランカスター大学の移動研究センターは 2003 年に設立された。同センターは地球規模，国家規模，ローカルな規模の人的移動について研究している（CeMoRe: web）。学術研究にとって，出版は重要である。ドレクセル大学の移動研究・政策センターは 2006 年以降，『Mobility』誌を刊行している（mCenter: web）。

2-2. 古代の人的移動

原始的な人類はアフリカから移動し，地球中をカバーするようになった。人類の移動の歴史は極めて長い。氷河期には，人類はベーリング地峡を徒歩で渡った。狩猟採集の追跡により，場所の移動は極めて自然なことであった。遊牧民や交易民にとってもまた，移動は生活のために必要である。もし訪問先が

a human investment and economic trade (Sato: 41-43). Yamada (2009) suggests the importance of national policy on high-skilled immigrants. After the introduction of its open-door policy of 1978, China became a source country of high-skilled emigrant workers, who especially went to the United States and to well-known academic institutions all over the world. However, due to economic growth and the promulgation of the *haigui* (sea turtle) policies, which we treat in more detail below, many high-skilled workers returned to China to earn good incomes (Yamada: 471-477).

Due to the sufficient number of previous studies, works on human mobility are readily available. Aoki and Inamura (1997) reviewed many studies related to migration and categorized them. They categorized analyses of historical trends in migration, analyses of migration flow, and work on area-based migration patterns (Aoki and Inamura: 224). Shigematsu (1995) reviewed migration studies; especially those focused on South Asia, and categorized their approaches, including the classical push-pull theory and the modern world system theory (Shigematsu: 268-269). Takahashi (2014) reviewed migration papers related to transnationalism, especially focusing on Europe after the Cold War (Takahashi: 49-50).

Academic research often develops from the individual level to the organizational. The Center for Mobilities Research at Lancaster University was established in 2003. It examines the analysis of the global, national, and local movements of people (CeMoRe: web). For academic research, publication is important. The Mobilities Research and Policy Center at Drexel University has been publishing the journal *Mobility* since 2006 (mCenter: web).

2-2. Ancient Human Mobility

Primitive human beings moved out from Africa to cover the entire earth. The history of human mobility is quite long. During the Ice Age, human beings also crossed the Bering Isthmus on foot. In the pursuit of hunting and gathering, mobility from place to place was quite natural. For nomadic people and traders, mobility is also needed to

無人であったり，敵が存在しなかったりした場合，これらの移動は平和裏に行われた。地理的な制限により国境が発生する前，人々の移動は自由だった。吉澤（2007）はホモ・サピエンスをホモ・モビリタス（移動する人）と呼んでいる（吉澤：ii）。

　しかしながら，季節的に厳しい地方（雪，低温，乾季，その他の障害）に住む人々を除き，農耕民にとって居住地から非日常的な新たな場所に移動するのは特別なことであった。居住地のいくつかは町や都市に発展した。季節的に移動しなくても良い農耕社会の人々にとって，旅の目的は移動を促すために重要なことである。しかし，政治権力を有する文明もまた，人的移動を促す。領土を維持するために，支配者は政治的にあるいは軍事的に人々を強制的に移動させた。時には支配者もまた移動することがあった。

　多くの古代・中世の社会では，政治，宗教，教育，および哲学が関連していた。Xiang（2009）によると，泰山への巡礼は遅くとも紀元前1000年には行われていた。秦の始皇帝が紀元前219年に泰山で封禅の儀式を行ったように，伝説では72人の中国の諸皇帝たちが即位した時に封禅した（Xiang：82）。山岳信仰は中国各地で行われていたが，始皇帝訪問後，泰山は道教にとっても重要な聖地になった。

　西洋のキリスト教のように，仏教はアジアにおいて文化を越えて存在している。吉澤（2007）によると，インドのバラナシは遅くとも紀元前6世紀にはバラモン教の聖地であった。バラモン教の巡礼に続き，アショカ王は紀元前3世紀ごろ，ルンビニ（現在はネパール領）を含む仏教の巡礼を導入した（吉澤：9-10）。中国は法顕や義浄などの僧侶をナーランダやヴィクラマシーラなどの仏教機関に送り，玄奘三蔵は唐王朝の許可を取らずにインドを訪問した（Sen 2006：24）。日本は最澄や空海などの僧侶を中国に送った。道教との結びつきにより，中国の現地化した仏教は伝来後の日本に強い影響を及ぼした。（吉澤：11-12）。

live. If there were no people or no enemies in the places visited, these movements would be peaceful. Before the existence of any borders apart from geographical limitations, people could go everywhere. Yoshizawa (2007) calls *Homo sapiens* as *Homo mobilitas* (Yoshizawa: ii).

However, moving from the place of residence to a new, unusual place is a special event for agricultural people, except for those who live in seasonally difficult areas (with snow, low temperatures, dry seasons, or other natural obstacles). Some permanent settlements developed into towns and cities. For people in agricultural societies who do not need to migrate seasonally, the purpose of travel was an important stimulus to moving. However, civilizations with political power also supported human mobility. To maintain their territories, rulers forced people to move through politics or the military. Sometimes rulers also participated in activities of motion.

In many ancient and medieval societies, politics, religion, education, and philosophy were related. According to Xiang (2009), pilgrimages to Mt. Taishan began by 1000 BC at the latest. As Emperor Qin Shi Huang visited Mt. Taishan in 219 BC for his coronation ceremony, 72 legendary Chinese emperors held their own ceremonies there when they came to the throne (Xiang: 82). Mountain-dwelling religions existed locally in China; however, after Emperor Qin Shi Huang's visit, Mt. Taishan became an important holy place for Taoism as well.

Like Western Christianity, Buddhism has a cross-cultural existence in Asia. According to Yoshizawa (2007), Varanasi in India has been a holy place for Brahmanism since the sixth century BC at the latest. Following the Brahmanist pilgrimage, King Asoka initiated a Buddhist pilgrimage that included Lumbini (currently in Nepal) around the third century BC (Yoshizawa: 9-10). China sent monks such as Faxian and Yijing to Indian Buddhist institutions such as Nalanda and Vikramashila, whereas Xuanzang left Tang Dynasty China without permission to visit India (Sen 2006: 24). Japan sent monks such as Saicho and Kukai to China. Combined with Taoism, the localized Buddhism of China had a strong influence on Japan after it

同じような人的移動はヨーロッパでも見ることができる。プラトンやアリストテレスのような偉大な思想家は古代ギリシアに哲学の学校を設立した。ギリシアの学者たちは他の地域にも影響を及ぼした。著名なローマの作家であるキケロは哲学や修辞学，他の学問を学ぶためにギリシアを訪問した（的射場2010：107）。ローマ帝国の拡大により，ギリシア哲学はラテン語に翻訳され，380年にキリスト教がローマ帝国の国教となるまで広まっていった。ローマ帝国の没落後，アル・カラウィーイーンやアル・アズハルのようなイスラム系の教育機関がギリシア語のテキストをアラビア語に翻訳した（University of Al-Azhar: web）。

2-3. 中世の人的移動

　インドのナーランダやエジプトのアル・アズハルの学生のケースのように，宗教目的の学生の移動はヨーロッパでも起こった。キリスト教の修道院はヨーロッパ中に作られ，中世大学が発展するまでラテン語教育機関として重要な役割を演じてきた。ボローニャ大学の設立に続き，キリスト教世界の視点をラテン語で教える高等教育機関として，パリ大学，オックスフォード大学，ケンブリッジ大学，サラマンカ大学などが11-15世紀の間に設立された。

　世俗的な旅もまた大きく発展した。大規模な教育旅行として，いわゆるグランド・ツアーがイギリスの上流階級の間で普及していった。その多くは，14-16世紀当時の先進地域であったイタリアやフランスに訪問した（山村2010：7）。17世紀になると，イギリスの貴族にとって学ぶために旅することは必須になり，彼らは従者を伴い先進地域を訪問した（Boyer 2006：96-97）。

　しかしながら，中世の時代，封建社会における農民は地元の支配者により旅を禁じられていた。封建社会は農業に依存しており，農業からの安定した収入は地元の支配者にとって必要であった。ただし，巡礼は例外であり，農民は巡

was imported (Yoshizawa: 11-12).

Similar occurrences in human mobility were seen in Europe. Great thinkers such as Plato and Aristotle established schools of philosophy in ancient Greece. Greek scholars had a strong influence on other regions. The famous Roman writer Cicero went to Greece to study philosophy, rhetoric, and other fields (Matoba 2010: 107). Under the expansion of the Roman Empire, Greek philosophy translated into Latin was disseminated until Christianity became the official religion of the Roman Empire in 380. After the fall of the Roman Empire, Islamic educational institutions such as Al-Quaraouiyine and Al-Azhar, produced translations of Greek texts into Arabic (University of Al-Azhar: web).

2-3. Medieval Human Mobility

As was the case with students at Nalanda in India and Al-Azhar in Egypt, the mobility of religious students also occurred in Europe. Christian monastic schools were established around Europe and played a significant role as educational institutions, teaching in Latin, until the development of the medieval universities. Following the University of Bologna, higher educational institutions whose functioning was based on a Christian worldview and teaching in Latin, such as the universities of Paris, Oxford, Cambridge, and Salamanca, were established in the eleventh to fifteenth centuries.

Secular travel also developed to a great extent. Large-scale educational tours, the so-called Grand Tour, became common among the British upper classes. Many visited Italy and France, which were advanced areas in the fourteenth to sixteenth centuries (Yamamura 2010: 7). From the seventeenth century, travel to study became a must for British aristocrats, and they visited advanced areas together with their servants (Boyer 2006: 96-97).

However, during medieval times, farmers in feudal societies were prohibited to travel by local rulers. In feudal societies, which rely on agriculture, stable revenues from agriculture were necessary for local rulers. Pilgrimage was an exception; farmers

礼目的の旅を許されていた。サンティアゴ・デ・コンポステーラは 11-12 世紀の間に重要な巡礼地になった。すでに富裕層にとって人気のある巡礼地であったエルサレムやローマに加え，スペインやフランスからサンティアゴ・デ・コンポステーラへの巡礼者は増加した（岡本 2012：127-128）。イギリス人の巡礼者はカンタベリーやオックスフォード，その他のローカル・サイトにも訪問した（Yamashiro 2003：50）。

　同様の現象は日本でも見られた。奈良や京都などの古都を含む関西にはたくさんの寺院がある。聖職者の幾人かは宗教的な目的で訪問したが，10 世紀ごろには宗教以外の目的の訪問もみられるようになった（林 2012：13）。西国三十三所参拝やお伊勢参り，四国のお遍路などの巡礼が日本各地に生まれた。伊勢では，非聖職者による巡礼が近隣の関西から室町時代に広まっていった（新田 2014：34）。しかしながら，ガイド付きパッケージツアーの普及により，江戸時代後期には伊勢参りは国中に広まっていった。

　モンゴル帝国の拡大もまた，人的な移動の転機になった。世俗的なモンゴル帝国の支配のもと，近隣諸国との武力衝突にもかかわらず，ユーラシア大陸を跨いでの旅は容易になった（小沢 2012：184-185）。プラノ・カルピニは伝道者として旅し，マルコ・ポーロはビジネスのため旅立った。イブン・バットゥータはハッジによるメッカ巡礼のため旅を始めたが，多大なる旅の延長により，世界で最も知られた観光客の一人になった（Chanda 2009：299-300）。チャンダによると，アフガニスタンから北京の旅はラクダで 1 年かかったとされるが，最小限の警護付の休息所の整備により，他の時代よりも安全に旅を行うことができた（Chanda：92-93）。

　1492 年にイベリア半島においてレコンキスタが終わったこともまた，人的移動にとって転換点になった。同じ年，クリストファー・コロンブスは大西洋を横断した。彼の西半球到達により，ヨーロッパにおける地理的な知識は拡大

were allowed to travel for this reason. Santiago de Compostela became an important pilgrimage destination in the eleventh and twelfth centuries. In addition to Jerusalem and Rome, which were already major destinations for the rich, pilgrimages from Spain and France to Santiago de Compostela increased (Okamoto 2012: 127-128). English pilgrims could visit Canterbury, Oxford, and other local sites (Yamashiro 2003: 50).

Similar phenomena could be seen in Japan. In the Kansai region, which includes the old capital cities of Nara and Kyoto, there are many temples. Some priests visited these temples for ascetic purposes; however, non-monastic visits began to occur around the tenth century (Lin 2012: 13). Thirty-three pilgrimage sites were established gradually at Saigoku, and similar journeys were established for Ise, Shikoku, and other parts of Japan. In Ise, a non-monastic pilgrimage from the neighboring Kansai region gradually developed during the Muromachi Period (Nitta 2014: 34). However, due to the development of a guided package tour, the Ise pilgrimage expanded widely throughout the nation during the late Edo Period.

The expansion of the Mongol Empire was also a turning point for human mobility. Under the rule of the secular Mongol Empire, despite the existence of military struggles with neighboring countries, travel across the Eurasian continent became easy (Ozawa 2012: 184-185). Plano Carpini traveled as missionary and Marco Polo went on business. Ibn Battuta started his travel as Hajj pilgrimage to Mecca; however, due to the very great extent of his travels, he became one of the most famous tourists in the world (Chanda 2009: 299-300). According to Chanda, travel from Afghanistan to Beijing took one year by camel; however, due to the existence of rest places with minimal guards, travel was safer than it had been in other ages (Chanda: 92-93).

The end of the Reconquista in the Iberian Peninsula in 1492 was a turning point for human mobility. That same year, Christopher Columbus voyaged across the Atlantic Ocean. Due to his arrival in the Western Hemisphere, geographical knowledge

した。ポルトガルとスペインは大西洋の反対側を征服し，植民地化した。この植民地化の後，いわゆる新世界と呼ばれる場所へ，アフリカから奴隷が強制的に移動された。ポルトガルとスペインに続き，フランスやオランダ，イギリスなどのヨーロッパ諸国が植民地を設立した。

2-4. 近代化と人的移動

　産業の近代化もまた人的移動の主要な要素である。イギリスでは，1769 年のジェームス・ワットの蒸気機関の改良により，多くの工場が開発された。工場はたくさんの人々を雇用するため，農業社会よりも工業化によって都市化が進んだ。技術が急速に発展し，蒸気機関はより強力になり，より小型化した。ロバート・フルトンは蒸気機関を船に設置し，1807 年に蒸気船を開発した。ジョージ・スチーブンソンは 1825 年に乗客向けの蒸気機関車を生み出し，旅の形態を大きく変化させた（蛭川 2008：59-60）。

　ソフトウェアもまた旅にとって重要である。トーマス・クックは近代的な交通手段とガイド付きパッケージツアーを結びつけた。1841 年にクックはレスターとラフバラ間の旅客のための割引運賃を鉄道会社に交渉した（蛭川：11-13）。パッケージツアー自体は日本やオスマン帝国にすでに存在していたが，クックは近代的な交通機関を用いての旅行と団体割引を発展させた。最初のツアーの成功に続き，クックは世界で最も知られた旅行会社の一つを設立した。団体パッケージ旅行は世界中に広がっていった。

　近代化はイギリスから他の国々へ広まり，それらの国々を変化させた。たとえば，近代的な輸送システムはオスマン帝国での巡礼を変化させた。坂本（1990）によると，蒸気船と鉄道の導入は巡礼ルートを変え，メッカへの巡礼のためのラクダによるキャラバンに依存していた伝統的な町を変えた（坂本：212）。西洋の会社もまた時にはイスラム教徒の顧客を得た。チャンダ（2009）によると，オランダの蒸気船により，インドネシアからメッカへの巡礼者は1850 年代の年間 2000 人から，1900 年代には年間 7000 人に増加した（Chanda：259）。

in Europe expanded. Portugal and Spain conquered the opposite shores of the Atlantic and colonized them. After this colonization, slaves were forced to move from Africa to the so-called New World. Following Portugal and Spain, other European countries such as France, the Netherlands, and Great Britain set up colonies.

2-4. Modernization and Human Mobility

The modernization of industry is a key factor in human mobility. In the UK, due to the renovation of steam engine by James Watt in 1769, many factories developed. Because factories employed many workers, urbanization developed more in industrial than in agricultural societies. Technology developed rapidly and steam engines became stronger and more compact. Robert Fulton attached a steam engine to a ship and created a steamship in 1807. George Stevenson created locomotion for passengers in 1825, which changed travel dramatically (Hirukawa 2008: 59-60).

Software was also important for travel. Thomas Cook organized a guided package tour with modern transportation. In 1841, Cook negotiated with a railway company to bring passengers from Leicester to Loughborough at a reasonable price (Hirukawa: 11-13). Package tours already existed in Japan and the Ottoman Empire; however, Cook improved travel by modern transportation with the introduction of the group discount. Following the success of his first tour, he created one of the best-known travel companies in the world. Group package tours expanded around the globe.

Modernization also expanded from the UK to other countries and changed each one. For example, the modern transportation system changed the pilgrimage system under the Ottoman Empire. According to Sakamoto (1990), the initiation of steamships and railways changed pilgrimage routes and also changed the traditional towns that relied on camel-caravan pilgrimages to Mecca (Sakamoto: 212). Western companies had occasional Islamic customers. According to Chanda (2009), thanks to Dutch steamships, pilgrimages from Indonesia to Mecca increased from 2000 a year in the 1850s to 7000 in the 1900s (Chanda: 259).

近代的な輸送は日本における巡礼も発展させた。日本初の商業化された鉄道が横浜と新橋の間に 1872 年に開業された。對馬（2012）によると，明治と大正の間に，多くの私鉄が巡礼地のアクセスのため路線を開き，訪問者増に貢献した（對馬：42）。時に，神社や寺院は新路線の開発のための資金援助も行った（對馬：48）。神社や寺院は鉄道の建設後により多くの巡礼者を得ることができたので，これは win-win の関係だった。

思想の開化と新たな社会システムもまた近代化にとって重要である。先進国にとって，新たな産業のために体系化された教育が必要である。近代化された教育機関は技能のある人材を輩出するようになった。ドイツはフランスやイギリスと比べると後進国であったため，先進国に追いつくために近代的な教育が必要であった。ラテン語ベースのヨーロッパの中世大学とは異なり，近代の大学は現地語が分かれば多くの人に開かれていた。たとえば，1810 年に開学されたベルリン大学（現フンボルト大学）はヴィルヘルム・フォン・フンボルトの主導により，近代化のための人材を教育した（Humboldt Universität: web）。

他の国々もベルリン大学による教育の近代化の成功に続いた。たとえば，ジェレミー・ベンサムの支援のもと，世俗的なロンドン大学（現ユニバーシティ・カレッジ・ロンドン：UCL）が 1826 年に設立された。UCL は宗教や人種，階級にかかわらず，あらゆる学生を受け入れた。徳川幕府に留学が禁じられていたのにもかかわらず，伊藤博文は 1863 年に UCL で非合法に政治学を学び，後に日本の初代総理大臣になった（UCL: web）。明治憲法が制定される前，伊藤博文は法律を学ぶために，1882 年から 1883 年までベルリン大学やほかのヨーロッパの諸大学もまた訪問した（瀧井 1997：42-43）。

歴史的に見れば，日本は留学生の受け入れ国ではなく，送り出し国であった。しかし，日本の近代化が西洋的な教育システムを発展させたため，近隣諸国からの留学生が増加した。1881 年に，慶應義塾大学の創設者である福沢諭吉は，

Modern transportation allowed the further development of pilgrimages in Japan. The first commercialized railway line in Japan was established between Yokohama and Shinbashi in 1872. According to Tsushima (2012), during the Meiji and Taisho periods, many private railways were built to access pilgrimage venues, and this contributed to increase the number of visitors (Tsushima: 42). Sometimes shrines and temples financially supported railway companies to develop new lines (Tsushima: 48). Because shrines and temples received many more pilgrims after the construction of the railway, it was a win-win proposition.

The enlightenment of thought and newer social systems are also important in modernization. For modernized countries, systematic education for newer industries is needed. Modern educational institutions came into being to develop skilled human resources. Because Germany was less developed than France and Great Britain at that time, modernized education was needed to catch up. Unlike with Latin-based medieval universities in Europe, modern universities were opened to everyone if they could understand the local language. For example, Berlin University (now Humboldt Universität) was established in 1810 to educate human resources for modernization, thanks to the initiative of Wilhelm von Humboldt (Humboldt Universität: web).

Other countries followed the success in educational modernization of Berlin University. For example, supported by Jeremy Bentham, the secular London University (now University College London: UCL) was established in 1826. UCL accepted students regardless of religion, race, and class. Despite the prohibition of the Tokugawa government against study abroad, Ito Hirobumi studied politics illegally in UCL in 1863, later becoming the first Prime Minister of Japan (UCL: web). Ito Hirobumi also visited Berlin University and other European universities to learn law from 1882 to 1883 when the Meiji Constitution was under development (Takii 1997: 42-43).

Japan was historically a student-sending country, rather than a student-receiving one. However, as Japan's modernization arrived at the development of a Western-type education system, international students from neighboring countries came in increasing

彼の私塾に朝鮮半島からの学生を受け入れた。1896 年に清朝政府は国費留学生として 13 人の中国人学生を日本に送った（島津 2007：53）。後に有名な作家になる魯迅は 1902 年に清国政府国費留学生として来日している。清朝中国からの政府奨学金は増加し，1906 年には 1 万 2000 人が日本に留学した（孫 2003：49-50）。ドイツ，イギリス，日本では，先進的な教育が世界的に学生を引き寄せるようになった。さらに，現地語で提供されている，国家によって統一された教育システムは，ナショナル・アイデンティティを生み出すようになった。

第 2 章のおわりに

　この章では人的移動の歴史的変遷について手短にまとめた。諸文献から，古代や中世の旅は生活に関わっていたが，教育のための旅もまた存在していたことが分かる。教育と宗教は関連しているが，教育のための旅については第 5 章で述べる。

参考文献

AOKI, Toshiaki and INAMURA, Hajime（1997）"An Overview of Migration Studies and Future Perspectives," *Doboku Keikakugaku Kenkyu Ronbunshu*, 14, pp. 213-224

ボワイエ マルク（2006）『観光のラビリンス』（成沢広幸訳）法政大学出版局

CeMoRe（n.d.）"website," http://www.lancs.ac.uk/fass/centres/cemore/，2017 年 4 月 6 日閲覧

チャンダ ナヤン（2009）『グローバリゼーション　人類 5 万年のドラマ』（友田錫，滝上広水訳）NTT 出版

蛭川久康（2008）『トマス・クックの肖像』丸善

Humboldt-Universität（n.d.）"Short History," https://www.hu-berlin.de/en/about/history/huben_html，2017 年 4 月 6 日閲覧

Lancaster University（n. d.）"Professor John Urry", http://www. lancaster. ac. uk/fass/sociology/profiles/john-urry，2017 年 4 月 6 日閲覧

林薫如（2012）『日本における巡礼の成立』岡山大学

的射場敬一（2010）「共和制ローマとキケロ」『国士舘大学政治研究』2，107-135 頁

mCenter（n.d.）"website," http://mcenterdrexel.wordpress.com/，2017 年 4 月 6 日閲覧

numbers. In 1881, Fukuzawa Yukichi, the founder of Keio University, accepted Korean students at his private college. In 1896, the Qing government sent 13 Chinese students to Japan with governmental scholarships (Shimazu 2007: 53). In 1902, Lu Xun, later to become a well-known writer, visited Japan under a Qing government scholarship. The number of governmental scholarships from Qing China increased, reaching 12,000 in 1906 (Sun 2003: 49-50). In Germany, Great Britain, and Japan, advanced education was a magnet for students internationally. Further, a national unified education system based on the local language worked to create a national identity.

Conclusion of Chapter 2

This chapter briefly summarizes historic changes in human mobility. From the literatures, it is possible to see that ancient and medieval mobility were related to life, although travel for education also existed. Education and religion were also related to movement. Chapter 5 will focus on travel for education.

References

AOKI, Toshiaki and INAMURA, Hajime (1997) "An Overview of Migration Studies and Future Perspectives," *Doboku Keikakugaku Kenkyu Ronbunshu*, 14, pp. 213-224

BOYER, Marc (2006) *Le Tourisme de l'an 2000* (Japanese version), Hosei University Press

CeMoRe (n.d.) "website," http://www.lancs.ac.uk/fass/centres/cemore/, Accessed April 6 2017.

CHANDA, Nayan (2009) *Bound Together* (Japanese version), NTT Shuppan

HIRUKAWA, Hisayasu (2008) *Thomas Cook no Shouzou*, Maruzen

Humboldt-Universität (n.d.) "Short History," https://www.hu-berlin.de/en/about/history/huben_html, Accessed April 6, 2017

Lancaster University (n.d.) "Professor John Urry", http://www.lancaster.ac.uk/fass/sociology/profiles/john-urry, Accessed April 6, 2017

LIN, Huiju (2012) *Nihon ni Okeru Junrei no Seiritsu*, Okayama University

MATOBA, Keiichi (2010) "Kyouwasei Rome to Cicero," *Kokushikan Daigaku Seiji Kenkyu*, 2, pp. 107-135

mCenter (n.d.) "website," http://mcenterdrexel.wordpress.com/, Accessed April 6, 2017

新田功（2014）「観光の原点としての伊勢参宮についての経済的・統計的考察」『新情報』102，32-41頁

岡本亮輔（2012）「信仰なき巡礼者」山中弘編『宗教とツーリズム』世界思想社，126-148頁

小澤実（2012）「モンゴル帝国期以降のヨーロッパとユーラシア世界との交渉」『東洋史研究』71（3），181-196頁

坂本勉（1990）「巡礼とコミュニケーション」濱下武志編『移動と交流』岩波書店，197-222頁

佐藤仁志（2013）『国際的な労働移動と貿易』RITEI

SEN, Tansen（2006）"The Travel Records of Chinese Pilgrims Faxian, Xuanzang, and Yijing," *EDUCATION ABOUT ASIA*, 11（3），pp. 24-33

重松伸苛（1995）「国際移民研究の課題と動向」『国際開発研究フォーラム』2，265-276頁

嶋津拓（2007）「戦前戦中期における文部省直轄学校の特別予科制度について」『長崎大学留学生センター紀要』15，53-77頁

SMITH, Valene（n.d.）"homepage," http://valenesmith.com/，2017年4月6日閲覧

SMITH, Valene（1989）*Hosts and Guests: The Anthropology of Tourism*, University of Pennsylvania Press

孫長虹（2003）「魯迅の日本人観」『多元文化』3，49-69頁

TAKAHASHI, Kazu（2014）"Review of the International Migration," *YAMAGATA UNIVERSITY THE JOURNAL OF LAW AND POLITICS*, 58/59, pp. 43-69

瀧井一博（1997）「伊藤博文滞欧憲法調査の考察」『人文學報』80，33-78頁

對馬路人（2012）「鉄道と霊場」山中弘編『宗教とツーリズム』世界思想社，32-54頁

UCL: University College London（n.d.）"History," https://www.ucl.ac.uk/about/who/history，2017年4月6日閲覧

UNIVERSITY OF AL-AZHAR（n. d.）"Historical Background," https://web.archive.org/web/20040701101509/http://www.frcu.eun.eg/www/universities/html/azhar.html，2017年4月6日閲覧

URRY John（1990）*The Tourist Gaze: Leisure and Travel in Contemporary Societies*, Sage

URRY, John（1995）*Consuming Places*, Routledge

URRY, John（2000）*Sociology Beyond Societies: Mobilities for the Twenty-First Century*, Routledge

XIANG, Yixiao（2009）*Global-local Relationships in World Heritage: Mount Taishan, China*, University of Waterloo Ph.D Dissertation

NITTA, Isao (2014) "Kankou no Genten to shite no Ise Sangu ni tsuite no Keizaiteki-Toukeiteki Kousatsu," *Shin Jouhou*, 102, pp. 32-41

OKAMOTO, Ryousuke (2012) "Shinkou naki Junreisha," in Yamanaka, Hiroshi ed., *Shukyou to Tourism*, Sekai Shisou Sha, pp. 126-148

OZAWA, Minoru (2012) "Mongol Teikokuki Ikou no Europe to Eurasia Sekai no Koushou," *Touyoushi Kenkyu*, 71(3), pp. 181-196

SAKAMOTO, Tsutomu (1990) "Junrei to Communication," in Hamashita, Takeshi ed. *Idou to Kouryu*, Iwanami Shoten, pp. 197-222

SATO, Hitoshi (2013) *Kokusaiteki na Roudou Idou to Boueki*, RIETI

SEN, Tansen (2006) "The Travel Records of Chinese Pilgrims Faxian, Xuanzang, and Yijing," *EDUCATION ABOUT ASIA*, 11(3), pp. 24-33

SHIGEMATSU, Shinji (1995) "Kokusai Imin Kenkyu no Kadai to Doukou," *Kokusai Kaihatsu Kenkyu Forum*, 2, pp. 265-276

SHIMAZU, Taku (2007) "Senzen Senchuki ni okeru Monbusho Chokkatsu Gakkou no Tokubetsu Yoka Seido ni Tsuite", *Nagasaki Daigaku Ryugakusei Center Kiyou*, 15, pp. 53-77

SMITH, Valene (n.d.) "homepage," http://valenesmith.com/, Accessed April 6, 2017

SMITH, Valene (1989) *Hosts and Guests: The Anthropology of Tourism*, University of Pennsylvania Press

SUN, Changhong (2003) "Rojin no Nihonjinkan" *Tagen Bunka*, 3, pp. 49-61

TAKAHASHI, Kazu (2014) "Review of the International Migration," *YAMAGATA UNIVERSITY THE JOURNAL OF LAW AND POLITICS*, 58/59, pp. 43-69

TAKII, Kazuhiro (1997) "Ito Hirobumi Taiou Kenpou Chousa no Kousatsu," *The Zinbun Gakuhō: Journal of Humanities*, 80, pp. 33-78

TSUSHIMA, Michihito (2012) "Tetsudou to Reijou" YAMANAKA, Hiroshi ed. *Shukou to Tourism*, Sekai Shisousha, pp. 32-54

UCL: University College London (n. d.) "History," https://www.ucl.ac.uk/about/who/history, Accessed April 6, 2017

UNIVERSITY OF AL-AZHAR (n. d.) "Historical Background," https://web.archive.org/web/20040701101509/http://www.frcu.eun.eg/www/universities/html/azhar.html, Accessed April 6, 2017

URRY John (1990) *The Tourist Gaze: Leisure and Travel in Contemporary Societies*, Sage

URRY, John (1995) *Consuming Places*, Routledge

URRY, John (2000) *Sociology Beyond Societies: Mobilities for the Twenty-First Century*, Routledge

XIANG, Yixiao (2009) *Global-local Relationships in World Heritage: Mount Taishan, China*, University of Waterloo Ph.D Dissertation

山田敦（2009）「ハイテク移民研究序説」『一橋法学』8(2)，459-484頁

山村順次（2010）『観光地理学』同文舘出版

YAMASHIRO, Hiromichi（2003）"Pilgrimage in Medieval Europe," *Hiroshima Daigaku Daigakuin Bungakukenkyuka Ronshu*, 63, pp. 33-50

吉澤五郎（2007）『旅の比較文明学』世界思想社

YAMADA, Atsushi (2009) "High-tech Imin Kenkyu Jyosetsu," *Hitotsubashi Hougaku*, 8(2), pp. 459-484

YAMAMURA, Junji (2010) *Kankou Chirigaku*, Doubunkan Shuppan

YAMASHIRO, Hiromichi (2003) "Pilgrimage in Medieval Europe," *Hiroshima Daigaku Daigakuin Bungakukenkyuka Ronshu*, 63, pp. 33-50

YOSHIZAWA, Goro (2007) *Tabi no Hikaku Bunmeigaku*, Sekai Shisou Sha

第3章

現代における国際労働力移動の諸問題

第3章のはじめに

イブン・スィーナーが生涯を通して異なった支配者達に雇われ，イブン・バットゥータが世界旅行中に多くの地域で働いてきたように，中世では働く場所は柔軟であった。ジェノバ出身のクリストファー・コロンブスがスペインの支配者たちに雇われ，フィレンツェ出身のアメリゴ・ヴェスプッチもまたスペインのために働いていたように，近代化以前の国籍の概念は現在とは異なっていた。

ナショナル・アイデンティティと国境管理は時に関係している。富岡（1999）によると，1789年のフランス革命の後，1792年にフランス政府はパスポートを発行した（富岡：31-32）。国境管理を強化するため，フランス政府は1858年にビザ制度を導入した。当時パスポートとビザはヨーロッパでそれほど使われていなかったが，第一次世界大戦後，セキュリティの理由から，他の先進国もこれらの制度を導入した。人的移動をコントロールするため，ビザ制度はアメリカ合衆国で1917年，日本で1918年に導入された（富岡：41-42）。

3-1. 国際的な移動の背景

人的移動にはプッシュとプルの要因がある。アイルランドにおける1845年のジャガイモ飢饉は典型的なプッシュ要因である。飢饉により，難民のように，多くのアイルランドの人々は生きるために出国し，多くはカナダやアメリカ合衆国へ渡った。ナチス政権下のドイツやヨーロッパのその他の国々からユダヤ

Chapter 3

Contemporary Issues in International Labor Mobility

Introduction of Chapter 3

As seen in Avicenna, who was hired by different ruling families during his life, and as Ibn Battuta, who worked in many places during his world travels, workplaces were flexible during the Middle Ages. As Christopher Columbus from Genova was hired by the Spanish rulers, or as Amerigo Vespucci from Florence also worked for Spain, it can be seen that the concept of nationality before modernization was different from current one.

Sometimes national identity and border control are related. According to Tomioka (1999), the French government started to issue passports in 1792, just after the French Revolution of 1789 (Tomioka: 31-32). To strengthen border control, the French government implemented a visa system in 1858. At this time, passports and visas were not in wide use in Europe; however, after the First World War, other developed counties also put such a system into place, for security reasons. To control human mobility, the US put into place its own visa system in 1917 and Japan followed suit in 1918 (Tomioka: 41-42).

3-1. The Background of International Mobility

Human mobility has push and pull factors. The Potato Famine in Ireland in 1845 was a typical case of a push factor. Because of this famine, like refugees, a large number of Irish emigrated abroad to survive, and many of them arrived in Canada and the United States. The emigration of Jewish people during the period of Nazi power in Germany

系の人々が出国したのもプッシュ要因である。アルベルト・アインシュタインやピーター・ドラッカーのように，これらの出国者はアメリカ合衆国の科学の発展に貢献した。

ゴールド・ラッシュは典型的なプル要因である。1848年のカリフォルニアにおける金の発見により，1849年から大規模な人的移動が起こった。同じような現象はオーストラリアやニュージーランド，南アフリカでも起こっている。大規模な農業，巨大な工場の拡大，鉄道建設，特に大陸横断鉄道などは世界的に労働者を引き付けた。アメリカ合衆国では，中国系を含んだ移民労働者が大陸横断鉄道の建設に貢献し，1869年に両海岸がつながった。中国系移民の急増に対し，1882年には中国人排斥法が施行された（貫堂 1995：192-193）。

3-2. 国際労働者の歴史的トレンド

国際移住機関（IOM）によると，グローバリゼーションには3つの波があるとされる（表3-1）。第一の波では，新世界の多くの国々が農業労働力を必要としていたが，アメリカ合衆国では工場での労働者も求めていた。第二の波では，特に1970年代のオイルショック以前まで，工業の労働者が重要であった。第

表3-1　グローバリゼーションの3つの波

第一の波	1870年から1914年	アルゼンチンやオーストラリア，ニュージーランド，アメリカ合衆国など土地が豊富な国々へ移住
第二の波	1950年から1980年まで	先進国内で低賃金の地域に工業の再配分が行われた
第三の波	1980年から	多くの発展途上国が政策転換し，初めてグローバル市場に参入した（バングラデシュ，中国，インド，インドネシア，メキシコ，モロッコ，フィリピン，スリランカ，トルコを含む）

出典：International Organization for Migration（2008），*World Migration 2008: Managing Labor Mobility in the Evolving Global Economy*, IOM p. 25

and other European countries was likewise due to a push factor. Like Albert Einstein and Peter Drucker, these emigrants contributed to the development of the sciences in the United States.

The Gold Rush was a typical case of a pull factor. The finding of gold in California in 1848 prompted a mass migration movement that began in 1849. Similar phenomena also occurred in Australia, New Zealand, and South Africa. Agriculture on a mass scale, the expansion of large factories, and railway construction, especially on the intercontinental scale, attracted workers internationally. In the US, immigrant workers including Chinese contributed to the construction of the transcontinental railroad; the coasts were linked in 1869. In reaction to the rapid increase in number of Chinese immigrants, the Chinese Exclusion Act was enacted in 1882 (Kidou 1995: 192-193).

3-2. Historical Trends of International Workers

According to the International Organization for Migration (IOM), there have been three waves of globalization (Table 3-1). During the first wave, many countries in the New World experienced a need for agricultural workers; however, the United States also needed factory laborers. During the second wave, manufacturing laborers were

Table 3-1   Three Waves of Globalization

The first wave	between 1870 and 1914	People emigrated to land-abundant countries such as Argentina, Australia, New Zealand, and the United States.
The second wave	from 1950 to 1980	There was a redistribution of manufacturing within developed countries to lower-wage areas.
The third wave	began in 1980	Many developing countries changed their policies and broke into global markets for the first time (including Bangladesh, China, India, Indonesia, Mexico, Morocco, Philippines, Sri Lanka, and Turkey)

Source: International Organization for Migration (2008), *World Migration 2008: Managing Labor Mobility in the Evolving Global Economy*, IOM p. 25

三の波では，出身国と移民労働者のための仕事が多様化した。インドからのコンピュータ技術者やフィリピンからの看護師などが例としてよく知られている。

　これらの地球規模の動きに加え，地域的な人的移動もある。ある国の好景気は国際的に労働者を引き寄せる。たとえば，アメリカ合衆国のブラセロ・プログラムは好景気の時，メキシコからの農業労働者の受け入れをデザインしていた。このプログラムは 1942 年から 1964 年まで続き，1965 年の移民国籍法改訂により，移民の出身国の割り当て制度が廃止されるまで行われた（IOM 2013：38）。

　ヨーロッパにおける第二次世界大戦後の経済復興もまた人的移動を促した。パディアとカチャノスキー（2016）によると，1950 年から 1973 年の間，約3000 万人の外国人労働者が西ヨーロッパ，とくに西ドイツに移動した（パディアとカチャノスキー：142-143）。西ドイツのように，非熟練労働者のためのガストアルバイター（ゲストワーカー）制度がいくつかの国々に存在した。西ドイツのガストアルバイター制度は 1955 年から 1973 年まで続いた（IOM 2013：38）。

　歴史的に，アメリカ合衆国，カナダ，オーストラリア，ニュージーランドは移民の国として知られている。しかしながら，国際的な移民労働者は多くの賃金が高い国々へ移動する。図 3-1 は国別の移民の割合を示している。中東のいくつかの国々は 1973 年のオイルショック以降，移民にとって魅力的になった。南アジア諸国の労働者は中東，特に産油国へ移住している。

　歴史的に，大都市は移民の入国地点として重要な役割を果たしてきた。図3-2 によると，移民が多いオセアニアの諸都市に加え，ヨーロッパの諸都市やシンガポールもまた外国生まれの人口の割合が高い。

again important, especially before the oil crisis of the early 1970s. During the third wave, the source countries and the work for migrant labors were diversified. Computer engineers from India and nurses from the Philippines are well-known examples.

In addition to these global-scale movements, regional human mobility also exists. A booming economy in one country acts as a magnet to workers internationally. For example, the Bracero Program in the United States was designed for agricultural laborers from Mexico during a boom period of the economy. This program continued from 1942 to 1964, until the end of the system of quotas for immigrants, which were removed by the upcoming Immigration and Nationality Act Amendments of 1965 (IOM 2013: 38).

The recovering economy after the Second World War in Europe also stimulated human mobility. According to Padilla and Cachanosky (2016), from 1950 to 1973, approximately 30 million foreign workers moved to Western Europe, especially to West Germany (Padilla and Cachanosky: 142-143). As in West Germany, a *Gastarbeiter* (guest worker) system for low-skilled workers existed in some countries. The West German *Gastarbeiter* system continued from 1955 to 1973 (IOM 2013: 38).

Historically, the United States, Canada, Australia, and New Zealand have been known as immigrant countries. However, international migrant workers are moving toward many high-wage countries. Figure 3-1 shows the percentage of immigrants in the population by country. Some countries in the Middle East became attractive for immigrants after the oil crisis of 1973. Workers from South Asian countries are emigrating to the Middle East, especially oil-producing countries.

Historically, major cities played a key role of the entry points for immigrants. In addition to high-immigration cities in Oceania, cities in Europe as well as Singapore have high percentages of foreign-born populations according to Figure 3-2.

図 3-1　2015 年における国別全人口に対する移民の割合

出典：GMDAC（2017）*2015 Global Migration Trends Factsheet*, IOM, p. 6

図 3-2　2015 年における主要都市の外国生まれの人口

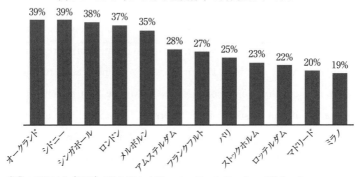

出典：GMDAC（2017）*2015 Global Migration Trends Factsheet*, IOM, p. 7

3-3. ターゲットとなる移民労働者

先進国において，シェンゲン条約諸国を除けば，入国管理はよく整備され，

50　第 3 章　現代における国際労働力移動の諸問題

Figure 3-1 Share of Immigrants as a Percentage of Total Population of Country of Destination, 2015

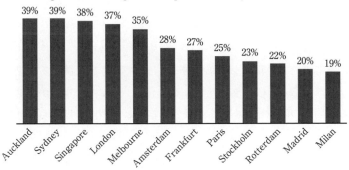

Source: GMDAC (2017) *2015 Global Migration Trends Factsheet*, IOM, p. 6

Figure 3-2 Foreign-born Population in Major cities, 2015

Auckland 39%, Sydney 39%, Singapore 38%, London 37%, Melbourne 35%, Amsterdam 28%, Frankfurt 27%, Paris 25%, Stockholm 23%, Rotterdam 22%, Madrid 20%, Milan 19%

Source: GMDAC (2017) *2015 Global Migration Trends Factsheet*, IOM, p. 7

3-3. Targeted Immigrant Workers

In developed countries, excluding Schengen agreement countries, border control is

Chapter 3 Contemporary Issues in International Labor Mobility 51

入国はコントロールされている。この管理により，ターゲットが選抜された人的移動が可能になっている。アメリカ合衆国では，H2-A ビザが主に農業，H2-B ビザが主に建築や道路建設，インフラ整備のために用いられている（パディアとカチャノスキー：146-147）。公的には，日本とオーストラリアは非熟練労働者の受け入れは行っていない。しかしながら，日本における国際的な技術インターンシップの研修生または技能実習生（旗手 2009：94-95）やオーストラリアにおけるワーキングホリデー参加者は事実上低賃金労働者として働いている（海野 2017：web）。

多くの先進国は石油ショック後も国際的な能力のある人々を引き付けてきた。ビジネス移民やハイテク移民制度はオーストラリアやニュージーランドなど多くの国々で見られる。アメリカ合衆国では，EB カテゴリーのビザが同じようなパターンである。たとえば，起業家のための EB-5 ビザは 50 万ドルの投資と 10 人の雇用を最低限求められている。定住は求められていないが，技術労働者のための H-1 ビザ（特に 1990 年に導入された H-1B ビザ）もまたアメリカに存在する（ヴェダー 2016：189）。

アメリカ合衆国のように，日本においても技術者移民は好意的に見られている。オーストラリアやニュージーランドに続き，日本も技術者移民のためのポイントシステムを導入した。たとえば，学術研究者の場合，学位，研究歴，年齢などが選考のための重要な基準である。日本や日本語に関する知識は補助的に重要な基準である。表 3-2 で見られるように，若くて日本語が話せ，博士号を有する長期間の研究歴のあるものは，日本のビザ制度では求められている。

高等教育と高度技能労働者は強い関係がある。改革開放経済が導入された1978 年以降，中国政府は中国人学生を国外，特にアメリカの大学に送り，教育を受けて帰国した人々を高給で迎えた。中国では，留学し，高度な技能を持っているものが *haigui*（ウミガメ）と呼ばれ，中国にてエリートになった。

relatively well organized and immigration is controlled. Thanks to this control, the targeting of selected human mobility is possible. In the US, the H2–A visa, used mainly for agriculture, and the H2–B visa, used mainly for construction of buildings, roads, infrastructure, and so on are common (Padilla and Cachanosky: 146–147). Officially, Japan and Australia do not accept low–skilled workers. However, international technical internship trainees (*kenshusei* and/or *ginou jisshusei*) in Japan (Hatate 2009: 94–95) and working holiday makers in Australia are hired as de facto low–wage labor (Unno 2017: web).

Many developed countries have also been working to attract international talent after the oil crisis. Business and high–tech immigrant schemes can be seen in many countries such as Australia and New Zealand. In the US, visas in the EB categories follow a similar pattern. For example, the EB–5 visa for entrepreneurs requires an investment of half a million dollars and the employment of more than ten workers. Although they do not provide permanent residency, however, H–1 visas (especially the H–1B visa, initiated in 1990) for skilled workers are also available in the US (Vedder 2016: 189).

As in the US, skilled workers are found to be preferable in Japan. Following Australia and New Zealand, Japan initiated a points system for skilled workers. In the case of academic researchers, for example, degree, research experience, and age are important criteria for selection. Knowledge of Japan and the Japanese language are also important supplementary criteria. As can be seen in Table 3–2, a younger Japanese–speaking doctoral holder with longer research experience is preferred by Japan's visa system.

Higher education and high–skilled workers are cross related. Since the beginning of the open–door policy of 1978, the Chinese government has sent Chinese students to foreign universities, especially in the US, and received returning educated citizens who could obtain higher salaries. In China, those who studied abroad and have high skill levels are called *haigui* (sea turtle), and they are part of the elite in China.

Chapter 3   Contemporary Issues in International Labor Mobility   53

表 3-2　日本における学術研究者のためのポイントシステム

基準点	学位（博士号：30 点，修士号：20 点） 研究歴（7 年以上：15 点，5-7 年：10 点，3-5 年：5 点） 年齢（29 歳まで：15 点，30-34 歳：10 点，35-39 歳：5 点）
ボーナス点	海外での仕事に関する資格：5 点 日本における高等教育機関での学位：10 点 日本語能力試験 1 級：15 点

出典：Immigration Bureau of Japan（2015）"Points-based Preferential Immigration Treatment for High-skilled Foreign Professionals," http://www.immi-moj.go.jp/ newimmiact_3/en/pdf/150406-6.pdf, Accessed April 19, 2017

　しかしながら，需要と供給のバランスの影響は高度技能移民にも及ぶ。図 3-3 によると，留学する中国人の学生は増加している。高度な教育を受けた帰国移民の増加により，多くの *haigui* は高度な技能を持つ失業者である *haidai*（昆布）になった（CLAIR 北京事務所 2015：19）。

図 3-3　留学する中国人学生（単位 10,000 人）

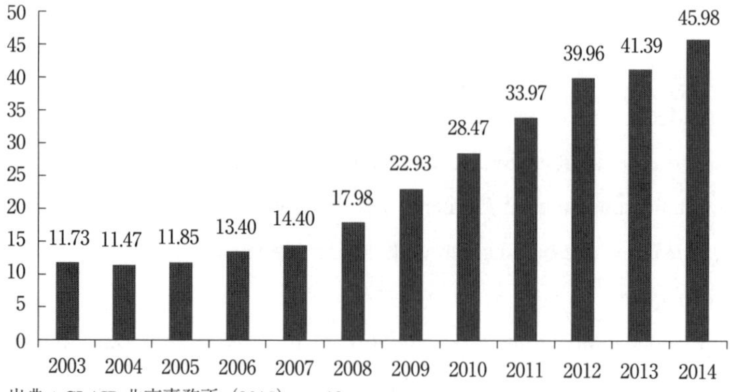

出典：CLAIR 北京事務所（2015），p. 12

Table 3-2 Points System for Academic Researchers in Japan

Basic Points	Degree (Doctoral Degree 30, Master's Degree 20) Research Experience (seven years or more 15, five to seven years 10, three to five years 5) Age (up to twenty-nine years old 15, between thirty and thirty-four years old 10, between thirty-five and thirty-nine years old 5)
Bonus Points	Foreign work-related qualification 5 Degree at a higher education institution in Japan 10 N1 of the Japanese Language Proficiency Test 15

Source: Immigration Bureau of Japan (2015) "Points-based Preferential Immigration Treatment for High-skilled Foreign Professionals," http://www.immi-moj.go.jp/newimmiact_3/en/pdf/150406-6.pdf, Accessed April 19, 2017

However, the balance of demand and supply influences highly-skilled immigrants. According to Figure 3-3, the number of Chinese students who are studying abroad is increasing. Due to the increase in number of highly educated returning migrants, many of *haigui* have become *haidai* (kelp), that is, the high-skilled unemployed (CLAIR Beijing Office 2015: 19).

Figure 3-3 Chinese Students Studying Abroad (Unit: 10,000 people)

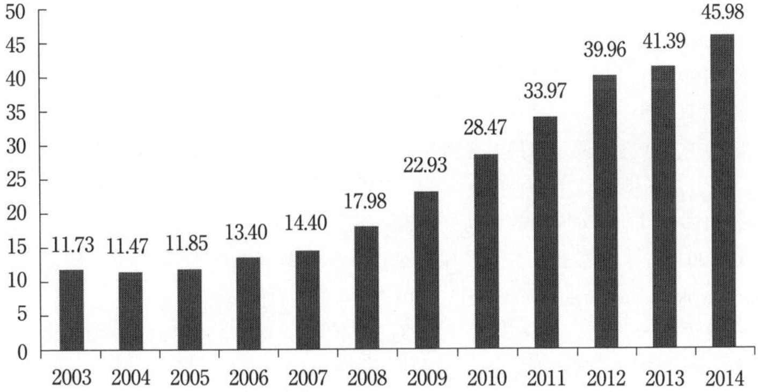

Source: CLAIR Beijing Office (2015), p. 12

Chapter 3　Contemporary Issues in International Labor Mobility　55

第3章のおわりに

第二次世界大戦後，アメリカと西ドイツではたくさんの非熟練労働者が求められていた。近年では起業家と高度な技術を持つ労働者が多くの国々に求められている。高度な技能を持つ労働者は高等教育によって生み出されており，彼らは移住する可能性がある。中国での留学ブームにより，学生の国際移動は増加している。日本の類似したケースは，第6章にて述べる。

参考文献

CLAIR 北京事務所（2015）『中国の教育制度と留学事情』CLAIR

GMDAC（2017）*2015 Global Migration Trends Factsheet*, IOM

旗手明（2009）「外国人研修・技能実習制度をどうするか」外国人研修生問題ネットワーク編『外国人研修生　時給300円の労働者』明石書店，83-97頁

Immigration Bureau of Japan（2015）"Points-based Preferential Immigration Treatment for High-skilled Foreign Professionals," http: //www. immi-moj. go. jp/newimmiact_3/en/pdf/ 150406-6.pdf, 2017年4月19日閲覧

International Organization for Migration（2008），*World Migration 2008: Managing Labor Mobility in the Evolving Global Economy*, IOM

International Organization for Migration（2013）*Migration and the United Nations Post-2015 Development Agenda*, IOM

貴堂嘉之（1995）「「帰化不能外人」の創造」『アメリカ研究』29，177-196頁

パディア アレクサンドル，カチャノスキー ニコラス（2016）「雇用ビザ：国際比較」パウエル ベンジャミン編『移民の経済学』（藪下史郎他訳）東洋経済新報社，123-176頁

富岡宣之（1999）『ひとの国際的移動』嵯峨野書院

海野麻美（2017）「「出稼ぎ日本人」も無縁じゃない豪州のひずみ」『東洋経済 ONLINE』 http://toyokeizai.net/articles/-/166615, 2017年4月7日閲覧

ヴェダー リチャード K.（2016）「穏当な移民改革案」パウエル ベンジャミン編『移民の経済学』（藪下史郎他訳）東洋経済新報社，177-207頁

Conclusion of Chapter 3

Just after the Second World War, many low-skilled workers were needed in the US and West Germany. Currently, entrepreneurs and high-skilled workers are preferable for many countries. High-skilled workers are a product of higher education, for which they may migrate. In tandem with the study abroad boom in China, international student mobility is increasing. Similar cases of Japan will be treated in chapter 6.

References

CLAIR Beijing Office (2015) *Chugoku no Kyouiku Seido to Ryugaku Jijou*, CLAIR

GMDAC (2017) *2015 Global Migration Trends Factsheet*, IOM

HATATE Akira (2009) "Gaikokujin Kenshu / Ginou Jisshu Seido wo Dousuru ka" in Gaikokujin Kenshusei Mondai Network ed., *Gaikokujin Kenshusei Jikyuu 300 Yen no Roudousha*, Akashi Shoten, pp. 83–97

Immigration Bureau of Japan (2015) "Points-based Preferential Immigration Treatment for High-skilled Foreign Professionals," http: //www. immi-moj. go. jp/newimmiact_3/en/pdf/ 150406-6.pdf, Accessed April 19, 2017

International Organization for Migration (2008), *World Migration 2008: Managing Labor Mobility in the Evolving Global Economy*, IOM

International Organization for Migration (2013) *Migration and the United Nations Post-2015 Development Agenda*, IOM

KIDOU Yoshiyuki (1995) "Kika Funou Gaijin no Souzou," *America Kenkyu*, No.29, pp. 177-196

PADILLA Alexandra and CACHANOSKY Nicolas (2016) "Employment Visas," in POWELL Benjamin ed., *The Economics of Immigration* (Japanese Version), Toyo Keizai Shinpousha, pp. 123-176

TOMIOKA Nobuyuki (1999) *Hito no Kokusaiteki Idou*, Sagano Shoin

UNNO Asami (2017) "Dekasegi Nihonjin mo Muen ja nai Goushu no Hizumi," *Toyo Keizai Online*, http://toyokeizai.net/articles/-/166615, Accessed April 7, 2017

VEDDER Richard K. (2016) "Immigration Reform," in POWELL Benjamin ed., *The Economics of Immigration* (Japanese Version), Toyo Keizai Shinpousha, pp. 177-207

第4章

日本から／への労働者の移動のトレンドと社会背景

第4章のはじめに

　この章では日本人労働者の海外移住と日本における外国人労働者のトレンドについて考察する。明治時代（1868-1912），日本は移民の送り出し国だった。しかしながら，1980年代以降，日本は多くの外国人労働者を受け入れている。1990年代初頭からの不景気にもかかわらず，日本における外国人労働者はいまだに増加している。

　時代を通じて，外国人労働者のタイプは変わってきた。明治政府は外国人の学者や技術者を高給で雇ったが，同じころ日本からの移民の多くは海外で農民として働いた。近年，日本は高齢化と人口減少に直面し，以前の高度人材に加え，介護や製造業，建設業，農業など，様々な分野で外国人労働者を受け入れている。

4-1. 日本から／への人的移動：文献レビュー

　統計は近年度マクロ・トレンドを理解するのに役立つため，著者は普段国際機関や政府が発行する人的な移動に関する統計を使っている。この章では，日本の外務省や法務省が発表した統計データを使っている。

　しかしながら，統計は最新のトレンドをカバーしていない時もある。このような場合，研究報告書の利用が重要である。たとえば，藤岡（2017）はエスノグラフィーの手法を使い，オーストラリアにおける非エリートの日本人労働者

Chapter 4

Migration Trends and Social Backgrounds of International Migrant Workers from and to Japan

Introduction of Chapter 4

This chapter analyzes of international migration trends of Japanese workers abroad and foreign workers in Japan. During the Meiji period (1868-1912), Japan was an immigrant sender. However, since the 1980s, Japan has been receiving many foreign workers. Despite the economic slump Japan has experienced since the early 1990s, the number of foreign workers in Japan is still increasing.

The types of foreign migrant workers have also changed over time. The Meiji government hired highly-skilled and highly paid foreign academics and engineers, while during the same period, many of Japanese nationals immigrated overseas to work as farmers. Currently, Japan is facing an aging population and overall depopulation and requires foreign workers for the care, manufacturing, construction and agriculture industries, in addition to previously mentioned high-skilled workers.

4-1. Human mobility from and to Japan: Literature Review

Statistics are useful for understanding recent macro-trends; the author of this paper has typically used human mobility statistics published by international organizations and governments. In the case of this chapter, the author has relied on statistics from Japan's Ministry of Foreign Affairs (MOFA) and Ministry of Justice.

However, sometimes statistics are not able to encapsulate newer trends. In these cases, the use of research papers is important. For example, Fujioka (2017) has studied non-elite Japanese workers in Australia using an ethnographical approach. Nakazawa

を調べた。中澤（2016）は多くの中間層の日本人女性が海外で働いていることを指摘した。

　インタビューは社会問題を深く掘り下げる時に効果的である。出井（2016）は事実上の労働者である留学生や研修生／技能実習生などの日本居住の外国人について調査した。榑松（2008）は日本の様々な分野で働いている外国人技能実習生の諸問題についてまとめた。低賃金で，労働時間が長く，安定していない雇用であることが，これらの調査によって強調されている。

　文献調査は歴史的な背景を調べるうえで必須である。たとえば，植村（2008）は明治時代に日本政府や主要な会社に雇われた外国人労働者の個々の資料をまとめた。当時，日本は移民の送り出し国として知られていた。日本の出国移民に関する歴史的な研究は数多い（飯田 1994，福井 2003 および 2014）。外国から日本への出戻り移民もある。丹野（2013）は海外生まれの日系人や日本で生まれた外国にルーツを持つ者などを含んだ日本の国籍について歴史的に調査した。

4-2. 日本の入国移民と出国移民の歴史的背景

　歴史的に，日本は高度人材の移民労働者を受け入れてきたが，第二次世界大戦の終了で失った植民地を除き，公的には非熟練の外国人労働者を受け入れなかった。植村（2008：2）によると，江戸時代末期から明治時代の初期に 2936 人の高給で招聘された外国人（お雇い外国人）の記録が残っている。彼らの多くはイギリス，アメリカ合衆国，フランス，ドイツ，オランダの出身であった。彼らの仕事は日本の近代化に貢献した（植村 2008：8）。

　しかしながら，明治時代からの高い人口増により，戦前の日本は移民の送り出し国になり，アメリカ合衆国やペルー，ブラジルなどに移民を送るように

(2016) has also noted that many middle-class Japanese women are working abroad.

The interview approach is effective in offering a deep understanding of social problems. Idei (2016) has reported on foreign residents living in Japan as de facto workers, such as international students and trainees. Kurematsu (2008) has also reported the problems associated with international trainees in various industries in Japan. Low-wages, long working hours, and unstable employment are often among the issues highlighted in these reports.

Literature review is also essential to studying an issue's historical background. For example, Uemura (2008) has summarized the personal documents of foreign workers hired by the Japanese government and major companies during the Meiji era. In this period, Japan was known as an emigration country. There are many historical studies related to Japanese emigrants (Iida 1994, Fukui 2003 and 2014). Return migration back to Japan via foreign countries is also possible. Tanno (2013) has studied the historical change of Japanese nationalities, including Japanese descendants born overseas, and foreign descendants born in Japan.

4-2. The Historical Backgrounds of Japanese Immigrants and Emigrants

Historically, Japan has accepted high-skilled immigrant workers; however, with the exception of Japanese colonies up to the end of WWII, Japan did not officially accept receive low-skilled foreign workers. According to Uemura (2008: 2), 2936 invited, highly paid foreigners (Oyatoi Gaikokujin) were recorded from the end of Edo period to the early Meiji period. Many of these workers were from the UK, the USA, France, Germany, and the Netherlands. Their work contributed to the modernization of Japan (Uemura 2008: 8).

However, due to Japan's higher population growth since the Meiji era, Japan became an immigrant sender during the pre-WWII period, with Japanese nationals

なった。近代化にもかかわらず，明治時代の工業化は限られており，引き続き
農業が主要な仕事であった。

　明治元年（1868），153人の日本人が，明治政府の許可なしで，農民としてハ
ワイに移住した（飯田 1994：87）。この非公式な労働者としての出国移民に続
き，1885年から1893年まで29,069人の公的な移民労働者が明治政府の支援の
下，ハワイに渡った（飯田 1994：87）。私費で日本からハワイに移住する人々
も続いた。1924年にアメリカ合衆国が日本人移民の受け入れを禁止した時，
約20万人の日本からの移民がハワイに住んでいた（飯田 1994：87）。

　北アメリカにおける20世紀初頭の日本からの移民制限のため，日本からの
移民は南アメリカ，特にペルーとブラジルに目的地が変わった。1899年に790
人の日本人が佐倉丸でペルーに移住した（福井 2003：36）。ブラジルへは日本
からの最初の移民団が1908年に笠戸丸で到着した（福井 2014：67）。これらの
移民は農民としての契約であったが，時と共に，仕事が多様化していった。第
二次世界大戦中，多くの国々は日本からの移民を禁止したので，日本は植民地
へ移民を送った。

　第二次世界大戦後日本は植民地を失ったので，日本列島は再び人口過剰に
なった。江原（2007：24）によると，1945年に旧植民地から630万人以上の
人々が日本に戻ってきたとされる。日本から南アメリカへの移民がこのころ再
開されている。ブラジルへの日本人移民は1953年に再開され，日系機関もま
たブラジルの農地を開発した（福井 2014：70）。

4-3. 移民受け入れ国としての日本
　近年，日本は高齢化と人口減少に面している。1960年代の高度経済成長は
多くの工場労働者を必要とした。日本経済は1973年の第一次石油ショックか
ら素早く立ち直り，1980年代後半にはバブル経済の好景気を迎えた。しかし

travelling to the US, Peru, Brazil and other countries. Despite modernization, the industrialization of Japan during the Meiji period was limited and farming continued to be a main occupation.

In the first year of the Meiji period (1868), 153 Japanese workers visited Hawaii to work as farmers without permission from the Meiji government (Iida 1994: 87). Following this unofficial emigration of migrant workers, from 1885 to 1893, 29,069 official migrant workers, supported by the Meiji government, travelled to Hawaii (Iida 1994: 87). Private Japanese immigration to Hawaii also continued. When Japanese immigration to the US was banned in 1924; approximately 200,000 Japanese immigrants lived in Hawaii (Iida 1994: 87).

Due to these early 20th century restrictions on Japanese immigration to North America, the major destination for Japanese migrants then changed to South America, particularly Peru and Brazil. In 1899, 790 Japanese nationals immigrated to Peru on the ship Sakura-maru (Fukui 2003: 36). The first group of Japanese immigrants to Brazil arrived in 1908 on the Kasato-maru (Fukui 2014: 67). These migrants contracted to work as farmers; however, over time, their sources of work shifted. During WWII, when many countries banned immigration from Japan, Japan sent immigrants to its colonies instead.

As Japan lost its colonies after WWII, the Japanese islands once again faced overpopulation. Ehara (2007: 24) notes that 6.3 million Japanese nationals from former Japanese colonies returned to Japan in 1945. Immigration from Japan to South America began again during this period. Japanese immigration to Brazil resumed in 1953 with Japanese agents also developing Brazilian farmland (Fukui 2014: 70).

4-3. Japan as an Immigrant Destination Country

Currently, Japan is facing an aging population and overall depopulation. Japan's rapid economic growth in the 1960s required many factory workers. The Japanese economy quickly recovered from the first oil crisis in 1973, with the bubble economy boom

ながら，1970年代後半から出生率は低いままであった。

若年層の工場労働者の不足により，1989年に日本政府は移民法の緩和を行い（1990年に施行），ブラジルやペルー，その他の南アメリカ諸国からの日系三世を移民労働者として受け入れるようになった（DIR 2014：4-5）。

1990年以降，在日外国人の数は増加している（図4-1）。しかしながら，2015年現在，日本における外国人居住者の割合は低く，およそ220万人の外国籍の人々が日本に住んでいる。しかしながら，この図は日本に帰化した者を含んでいないため，実際の日本はより多様的である。

図4-1 在日外国人数と日本の総人口に占める外国籍の人々の割合の変化

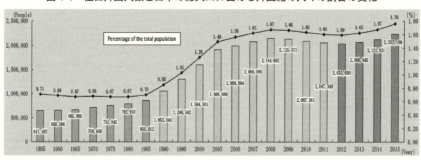

出典：Ministry of Justice（2017）*2016 Immigration Control*, p. 20

日本における外国人居住者のトレンドは変化している（図4-2）。1990年以降，在日コリアンの人口が減っている。在日ブラジル人の人口は2007年まで増えたが，2008年以降減少している。在日チャイニーズの人口は2010年まで増加したが，近年では停滞している。在日フィリピン人の数は徐々に増加しており，在日ベトナム人の数は急増した。

occurring in the latter part of the 1980s. On the other hand, since the latter part of the 1970s, the birth rate remained low.

Due to the shortage of younger factory workers, in 1989, the Japanese government relaxed immigration law (the law became official in 1990) and began receiving 3rd generation Japanese descendants (Nikkei Sansei) as immigrant workers from Brazil, Peru and other South American countries (DIR 2014: 4-5).

The number of foreign residents in Japan has increased since 1990 (Figure 4-1). As of 2015, however, the percentage of foreign residents in Japan remains low, with about, 2.2 million foreign nationals living in Japan. However, Japan is more diverse than this figure suggests, as this figure does not include those who have gained Japanese citizenship.

Figure 4-1 Changes in the number of foreign residents, and changes in the number of foreign residents as a percentage of the total population of Japan

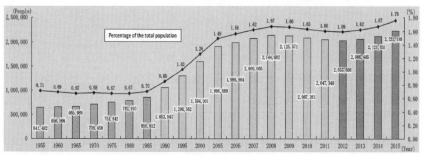

Source: Ministry of Justice (2017) *2016 Immigration Control*, p. 20

Trends in foreign residents in Japan are changing (Figure 4-2). The number of Korean residents in Japan has been decreasing since 1990. The number of Brazilian residents increased until 2007, but has been decreasing since 2008. The number of Chinese residents increased until 2010 but has recently stabilized. The number of immigrants from the Philippines has increased gradually, while the number of Vietnamese residents in Japan has grown rapidly.

図 4-2　主要国／地域別の外国人居住者数の変化

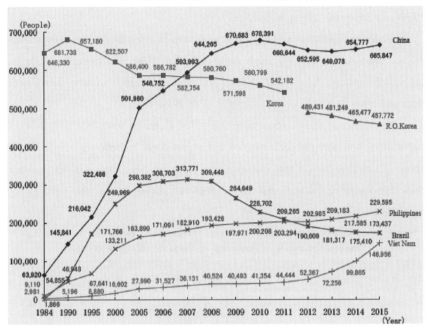

出典：Ministry of Justice（2017）*2016 Immigration Control*, p. 21

　1991 年のバブル経済の終焉にもかかわらず，日系人労働者の数は 1990 年代に増加した。バブル経済の終了まで，日本企業は終身雇用制度を発達させた。バブル崩壊後，小規模な製造業者はこの制度を維持できなくなり，短期の契約である派遣社員が広まっていった。丹野（2013：220-222）によると，多くの日系人労働者は小規模な工場で不安定な派遣制度で雇われた。

　2008 年のリーマンショックの後，日系人を含む多くの派遣社員は解雇（いわゆる派遣切り）された。その時，派遣社員の代わりに，いくつかの工場では，日本人や日系人よりも安く雇うことができる研修生・技能実習生を用いるようになった（丹野 2013：234-235）。自動車から弁当まで，多くの工場では技能実習生が事実上の労働者として働いている（樽松 2008：130-132）。

Figure 4-2 Changes in the number of foreign residents by major nationality/region

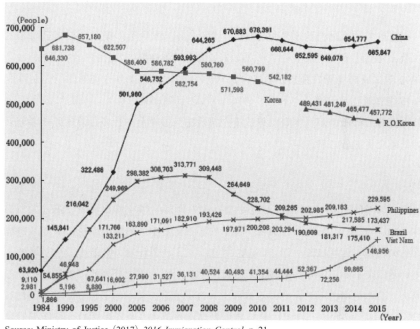

Source: Ministry of Justice (2017) *2016 Immigration Control*, p. 21

Despite the end of the bubble economy in 1991, the number of Nikkei workers increased during the 1990s. Until the end of bubble economy, Japanese companies developed a tenured employed system. After the bubble burst, smaller manufacturing companies could not retain this system and the use of short-term contract workers (Haken Shain) became more widespread. According to Tanno (2013: 220-222), many Nikkei workers were employed in small factories under this unstable contract scheme.

After the 2008 financial crisis (called "Lehman Shock" in Japanese), many contact workers, including the Nikkei were fired (referred to "Haken Giri" in Japanese). At this time, instead of contract workers, some factories began using international trainees (Kenshu-sei and/or Ginou Jisshu-sei), who can be paid less than local Japanese and Nikkei workers (Tanno 2013: 234-235). From factories

従来の外国人研修生制度は 1981 年に始まり，大企業の優れた技術を研修生に教えることが目的であった（外国人労働者問題 2009：211）。しかしながら，1990 年に研修場所の種類が広まり，1993 年には従来よりも長期間研修が可能な技能実習制度が導入された（外国人労働者問題 2009：211）。公的には実習生は労働者ではないが，実際は製造業，建設業，農業を含む多くの分野で事実上の低賃金労働者の供給源になっている。

　2010 年前後，日本における主要な外国人研修生は中国出身者であった（出井 2016：96-98）。しかしながら，日本の不景気と中国の経済成長により，中国からの技能実習生は減少している。近年，ベトナム出身の技能実習生が増加している（図4-3）。出井が示唆するには，ベトナムもまた経済的に成長しているため，日本で働こうとしているベトナム人労働者の質が低下しているとされる（出井 2016：98-100）。日本における労働環境が改善されなければ，技能実習生の供給源はさらに変わり続けるだろう。

　日本における高齢化は看護師やその他のケアワーカーの需要を高めている。EPA（Economic Partnership Agreement）制度により，日本政府はインドネシア（2008），フィリピン（2009），ベトナム（2014）年からの看護師・介護士研修生を受け入れている。看護師・介護士の研修は 3 年契約である。3 年後に引き続き日本で働きたい場合，日本の国家資格が必要である。2010 年には 3 人の外国人研修生が看護師試験に合格し，2012 年には 36 人が介護士試験に合格した（出井 2016：114-116）。

　外国人看護師・介護士の受け入れ制度にはいくつか問題がある。先進国において，ケアワーカーの不足は共通の問題である（柄谷 2016：50-55）。ケアワーカーの多くは発展途上国出身の女性であり，母国の家族と離れることが社会問

producing cars to those making lunchboxes, many factories now hire international trainees as de facto workers (Kurematsu 2008: 130-132).

When the former international trainee (Kenshu-sei) system began in 1981, its aim was to teach advanced technology to trainees at large companies (Gaikokujin Roudousha Mondai 2009: 211). However, the types of sites for this international internship scheme expanded in 1990, and a longer internship scheme (Ginou Jisshu) than that of the previous system was initiated in 1993 (Gaikokujin Roudousha Mondai 2009: 211). Officially, trainees are not workers; in actuality, however, they are currently de facto cheap sources of labor in various fields including, manufacturing, construction, and agriculture.

In about 2010, the majority of international trainees to Japan were from China (Idei 2016: 96-98). However, as Japan's economic depression and China's economic growth, the number of Chinese trainees has been decreasing. Currently, the number of trainees from Vietnam is increasing (Figure 4-3). Idei suggests that as Vietnam is also experiencing economic growth, the quality of Vietnamese workers who would like to work in Japan is decreasing (Idei 2016: 98-100). Without an improvement to working conditions in Japan, sources of international trainees will continue to change.

The aging of the Japanese population has also required nurses and other care workers. Under the EPA (Economic Partnership Agreement) scheme, the Japanese government has accepted international care trainees from Indonesia (since 2008), the Philippines (since 2009), and Vietnam (since 2014). Care trainees work under three year contracts. If they aim to continue to work in Japan after this three year period, Japanese national certificates are required. Three international nurses were successful in passing the Japanese certificate exam in 2010 and 36 international care workers were successful in 2012 (Idei 2016: 114-116).

This international care worker employment system has several problems. A shortage of care workers is a common problem in developed countries (Karatani 2016: 50-55). The majority of care workers are women from developing countries and

図4-3 主要国／地域別の来日技能実習生（入門レベル）の変化

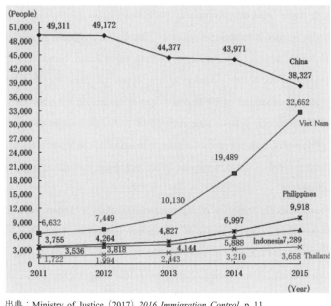

出典：Ministry of Justice（2017）*2016 Immigration Control*, p. 11

題になっている。カナダのケアギバー制度では，外国人ケアギバーが永住権を持ち，家族と暮らすことができる（出井 2016：123-124）。日本もケアワーカーの家族を受け入れることができるが，ケアワーカーは国家試験に合格しなければならず，研修期間中は家族と住むことができない（森 2008：25）。

ケアワーカーをめぐる他の種類の国際競争もある。たとえば，ドイツは日本と同じような研修制度を 2013 年に開始し，ベトナムやフィリピンから看護師を受け入れている（出井 2016：126-127）。この制度では口頭でのコミュニケーションのための国家試験が外国人看護師に求められている。日本の国家試験は筆記であり，一般の日本人が分からないような医療日本語で書かれている（出井 2016：127-128）。

Figure 4-3 Changes in the number of foreign nationals newly entering Japan with a "Technical Intern Training (basic level)" residence status, by major nationality/region

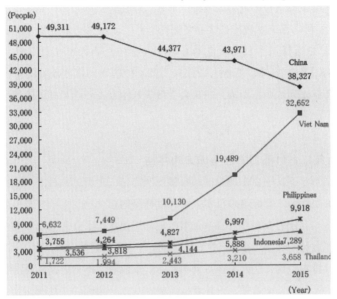

Source: Ministry of Justice (2017) *2016 Immigration Control*, p. 11

separation from families in home countries becomes a social issue. In Canada's "caregiver" scheme, international caregivers eventually obtain permanent residency status and live with their families (Idei 2016: 123-124). Japan also accepts care workers' families; however, care workers have to first-pass the national exam, and cannot stay with their family during the internship period (Mori 2008: 25).

Other types of international competitions for care workers also occur. For example, Germany began a similar care trainee system to that of Japan in 2013, and has been accepting nurses from Vietnam and the Philippines (Idei 2016: 126-127). This system requires international nurses to take a national exam for verbal communication. The national exam in Japan is written, and based on medical Japanese, which is difficult to understand for ordinary Japanese speakers (Idei 2016: 127-128).

工場労働者やケアワーカーに加え，日本の不景気にもかかわらず，その他の分野でも労働力が不足している。移住のためのポイントシステムは特定の移民労働者や起業家の選抜のために有効である。移民選抜のためのポイントシステムは1960年代にカナダ政府によって開発され，オーストラリアやニュージーランドなどでも採用された。日本も高度人材のためのポイントシステムを2012年に導入している。しかしながら，多くの国々が高度な技能を持った外国人労働者を求めているため，将来の受け入れ国となるための国際競争は激しい。

4-4. 近年における日本からの人的移動

古典的なプッシュ―プル理論は国際移民研究にて主流である。第二次世界大戦前と戦争が終わった直後の日本人移民は経済的なプッシュ―プルのケースと考えられる。しかしながら，日系企業の地球規模化により，異なった人的移動のトレンドも見られる。

図4-4は日本の外に住んでいる日本人で，永住者，あるいは長期滞在者を示している。外務省によると，永住者は，アメリカ合衆国のグリーンカード保持者のように，特定の国で永住を許可されている者を指す。長期滞在者は3か月以上の滞在者で，永住権を持っていない者を指す。これらのカテゴリーには，移住により，日本国籍を失った者は含まれていない。日本の総人口が減少しているのにもかかわらず，海外で暮らす日本人の数は増えている。

海外で生活している日本人のトレンドは変化している。表4-1によると，ブラジルは日本人居住者の数が1996年では2番目に多かったが，年々順位を落としている。表4-2によると，中国が2006年に日本人受け入れの2位になり，2016年でも2位を維持している。2016年にはオーストラリアの人気が高まり，3位になった。オーストラリアのように，タイの人気も高まり，2016年に4位になった。

In addition to factory workers and care workers, and despite Japan's economic depression, there remains a shortage of workers in other industries. A points system for immigration is effective in selecting specific immigrant workers and entrepreneurs. The points system for immigrant selection was originally developed by the government of Canada in the 1960s, and has been adopted by other countries such as Australia and New Zealand. Japan introduced a points system for high-skilled workers (Koudo Jinzai) in 2012. However, there is fierce competition between potential host countries, as many countries aim to recruit high-skilled foreign workers.

4-4. Current Issues in Human Mobility from Japan

Classical push-pull theory has dominated international migration research. Japanese migrants during the pre-WWII period, and just after WWII, were considered economic push-pull cases. However, due to the globalization of Japanese companies, different trends human mobility can also be observed.

Figure 4-4 shows the number of Japanese people living outside of Japan, who are categorized as permanent residents and long-term visitors. According to MOFA, permanent residents are defined as emigrants who have been permitted to live permanently in a particular country, such as green card holders in the US. Long-term visitors are defined as visitors who stay longer than 3 months but do not have permanent residency. These categories do not include those who lost Japanese citizenship due to emigration. Despite the continual decrease of the total population of Japan, the number of Japanese nationals living outside of Japan is increasing.

Trends in Japanese nationals outside of Japan are changing. According to Table 4-1, Brazil was the second largest receiver for Japanese nationals in 1996; however, this ranking is decreasing year by year. According to Table 4-2, China became the No. 2 receiver of Japanese nationals in 2006, and remains China No. 2 as of 2016; however, Australia is becoming a more popular destination and ranked No. 3 in 2016. Like Australia, Thailand is becoming more popular and ranked No. 4 in 2016.

Chapter 4   Migration Trends and Social Backgrounds of International Migrant Workers from and to Japan   73

図 4-4 日本からの長期滞在者と永住者（単位：人）

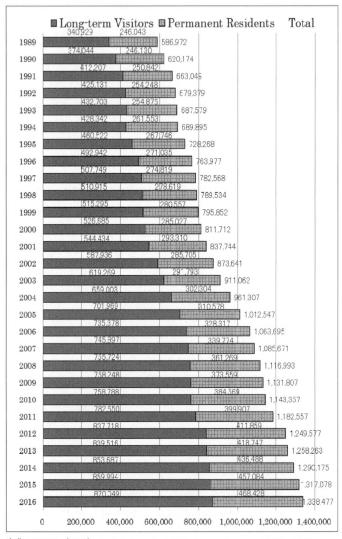

出典：MOFA（2017）*Annual Report of Statistics on Japanese Nationals Overseas*, MOFA, p. 20

Figure 4-4 Long-term Visitors and Permanent Residents from Japan
(Unit: Number of people)

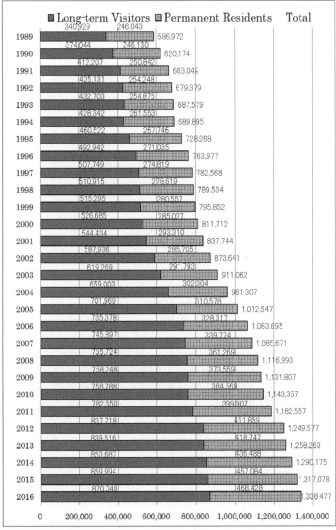

Source: MOFA (2017) *Annual Report of Statistics on Japanese Nationals Overseas*, MOFA, p. 20

表 4-1　1996 年の海外居住の日本人
（単位：人）

1	アメリカ合衆国	273,779
2	ブラジル	89,005
3	イギリス	55,372
4	カナダ	26,545
5	オーストラリア	25,688
6	シンガポール	25,355
7	香港	24,500
8	ドイツ	24,117
9	タイ	23,292
10	フランス	20,060

出典：MOFA 1997 web

表 4-2　2006 年の海外居住の日本人
（単位：人）

1	アメリカ合衆国	370,386
2	中国	125,417
3	ブラジル	64,802
4	イギリス	60,751
5	オーストラリア	59,285
6	カナダ	44,158
7	タイ	40,249
8	ドイツ	33,608
9	フランス	30,863
10	シンガポール	26,370

出典：MOFA 2007, p. 14

表 4-3　2016 年の海外居住の日本人
（単位：人）

1	アメリカ合衆国	421,665
2	中国	128,111
3	オーストラリア	92,637
4	タイ	70,337
5	カナダ	70,174
6	イギリス	64,968
7	ブラジル	53,400
8	ドイツ	44,027
9	フランス	41,641
10	韓国	38,045

出典：MOFA 2017, p. 28

　アメリカ合衆国は日本からの移民受け入れの長い歴史を持っている。戦前の日系移民の子孫の多くはアメリカの市民権を持っている。日本国籍を持っているアメリカ居住者はアメリカ合衆国における日本企業で働くもの，研究者，学生など，多様である。20 世紀の間，ブラジルは日本からの移民の最大の受け

Table 4-1 Japanese Nationals Overseas, 1996 (Unit: Number of people)

1	USA	273,779
2	Brazil	89,005
3	UK	55,372
4	Canada	26,545
5	Australia	25,688
6	Singapore	25,355
7	Hong Kong	24,500
8	Germany	24,117
9	Thailand	23,292
10	France	20,060

Source: MOFA 1997 web

Table 4-2 Japanese Nationals Overseas, 2006 (Unit: Number of people)

1	USA	370,386
2	China	125,417
3	Brazil	64,802
4	UK	60,751
5	Australia	59,285
6	Canada	44,158
7	Thailand	40,249
8	Germany	33,608
9	France	30,863
10	Singapore	26,370

Source: MOFA 2007, p. 14

Table 4-3 Japanese Nationals Overseas, 2016 (Unit: Number of people)

1	USA	421,665
2	China	128,111
3	Australia	92,637
4	Thailand	70,337
5	Canada	70,174
6	UK	64,968
7	Brazil	53,400
8	Germany	44,027
9	France	41,641
10	S. Korea	38,045

Source: MOFA 2017, p. 28

The United States has a long history as a Japanese immigrant receiver country. Many descendants of pre-WWII Japanese immigrants are American citizens. Japanese nationals in the USA are a diverse group of workers in Japanese companies in the US, researchers, and students. During the 20th century, Brazil was the largest emigration

入れ国であり，多くの日系一世と幾人かの日系二世は日本国籍を持っていた。

　他の国々は歴史的には日本国籍者にとって主要な受け入れ国ではなかったが，現在ではこれらの国々に進出した日系企業が多くの日本人を雇用している。中国は，海外での日系企業が日本人労働者を雇用し，増加している典型的な例である。バブル経済崩壊後の日本では，「ABROADERS」や「Working Abroad」，「World Post」，「Kamome Asia」など，日本人向けの海外求人サイトが発展し，日本から中国やその他のアジア諸国への日本人労働者をリクルートしている。

　日本国籍者はオーストラリアやヨーロッパ諸国へ学生としても渡航している。留学の主な目的は公的には学ぶことである。しかしながら，日本の高等教育でのコストにより，奨学金を提供し，授業料を免除し，労働を許可し，卒業後の仕事の機会に恵まれた国々は若い世代の日本人にとって魅力的になった。

4-5. 海外における日本国籍者のジェンダーの差異

　プッシュ―プルやグローバル化のアプローチに加え，ワークライフバランスのアプローチもまた徐々に知られるようになった。中澤他（2008）はシンガポールにおける日本人女性について調査している。日本人女性にとって，国際的な就労場所のトレンドは 1990 年代の香港，2000 年代の上海，そしてシンガポールと変化してきた。中澤他が 2006 年にシンガポールで働く 26 人の日本人女性にインタビューしたとき，19 人は大卒であった。

　中澤による海外で働く日本人女性のケーススタディでは，「自主的な駐在員」としての女性労働者を示唆している（中澤　2016：80-81）。日本企業の海外支店で多くの女性が働いているのにもかかわらず，彼女らの傾向は日本の本社から送られてきた日本人労働者と異なっている。幾人かの女性労働者はまた，い

country from Japan and many of the 1st generation of Japanese immigrants (Nikkei Issei) and some of the 2nd generation of Japanese descendants (Nikkei Nisei) have retained Japanese citizenship.

Other countries have historically constituted non-major immigration countries for Japanese national; however, Japanese companies in these countries are now hiring many of Japanese workers. China is a typical case that reflects growing number of the Japanese workers in Japanese companies abroad. After the burst of the bubble economy in Japan, job-hunting websites for Japanese people, such as "ABROADERS," "Working Abroad", "World Post", and "Kamome Asia," emerged especially to recruit Japanese workers to China and other Asian countries.

Japanese nationals are travelling as students to Australia and other European countries. The primary purpose of study abroad is officially education. However, due to the cost of Japanese higher education, countries which offer scholarships, tuition exemptions, work permissions, and job opportunities after graduation have become attractive for younger generations of Japanese nationals.

4-5. Gender Differentiations of Japanese Citizens outside of Japan

In addition to the push-pull and globalization approaches, newer work-life balance approaches are gradually becoming more common. Nakazawa et al. (2008) have conducted a study of Japanese women working in Singapore. For Japanese women, international work destination trends have shifted from Hong Kong (1990s), Shanghai (2000s) and Singapore (Nakazawa et al. 2008: 97). When Nakazawa et al. interviewed 26 Japanese women working in Singapore in 2006, 19 of their subjects were university graduated.

Nakazawa's case studies of Japanese women working outside of Japan suggest that some of these women work as "self-initiated expatriates" (Nakazawa 2016: 80-81). Even though many of the women work in branch offices of Japanese companies, their attitudes are different from those of Japanese workers send from the

くつかの国々を移動している。

　ワークライフバランスの研究は地理学者や文化人類学者，社会学者などにより，質的調査が行われてきた。1990年代の時点では，外務省によって公開された海外雇用の日本人の統計情報が十分ではなかったため，量的なアプローチは困難であった。しかしながら，研究機関や個人の研究者によるサンプル調査が2000年代に見られるようになった。

　労働政策研究・研修機構（JILPT 2008：28）によると，2006年における日本の会社から海外に派遣された日本人労働者の98.2％は男性であった（N＝1,565人）。JILPT（2016：50）による類似したサンプル調査によると，観光産業を除き，2010年から2015年まで日本企業から海外へ派遣された日本人労働者のほとんどが男性だった（N＝15社）。白木（2012：10）によると，2012年に日本から中国へ派遣された98.9％（N＝528人），ASEANへ派遣された98.8％（N＝516人）が男性であった。

　これらの性差を用い，日本企業によって現地職員として雇用された日本人女性の数を推計したいくつかの研究がある。細萱他（2017：46-48）は夫を同伴していない日本人女性に注目し，海外で自主的に駐在している日本人の数を推計した。同様の手法で，丹羽他（2016：216-220）はデュッセルドルフにて現地で雇われ，働いている日本人の数を推計している。

　アメリカ合衆国や中国，ヨーロッパと比べると，オーストラリアにおける日系企業の数は少ない。しかしながら，先述のように，オーストラリアは海外居住の日本人にとって第3位の人気がある。エスノグラフィーの手法を使い，藤岡（2017：460-464）はオーストラリアにてワーキングホリデー・ビザを用いて滞在する非エリートの日本人を調査した。彼は43人の男性と41人の女性を2007年から2009年の間にオーストラリア，主にメルボルンで調査した。男性の場合，43人中14人が大卒であった。女性の場合，41人中17人が大卒，12人が短大卒であった。中澤がシンガポールで調査した結果と同様に，藤岡の調査から，海外で働いている日本人女性は高学歴の者が多いことが分かる。

company headquarters in Japan. Some female workers also move to several countries.

Work‒life balance research is usually undertaken by geographers, anthropologists and sociologists and is qualitatively oriented. As statistics offered by Ministry of Foreign Affairs do not offer enough information about Japanese nationals hired abroad in 1990s, a quantity‒based approach was difficult. However, sample research by from research institutes and individual researchers has been available since the 2000s.

According to the Japan Institute for Labour Policy and Training (JILPT 2008: 28), 98.2% of Japanese workers outside of Japan sent by Japanese companies in 2006 were male (N=1,565 people). Similar sample research by JILPT (2016: 50) also shows that, except in the tourism industry, the majority of Japanese workers sent abroad by Japanese companies in 2010 to 2015 were male (N=15 companies). According to Shiraki (2012: 10), 98.9% of executives sent from Japan to China (N=528 people) and 98.8 % to ASEAN (N=516) in 2012 were male.

Using these gender differentiations, some researchers estimate the number of Japanese women workers who were hired by Japanese companies but as local workers. Hosogaya et al. (2017: 46‒48) focused on the number of Japanese women not accompanied by a husband and estimated the number of Japanese self‒initiated expatriates outside of Japan. Using a similar method, Niwa et al. (2016: 216‒220) tried to estimate the number of locally hired Japanese workers in Dusseldorf.

Compared to the US, China and Europe, the number of Japanese companies in Australia is relatively small. However, as mentioned above, Australia is currently the 3rd most popular destination for Japanese nationals outside of Japan. Using an ethnographic approach, Fujioka (2017: 460‒464) has studied young non‒elite Japanese people on a working holiday visa in Australia. He interviewed 43 men and 41 women in Australia from 2007 to 2009, mainly in Melbourne. In the case of men, 14 out of 43 interviewees were university graduates. Out of 41, 17 of the women were university graduates and 12 were junior college graduates. As indicated by Nakazawa's research in Singapore, Fujioka shows that Japanese women working outside of Japan are highly

さらに，藤岡（2017：287）によると，これらの非エリートの日本人は手ごろな価格で日本関係のサービスを提供するため，海外居住のエリート層の多くの日本人にとって，日本人ワーキングホリデー参加者は貢献している。全員ではないが，幾人かの海外居住の日本人エリートは赴任時に十分な現地語の能力を有していない。そのため，非エリートの日本人労働者で現地の知識がある者は役に立つ。しかしながら，大抵の場合，非エリートの日本人は現地の人々よりは言語スキルが低いため，非エリートの日本人は海外で日本関係の仕事に就くことが多い。藤岡（2017：418）によると，日本の本社から送られてきた管理職がこの労働市場ピラミッドの頂点に立ち，海外支店で雇われた日本人が中間層，サポート・スタッフのワーキングホリデー参加者が底辺に位置する。

若者向けに特化した労働ビザ制度はいくつかある。イギリスの「Youth Mobility Scheme」では，日本人は 2 年間滞在することができる。オーストラリアのワーキングホリデー・ビザ制度は 1 年間滞在できるが，地方での就労経験のあるものは 2 回目のワーキングホリデー・ビザを申請することができる。ニュージーランドでのワーキングホリデー・ビザも 1 年間だが，延長ビザやほかのタイプの就労可能なビザを申請できる。

日本における派遣労働は大抵の場合 1 年までの契約なので，これらのワーキングホリデー制度は外国へ入国するために試みてみる価値がある。藤岡（2017：258-261）は，日本において困難な仕事や長時間労働を強いる会社，いわゆるブラック企業についてもまた述べている。日本では非エリート層のキャリア上昇が困難であるため，ワーキングホリデーは希望のない生活をリセットするための道具として用いられている。海外の大学院に進学することは一般の日本人にとって大きなチャレンジであるが，ワーキングホリデーと英語学校の組み合わせはより現実的な選択である。

先述のように，日本人女性が海外で生活し，働いていることに関する研究は

82　第 4 章　日本から／への労働者の移動のトレンドと社会背景

educated.

Fujioka (2017: 287) also suggests that Japanese working holiday makers are contributing to the numbers of Japanese elites outside of Japan, because non-elite Japanese nationals offer services related to Japan at reasonable prices. Some (though not all) Japanese elites outside of Japan do not possess sufficient local language proficiency upon arrival. Non-elite Japanese workers who possess local knowledge thus prove useful. Yet, as non-elite Japanese workers typically have fewer language skills compared to locals in destination countries, due to competition for work with locals, the majority of workplaces for non-elite Japanese workers abroad are Japan-related. According to Fujioka (2017: 418), Japanese executives sent from headquarters in Japan are at top of this labor pyramid, while Japanese workers hired by local branches of Japanese companies are in the middle, and working holiday Japanese nationals working as support stuff are at bottom in the labor market.

There are a number of youth-specific working visa schemes. Under the UK's "Youth Mobility Scheme," Japanese people can stay in 2 years. The Australian working holiday visa scheme allows stays of up to one year; however, those with experience working in rural areas can apply for a second working holiday visa. Working holiday visas to New Zealand allow stays of up to 1 year; however, potential workers can apply for an extended visa and/or different types of work visas.

As the Haken contract in Japan is usually up to 1 year long, these working holiday schemes are worth trying as the basis for entrance to foreign countries. Fujioka (2017: 258-261) also describes companies who impose difficult work and longer working hours (called "Black Kigyou" in Japanese) in Japan. As career advancement is not easy for non-elites in Japan, a working holiday is used as a tool to reset a hopeless life. Admittance to a postgraduate school outside of Japan is a major challenge for ordinary Japanese citizens; however, a combination of a working holiday and an English language school is a much more realistic option.

The outstanding living and working trends of Japanese women have been

たくさんある。2015年からは，外務省もまた海外居住の日本人に関する統計データに年齢とジェンダーに関する項目を加えるようになった。図4-5は外務省の新しいバージョンの2016年における海外居住の日本人の年齢・ジェンダー別データである。19歳以下のデータを除き，ここからは年齢別の男女差が見られる。2016年10月1日現在，20歳から49歳までの海外居住者は，女性が男性を上回っている。20代の場合は留学も考えられるが，30代と40代は就労が必要であろう。日本国内における女性の就労率は30代と40代が低いが，海外での傾向は反対である。

図4-5　年齢とジェンダー別の海外居住の日本人
（2016年総計）（単位：人）

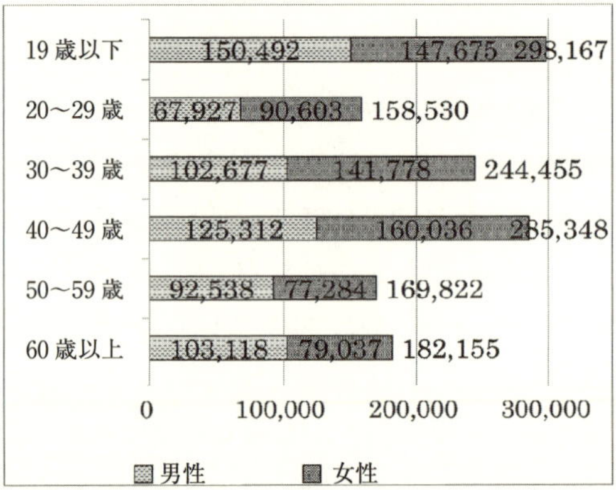

年齢	男性	女性	合計
19歳以下	150,492	147,675	298,167
20〜29歳	67,927	90,603	158,530
30〜39歳	102,677	141,778	244,455
40〜49歳	125,312	160,036	285,348
50〜59歳	92,538	77,284	169,822
60歳以上	103,118	79,037	182,155

出典：MOFA（2017）*Annual Report of Statistics on Japanese Nationals Overseas*, MOFA, p. 26

　このジェンダー別の差異は，いくつかの国々で特徴的である。図4-6は外務省の統計から作成したものであるが，2016年にアメリカ合衆国に居住している日本人を年齢とジェンダー別に分けたものである。アメリカ合衆国では，19歳以下を除き，日本人女性は男性よりも多い。このデータによると，労働年齢の女性の数は多く，40歳から49歳までが突出している。

thoroughly examined, as noted above. Since 2015, MOFA added age and gender data to its statistics on Japanese citizens overseas. Figure 4-5 was created from this newer version of the MOFA statistics and shows the number of Japanese nationals overseas in 2016, divided by age and gender. With the exception of those less than 19 years old, differentiation between men and women by age is now available. As of October 1, 2016, there were more women aged 20 to 49 abroad than men. People in their 20s are able to stay abroad as students; however, those in their 30s and 40s need jobs. While the percentage of women workers within Japan is low — in 30s and 40s — the overseas pattern is the inverse.

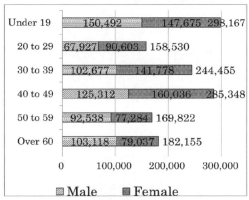

Figure 4-5 Japanese nationals overseas by age and gender (Totals, 2016) (Unit: People)

Source: MOFA (2017) *Annual Report of Statistics on Japanese Nationals Overseas*, MOFA, p. 26

This gender disparity can be found to a significant degree in some countries. Figure 4-6, created from the MOFA statistics, shows the number of Japanese nationals in the US in 2016, divided by age and gender. In the US, with the exception of those under 19 years old, the number of Japanese women is larger than men. As with the overall data, the number of women of working age is large and for those aged between 40 and 49, outstanding.

図 4-6 年齢とジェンダー別の海外居住の日本人（アメリカ合衆国 2016 年）（単位：人）

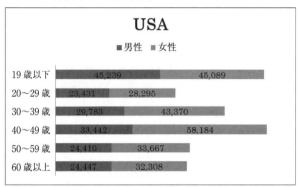

出典：Made from data from the MOFA（2017）*Annual Report of Statistics on Japanese Nationals Overseas*, MOFA, p. 61

図 4-7 はオーストラリアのケースである。アメリカ合衆国と同様に，19 歳以下を除くと，女性の数が男性を上回っている。しかしながら，いくつかの違いがある。日本女性の割合はオーストラリアの方がアメリカ合衆国よりも高い。さらに，ピークの年齢が 30-39 歳であり，アメリカ合衆国よりも若い。20-29

図 4-7 年齢・ジェンダー別の海外居住の日本人（オーストラリア 2016 年）（単位：人）

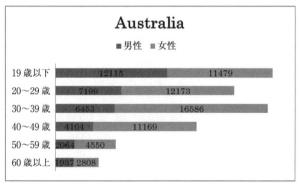

出典：Made from data from the MOFA（2017）*Annual Report of Statistics on Japanese Nationals Overseas*, MOFA, p. 77

86　第 4 章　日本から／への労働者の移動のトレンドと社会背景

Figure 4-6 Japanese nationals overseas by age and gender
(USA 2016) (Unit: Number of people)

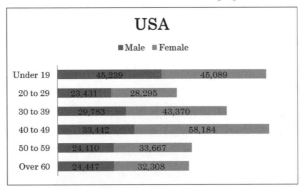

Source: Made from data from the MOFA (2017) *Annual Report of Statistics on Japanese Nationals Overseas*, MOFA, p. 61

Figure 4-7 is represents the case of Australia. As in the USA, the number of women is larger than men, with the exception of those under 19 years old. However, there are some differences. The percentage of Japanese women in Australia is higher than in the US. In addition, the peak age is between 30 and 39 years old and thus

Figure 4-7 Japanese nationals overseas by age and gender
(Australia 2016) (Unit: Number of people)

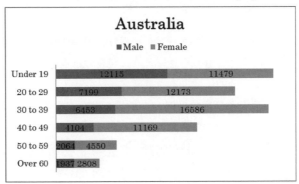

Source: Made from data from the MOFA (2017) *Annual Report of Statistics on Japanese Nationals Overseas*, MOFA, p. 77

歳の割合が高い理由の一つは，30歳未満の日本人に対してオーストラリアがワーキングホリデー・ビザを与えていることが考えられる。

　いくつかの場合，長期滞在者は地元の配偶者を有している。ワーキングホリデーは1～2年滞在するのに対し，日本国籍者（特に女性）は，地元の配偶者を有していれば，特定の国で長期間滞在できる。子供のためのガーディアン・ビザを有している国々では，（両）親もまた長期間滞在できる。日本国籍の場合，日本企業によって赴任した男性労働者は大抵の場合日本に帰国するが，女性の場合は子供と一緒に外国に残る場合もある。統計的な研究ではないが，濱野（2014：147）が2007～2008年にオーストラリアでの国際結婚を調査した時，28人の永住権被験者のうち，23人がオーストラリア人の夫を有していた。データは十分ではないが，先行研究から推測すると，海外で働く日本人女性に関して以下の仮説が考えられる：

　　1．女性にとって日本よりも海外のほうが働く機会に恵まれている。
　　2．女性にとって日本の労働状況は望ましくない。
　　3．日本における子育ては労働年齢の女性にとって望ましくない。
　　4．ある外国の国々の生活は女性にとってフレンドリーであり，魅力的である。

第4章のおわりに

　すでに述べてきたように，明治時代，日本は移民の送り出し国であった。しかしながら，人口減少と労働力不足により，現在の日本は事実上の外国人労働者を受け入れている。公的には日本は高度人材を受け入れているが，事実上，製造業，建築業，農業，福祉の分野での労働者が存在する。1990年代は南米出身の日系人が海外からの主な労働力流入であった。近年では，東アジアや東南アジアからの外国人研修生・技能実習生が事実上の労働者として働いている。

　しかしながら，海外で暮らす日本人の数は増加している。グローバリゼー

younger than that in the US. One of the reasons for a higher percentage of Japanese nationals in Australia between 20 and 29 is that Australia offers working holiday visas for Japanese nationals under 30.

In some cases, long-term visitors are able to stay with a local spouse. While a working holiday is 1 or maximum 2 years long, Japanese nationals (primarily women) who have a local spouse can stay longer in a particular country. In countries that offer a guardian visa for children, parent(s) can also stay longer. In the case of Japanese nationals, male workers sent by Japanese companies typically move back to Japan; however, some women stay in the foreign country with their children. While not statistical research, in a study of Japanese intermarriage in Australia between 2007 and 2008, Hamano (2014: 147) found that 23 Japanese women out of 28 permanent residents had an Australian husband. While there is not enough data, from previous research, the following hypothesis about Japanese women aiming to work abroad may be made:

1. There are greater opportunities for work abroad than in Japan for women.
2. Working conditions in Japan is not suitable for women.
3. Child care in Japan does not suit women of working age.
4. The ways of life of certain foreign countries are friendly and attractive for women.

Conclusion of Chapter 4

As noted above, during the Meiji period, Japan was an emigration country. However, due to depopulation and a shortage of workers, Japan now requires many de facto foreign workers. Officially, Japan is accepting high-skilled workers; however, de facto manufacturing, construction, agricultural, and care workers also exist. During the 1990s, the major influx of workers from abroad was constituted by Japanese descendants from South America. Currently, de facto workers are made up of international trainees from East and South East Asia.

Yet, the number of Japanese nationals outside of Japan continues to increase. Due

ションにより，日本企業の多くは海外に支社を作っている。しかしながら，国際移動にはジェンダーの差異が見られる。日本の企業は大抵の場合日本から海外支社に男性の管理職を送り，日本人女性の多くは海外支社に現地職員として採用されている。さらに，ニュージーランドやオーストラリアなどのいくつかの国々では，若年層向けに特化した労働ビザがある。このような国々では，若い日本人，特に女性を高い割合で受け入れている。

参考文献

ABROADERS（n.d.）"Homepage", https://career.abroaders.jp/search/PREF_0001，2017 年 9 月 1 日閲覧

大和総研［DIR］（2014）『日本の移民問題を考える』DIR

江原裕美（2007）「日本における外国人受け入れと子どもの教育」『帝京大学外国語外国文学論集』14，17-44

藤岡伸明（2017）『若年ノンエリート層と雇用・労働システムの国際化』福村出版

福井千鶴（2003）「南米移民と日系社会」『地域政策研究』5(3)，35-52

福井千鶴（2014）「100 年が経過する南米日系人社会の形成と変容」『国際関係研究』34(2)，67-76

外国人労働者問題とこれからの日本編集委員会編（2009）『研修生という名の奴隷労働』花伝社

濱野健（2014）『日本人女性の国際結婚と海外移住』明石書店

細萱伸子，新井範子，竹内（野木森）明香（2017）「女性のグローバルキャリア形成に関する意思決定とジョブ・サーチ行動」『上智経済論集』62(1/2)，45-60

出井康博（2016）『ルポ　ニッポン絶望工場』講談社

飯田耕二郎（1994）「ハワイにおける日本人の居住地・出身地分布」『人文地理』46(1)，85-102

JILPT（労働政策研究・研修機構）（2008）『第 7 回海外派遣勤務者の職業と生活に関する調査結果』JILEP

JILPT（労働政策研究・研修機構）（2016）『企業における転勤の実態に関するヒアリング調査』JILEP

Kamome Asia（n.d.）"Homepage", http://kamome.asia/，2017 年 9 月 1 日閲覧

to globalization, many Japanese companies are branching out internationally. There is, however, gender differentiation within this international migration. Japanese companies typically send male executives from Japan to overseas branches and many Japanese women are hired in these branches as local workers. Additionally, some countries, including the New Zealand and Australia, offer special working visa schemes for younger people. These countries have a higher percentage of young Japanese workers, especially women.

References

ABROADERS（n. d.）"Homepage", https: //career. abroaders. jp/search/PREF_0001, Accessed September 1, 2017

Daiwa Institute of Research［DIR］（2014）*Nihon no Imin Mondai wo Kangaeru*, DIR

EHARA Hiromi（2007）"Accepting and Educating Foreigners in Japan" *Teikyou Daigaku Gaikokugo Gaikokubungaku Ronshu*, 14, 17-44

FUJIOKA Nobuaki（2017）*Jakunen Non-elite Sou to Koyou/Roudou System no Kokusaika*, Fukumura Shuppan

FUKUI Chizuru（2003）"Nanbei Imin to Nikkei Shakai", *Chiiki Seisaku Kenkyu*, 5（3）, 35-52

FUKUI Chizuru（2014）"100 Nen ga Keika suru Nanbei Nikkeijin Shakai no Keisei to Henyou", *Kokusai Kankei Kenkyu*, 34（2）, 67-76

Gaikokujin Roudousha Mondai to Korekara no Nihon Henshu Iinkai ed.（2009）*Kenshu-sei to iu na no Dorei Roudou*, Kadensha

HAMANO Takeshi（2014）*Nihonjin Josei no Kokusai Kekkon to Kaigai Iju*, Akashi Shoten

HOSOGAYA Nobuko, ARAI Noriko, TAKEUCHI（NOGIMORI）Asuka（2017）"Josei no Global Career Keisei ni Kansuru Ishi Kettei to Job Search Koudou", *Jouchi Keizai Ronshu*, 62（1/2）, 45-60

IDEI Yasuhiro（2016）*Rupo Nippon Zetsubou Koujou*, Koudansha

IIDA Kojiro（1994）" A Study of Residence and Birthplace of the Japanese in Hawaii", *Jinbun Chiri*, 46（1）, 85-102

JILPT（Japan Institute for Labour Policy and Training）（2008）*Dai 7 Kai Kaigai Haken Kinmusha no Shokugyou to Seikatsu ni kansuru Chousa Kekka*, JILEP

JILPT（Japan Institute for Labour Policy and Training）（2016）*Kigyou ni okeru Tenkin no Jittai ni Kansuru Hearing Chousa*, JILEP

Kamome Asia（n.d.）"Homepage", http://kamome.asia/, Accessed September 1, 2017

柄谷理恵子（2016）『移動と生存』岩波書店

榑松佐一（2008）『トヨタの足元で』風媒社

Ministry of Foreign Affairs（1997）"Annual Report of Statistics on Japanese Nationals Overseas", http://www.mofa.go.jp/mofaj/toko/page22_000043.html, 2017 年 9 月 1 日閲覧

Ministry of Foreign Affairs（2007）*Annual Report of Statistics on Japanese Nationals Overseas*, MOFA

Ministry of Foreign Affairs（2017）*Annual Report of Statistics on Japanese Nationals Overseas*, MOFA

Ministry of Justice（2017）*2016 Immigration Control*, Ministry of Justice

森恭子（2008）「介護分野への外国人労働者の受入れについての検討」『人間科学研究』30, 21-29

中澤高志（2016）「グローバル中間層の国際移動と日本人の海外就職」『明治大学教養論集』512, 67-95

中澤高志，由井義通，神谷浩夫，木下礼子，武田祐子（2008）「海外就職の経験と日本人としてのアイデンティティ」『地理学評論』81(3)，95-120

丹羽孝仁，中川聡史，テーレン・ティモ（2016）「変容する海外で働く日本人」『埼玉大学紀要（教養学部）』51(2)，205-222

白木三秀（2012）「日本企業のグローバリゼーションと海外派遣者」『日本労働研究雑誌』623, 5-16

丹野清人（2013）『国籍の境界を考える』吉田書店

植村正治（2008）「明治前期お雇い外国人の給与」『流通科学大学論集　流通・経営編』21(1)，1-24

Working Abroad（n.d.）"Homepage", https://workingabroad.daijob.com/, 2017 年 9 月 1 日閲覧

World Post（n.d.）"Homepage", http://www.worldpost.jp/, 2017 年 9 月 1 日閲覧

KARATANI Rieko (2016) *Idou to Seizon*, Iwanami Shoten

KUREMATSU Saichi (2008) *Toyota no Ashimoto de*, Fubaisha

Ministry of Foreign Affairs (1997) "Annual Report of Statistics on Japanese Nationals Overseas", http://www.mofa.go.jp/mofaj/toko/page22_000043.html, Accessed September 1, 2017

Ministry of Foreign Affairs (2007) *Annual Report of Statistics on Japanese Nationals Overseas*, MOFA

Ministry of Foreign Affairs (2017) *Annual Report of Statistics on Japanese Nationals Overseas*, MOFA

Ministry of Justice (2017) *2016 Immigration Control*, Ministry of Justice

MORI Kyoko (2008) "Foreign migrant workers in Japan: The acceptance of nursing-caregivers for the elderly", *Ningen Kagaku Kenkyu*, 30, 21-29

NAKAZAWA Takashi (2016) "Global Chukansou no Kokusai Idou to Nihonjin no Kaigai Shushoku", *Meiji Daigaku Kyouyou Ronshu*, 512, 67-95

NAKAZAWA Takashi, YUI Yoshimichi, KAMIYA Hiroo, KINOSHITA Reiko, TAKEDA Yuko (2008) "Experience of International Migration and Japanese Identity",*Chirigaku Hyouron*, 81 (3), 95-120

NIWA Takahito, NAKAGAWA Satoshi, THELEN Timo (2016) "Changing of Japanese Working Abroad", *Saitama Daigaku Kiyou (Kyouyou Gakubu)*, 51(2), 205-222

SHIRAKI Mitsuhide (2012) "Nihon Kigyou no Globalization to Kaigai Hakensha", *Nihon Roudou Kenkyu Zassi*, 623, 5-16

TANNO Kiyoto (2013) *Kokuseki no Kyoukai wo Kangaeru*, Yoshida Shoten

UEMURA Shoji (2008) "Salaries of Oyatoi (Japan's Foreign Employees) in Early Meiji", *Ryutsu Kagaku Daigaku Ronshu Ryutsu Keiei Hen*, 21(1), 1-24

Working Abroad (n.d.) "Homepage", https://workingabroad.daijob.com/, Accessed September 1, 2017

World Post (n.d.) "Homepage", http://www.worldpost.jp/, Accessed September 1, 2017

第5章

国際学生移動の小史

第5章のはじめに

移民や観光のように，学生の教育的な移動も国内，国際に分けられる。さらに，留学生の移動はインバウンドとアウトバウンドに分けられる。さらに，これらのカテゴリーのトレンドもまた歴史的に変わってきた。たとえば，ルネッサンス期のイングランドは学生の送り出し国で，グランドツアーが目立つ存在であった。しかしながら，今日ではイギリスは有力な留学生の受け入れ国になっている。

5-1. 第5章の方法論

国際的な学生移動を歴史的に調べるため，文献を時系列に調べていくことは必要不可欠である。文献研究から，教育目的の人的移動の歴史から興味深いケースを見つけていくことは重要である。たとえば，1919年に設立されたIIE（国際教育協会）は1920年から雑誌を発行しており，これらの文献は歴史的なアプローチで研究するために役立つ資料である（IIE 1920：1）。

送り出し側，受け入れ側の両方から，留学に関する資料は集められている。社会学者は留学生へのインタビュー調査を行うが，現在どのような問題が起こっているのか調べるために重要な手法である。文化人類学では長期間の参与観察が特定のコミュニティを深く分析する上で効果的である。しかしながら，文献を比較分析することは要約するために必要であり，現在のケーススタディを一般化するために有効である。

94

Chapter 5

A Brief History of International Student Mobility

Introduction of Chapter 5

As with migration and tourism, student educational mobility can be categorized as either internal or international. International student mobility can be further categorized as inbound or outbound. In addition, the trends in these categories have historically changed. For example, England during the Renaissance Period was a student sender and the grand tour was one of its outstanding features. However, the UK is a major international student receiver now.

5-1. Methodology of Chapter 5

To study the history of the international student mobility, a chronological review of the literature is essential. The methodology of literature review, by which interesting cases from the history of educational human mobility might be found, is important. For example, the Institute of International Education (IIE), established in 1919, has been publishing its bulletins since 1920, and these documents are becoming useful research materials for our historical approach (IIE 1920: 1).

Written documents related to study abroad have been collected both on the sender's and the receiver's ends. As with sociologists, case studies that involve interviewing international students are another important way to learn about the issues as they currently exist. And, as in anthropology, long-term observations with participation are also effective ways to analyze a particular community in depth. However, a comparative literature review is still essential to fully summarize and make

さらに，量的に留学を研究することは，質的調査と同じぐらい重要である。
フランス，ドイツ，イギリスは近代において留学生の受け入れ国として知られ
るようになった。他方，アメリカ合衆国は第二次世界大戦後さらに多くの留学
生を受け入れるようになり，カナダやオーストラリア，ニュージーランドも急
激に留学生の数を増やしている。これらのトレンドを理解するためには，統計
的な研究が欠かせない。

統計的なアプローチのため，学生ビザの数が数量調査の基本であった。限定
された方法ではあるが，いくつかの短期交換プログラムや短期語学プログラム
では学生ビザが求められない。この場合，他のデータが求められるが，
ELICOS（留学生のための集中英語コース）の一員である English Australia は 1996
年から ELICOS で学ぶ学生の数を調査している（English Australia 2009：1）。さ
らに，オーストラリア国際教育（AEI）は ELICOS の市場を調べており（AEI
2009a：1，AEI 2009b：1），オーストラリア政府観光局（TA）は 2007 年にスタ
ディ・ツーリズム・レポートを出版している（Tourism Australia 2007：1-3）。

シンガポール，マレーシア，韓国，日本などのアジアのいくつかの国々もま
た統計的なアプローチを行うようになった。日本では文部科学省や日本学生支
援機構（JASSO）などの政府あるいは政府関連機関が留学生のための日本の大
学案内を出版し，留学生の数の統計調査も行うようになった。これらの案内書
や統計は現在の教育問題について基礎的な調査をする上で有効的である。日本
にとって国際教育が重要な産業になったため，いくつかの学術会社もまた情報
書籍や雑誌を出版している。

5-2. 古代と中世における学生移動

人的な移動は心理的，文化的，政治的に常に社会を変えてきた。行商は経済

useful generalizations of current case studies.

In addition, the quantity of study abroad is as important as the matter of quality. France, Germany and the UK have become widely known as student receivers during the modern era. On the other hand, the USA has welcomed many more international students since the end of WWII, and Canada, Australia and New Zealand are also rapidly increasing their numbers. Statistical research is essential to understanding these trends.

For the statistical approach, the number of student visas was a primary way of determining numbers. This is of limited use, though, as some short exchange programs and short language learning programs do not require a student visa. There are other sources of data, however, English Australia, a group of ELICOS (English Language Intensive Courses for Overseas Students) institutions, has been surveying the total number of ELICOS students since 1996 (English Australia 2009: 1). In addition, Australian Education International (AEI) has been surveying the ELICOS market (AEI 2009a: 1, AEI 2009b: 1), and Tourism Australia (TA) published its Study Tourism Report in 2007 (Tourism Australia 2007: 1-3).

Some Asian countries, such as Singapore, Malaysia, South Korea and Japan, are also following the statistical approach. In Japan, educational organizations established by or in cooperation with the government, such as MEXT (Ministry of Education, Culture, Sports, Science and Technology) and JASSO (Japan Student Service Organization), are publishing directories of Japanese universities for international students and also researching statistics regarding the number of international students. These directories and statistics are useful in the general study of educational current affairs. As international education becomes a major industry in Japan, some academic companies are also publishing informative books and magazines.

5-2. Ancient and Medieval Student Mobility

Human mobility has always changed society psychologically, culturally and politically.

的な目的による旅もあったが，教育的な目的の人的移動もあり，歴史的に多く
の社会に影響を及ぼしてきた。全てではないが，多くの留学生は名声とともに
母国に帰り，送り出し国に及ぼす影響も大きかった。

　学生の移動は長い歴史を持っている。春秋時代（722-476 BC）や戦国時代
（476-221 BC）のような内戦により中国が分裂していた時でも，これらの国家
間で学術交流が続いていた。「諸子百家」が生まれ，孔子や孟子，荀子などの
著名な学者を求めて多くの学生達が国境を越えた。

　古代ギリシアがいくつかの都市国家に分かれていた時もまた，国を越えた学
術交流が行われていた。多くの哲学者たちが学校を作り，国を越えた学術交流
は盛んだった。プラトンはアカデメイアを紀元前 387 年に設立し，アレクサン
ダー大王の師であるアリストテレスはリュケイオンを紀元前 335 年に設立した
（坂本と池谷 2010：7）。古代ギリシア語は後のローマ帝国（27 BC-395）でも学
術言語のひとつとして使われた。

　多くの宗教もまた教育機関を設立し，多くの宗教センターは国外からの学習
者のホストとなった。たとえば，紀元前 5 世紀にインドで設立されたナーラン
ダは中国やタイ，その他の国々から僧を受け入れ，後に彼らは母国にて仏教寺
院を建立した。中国は仏教の地域センターになり，韓国や日本からの僧を受け
入れた。
　イスラム教の教育機関であるマドラサもまた科学を生み出すのに重要な役割
を演じた。たとえば，10 世紀にエジプトで設立されたアル・アズハルは著名
な教育機関になった。イスラム教の影響の拡大に伴い，学生の移動を伴う知識
の拡散が起こった。言い換えれば，世界規模の宗教はしばしばコスモポリタン
な教育機関を設立した。
　ヨーロッパの中世の間（5-15 世紀），1088 年にボローニャ大学が設立され，

98　　第 5 章　国際学生移動の小史

Traders and merchants might travel with an economic goal in mind, but human mobility for educational purposes has also influenced many societies throughout history. Many (if not all) international students return to their home country with enhanced reputations, and so social influences on the sender country were strong.

Student mobility has a long history. When China split up into several nations during the eras of civil wars, such as during the Spring and Autumn Period (722-476 BC) and Warring States Period (476-221 BC), academic relationships between these nations still continued. The "Hundred Schools of Thought" was established, and many students crossed their borders to learn from famous scholars such as Confucius, Mencius and Xunzi.

When ancient Greece split into several city-states, interstate academic exchanges also existed. Many philosophers established schools, and interstate student mobility was active. Plato established the Platonic Academy (*Akademia*) in 387 BC and Aristotle, whose students included Alexander the Great, established the Lyceum (*Lykeion*) in 335 BC (Sakamoto and Iketani 2010: 7). The ancient Greek language also continued to be used as one of the educational languages of the later Roman Empire (27 BC-395).

Many religions have established educational institutes, and some religious centers host learners from other countries. For example, Nalanda, built in 5th century BC in India, received monks from China, Thailand and other countries who then established Buddhist temples in their own countries. China became one of the regional centers of Buddhism and received monks from Korea and Japan, as well.

Madrasah, Islamic educational institutions, also played an important role in the creation of sciences. For example, Al-Azhar, built in 10th century Egypt, became a renowned educational institution. Following the expansion of Islamic influence, this knowledge spread out with student mobility. In other words, world-wide religions often also established cosmopolitan educational institutions.

During the Medieval Period in Europe (5th-15th centuries), the University of

他の大学も続いた。ラテン語がリンガフランカだったため，国際的な学生移動が容易に行われた（江藤 2006：100）。ルネサンスの時代（14-16 世紀），人文学と科学が特にイタリアにて再興した。イギリスの若い上流階級の人々にとってグランドツアーが人気になり，当時先進的だったイタリアやフランスなどで教養のための旅を行った。

　大航海時代（15-17 世紀），スペインとポルトガルは領土を拡大し，影響力も広まった。世俗的なオランダとイギリスがヨーロッパの外に勢力を拡大する前，宗教と技術はしばしば結びついていた。世俗的なモンゴル帝国（13 世紀）の支配が終わった後，キリスト教の宣教師たちはアフリカやアジア，南北アメリカ大陸からの才能ある若者をヨーロッパへ引き付けるのに重要な役割を演じた。貿易商と共に，宣教師たちはしばしば薬や機械，時には火器を持ち込んだ。日本のキリシタン大名たちもまた若者をヨーロッパに送り，1582 年の天正使節団は大規模な事業になった（宮永 2001：171）。

5-3. 近代における留学

　狭義の「留学生」は近代的な国民国家が発展してから生まれた。ネイションは共通の文化と言語を用いる人々がおり，政治的な主権がある単位である。これらの国民国家は 18 または 19 世紀以降，国民とそうでない者を強く意識するようになった。フランスやドイツなどの国民国家は近代的な高等教育制度を設立し，同様に著名な国立の教育機関を設立した。いくつかの中世大学は国民国家によって再編され，現地の言語が教育の主要な言語になった。

　他方，アメリカ合衆国は単一のネイションによる国家ではない。しかしながら，高い識字率と効果的なメディアは「想像の共同体」を生み出し，政治的に統一されている。国民国家と同様に，これらの「想像の共同体」は共同体のメ

Bologna was established in 1088 and other universities followed. As the Latin language was a lingua-franca, international student mobility was more easily enabled (Eto 2006: 100). During the Renaissance Era (14th-16th centuries), humanities and sciences were revitalized, especially in Italy. The Grand Tour became popular among young upper-class British men of means, and they traveled to acquire knowledge in Italy, France and other advanced countries at that time.

During the Age of Exploration (15th-17th centuries), Spain and Portugal expanded their territories and their influence followed. Before the secular the Netherlands and the UK expanded their territories outside Europe, religion and technologies were often related. After the rule of the secular Mongolian Empire (13th century), Christian missionaries played an important role in attracting younger talents from Africa, Asia and the American continents to Europe. Along with traders, missionaries often brought medicine, machinery and sometimes firearms. Christianized Japanese Lords also sent young people to Europe, and the Tensho Embassy in 1582 was a significant event (Miyanaga 2001: 171).

5-3. Study Abroad in the Modern Era

The narrowing definition of "international students" is based on the development of modern nation states. A nation is defined as a unit that contains people with a common culture and language, and political sovereignty. These nation states have strictly recognized nationals as distinct from others since the 18th or 19th century. Nation states such as France and Germany established effective modern higher education systems and renowned national educational institutions as well. Some medieval universities were reconstructed by nation states, and local languages became dominant in education.

On the other hand, the USA is not a singular nation state. However, political unification with a high literacy rate and an effective media succeeded in creating an "imagined community". Like nation states, these "imagined communities" also

ンバーと他者を判別する。アメリカ合衆国では，教育は州や共同体の事項である。結果として，地元の住民と移民のために数多くの教育機関が設立された。しかしながら，特によく知られている私立の高等教育機関は次第に海外からの学生を引き付けるようになった。現地の言葉，この場合の英語は通常現地の学生と留学生の両者で使われている。

「先進」と「発展途上」は歴史的に相対的な用語である。産業革命以前，イギリスはヨーロッパ大陸から多くのことを学んだ。独立前のアメリカ合衆国はイギリスから知識を得た。国民国家が成立する前，ドイツはイタリアやフランスより後進国であった。ある時代における発展途上国からの学生は先進国の教育機関から知識を学び，時には母国にて教育機関を設立した。日本は留学生の送り出し国であったが，明治時代（1868-1912）にドイツ式の教育改革を行った後，留学生を受け入れるようになった。

これらの変化には，蒸気船や鉄道などの近代的な交通システムが旅を容易にしたことが関係しており，内燃機関と自動車の開発によりトレンドは加速化された。産業革命以降もたらされた交通機関の発達は，多くの人々をより速く，より安全に，より遠くに運ぶようになった。大陸を跨いでの留学が可能になり，宗教的な理由だけでなく，政治的，文化的，経済的な目的など理由が多様化した。

第一次世界大戦後，留学は政治的に重要になった。第一次世界大戦によるヨーロッパでのトラウマの後，教育は平和構築のために重要になった。平和な国際関係を築くため，相互理解は重要である。何人かのアメリカ人の教育者たちが IIE を 1919 年に設立し，特にヨーロッパからの留学生や学者を受け入れた（IIE n.d.a: web, IIE n.d.b: web）。同様に，現在ブリティッシュ・カウンシルとして知られている外国との関係のためのイギリスのコミッティが 1934 年に設立され，イギリスと諸外国との相互理解に努めた（British Council n.d.: web）。

distinguished their community members from other people. In the USA, education has been seen as a state or community matter. As a result, many educational institutions were established for local residents and immigrants. However, the more well-known private higher education institutions have gradually become magnets for students from overseas. The local language, in this case English, was usually used both for local students and international students.

"Developed" and "developing" are historically comparative terms. Before the industrial revolution, the UK learned a lot from the European continent. Before independence, the USA imported considerable knowledge from the UK. Before the nation state was established, Germany was less developed than Italy and France. Students from developing countries at a particular time have always acquired knowledge from educational institutions in developed countries, and some came back to establish educational institutions in their home country. Japan had been a net student sender, but began to accept international students after its German-modeled educational reformation in the Meiji Era (1868-1912).

On top of these changes, modern transportation systems such as steam ships and railways have made travel easier, a trend accelerated by internal-combustion engines and cars. The transportation systems developed since the industrial revolution meant that large groups of people could travel faster, safer and farther than ever before. Intercontinental study abroad was made possible not only for religious purposes, but also for diversified political, cultural and economic goals.

Since the end of First World War, study abroad has become an important political issue. After the trauma brought to Europeans by the First World War, education was seen as an increasingly important contributing factor to peace. For peaceful international relations, mutual understanding is vital. Some American educators established IIE in 1919, which received international students and visiting scholars from Europe in particular (IIE n.d.a: web, IIE n.d.b: web). Similarly, the British Committee for Relations with Other Countries, which was renamed the British

しかしながら，第二次世界大戦はさらに多くの被害を生み，平和のための文化・教育的な政策はより重要になった。国際的な教育を運用するため，UNESCO（国際連合教育科学文化機関）が 1945 年に設立された（UNESCO n.d.a: web）。第二次世界大戦の終了後，政治的な視点から留学はより重要になった。旧植民地の独立により，新国家の支配者たちにとって留学は重要だった。たとえば，フランスは旧フランス植民地から多くの留学生を受け入れた。

さらに，冷戦の時代（第二次世界大戦の後），アメリカ合衆国と旧ソビエト連邦は勢力を拡大し，教育は彼らの影響力を国際的に拡大するための主要な道具になった。「友好国」から若くて才能のある人々を引き寄せるため，フルブライト・プログラムが 1946 年に導入された（US Department of State n.d.: web）。日本と旧西ドイツは復興期に多くの学生をアメリカ合衆国に送り，両国は後に留学生の受け入れ国にもなった。

アメリカ合衆国において留学生が増加したことにより，選抜システムが重要になった。TOEFL（外国語としての英語テスト）や TOEIC（国際コミュニケーション英語能力テスト）などの英語試験を提供する ETS（教育試験サービス）が 1947 年に設立された（ETS n.d.: web）。留学生アドバイザーのための全国組織（NAFSA，1964 年に the National Association for Foreign Student Affairs と改名し，さらに 1990 年に the Association of International Educators と再度改名）が 1948 年に設立された（NAFSA n.d.: web）。

1970・80 年代，冷戦の影響は次第に弱くなっていった。政治的な問題に代わり，経済が重要な問題になった。アメリカ合衆国における大学は私学が優勢的で，裕福な留学生を容易に求めていた。さらに多くの留学生を受け入れるた

Council, was established in 1934 for the mutual understanding of the UK and other countries (British Council n.d.: web).

World War II brought yet more suffering, and cultural and educational policies for peace became still more important. To deliver international education, UNESCO (the United Nations Educational, Scientific and Cultural Organization) was established in 1945 (UNESCO n.d.a: web). Since the end of WWII, study abroad has become much more important from a political perspective. As many former colonies became independent, study abroad became important for rulers of the new nations. For example, France accepted international students especially from former French colonies.

In addition, during the Cold War (after the end of WWII), the USA and the former Soviet Union expanded their powers, and education became a key tool to expand their influence internationally. To invite younger talented people from "friendly countries," the Fulbright Program was launched in 1946 (US Department of State n.d.: web). Japan and the former West Germany sent students to the USA and when their economies recovered, they also became international student receivers themselves.

As the number of international students has increased in the USA, the selection system has become more important. The ETS (Educational Testing Service), which provides English language examinations such as TOEFL (Test of English as a Foreign Language) and TOEIC (Test of English for International Communication), was established to assist in this regard in 1947 (ETS n.d.: web). The National Association of Foreign Student Advisers (NAFSA, renamed as the National Association for Foreign Student Affairs in 1964 and re-renamed as the Association of International Educators in 1990) was then established in 1948 (NAFSA n.d.: web).

In the 1970s and 80s, the shadow of the Cold War faded. Instead of political affairs, economic issues came to the fore. Universities in the USA are run on a predominantly private basis, and it is easy for them to invite wealthy private

め（そしてアメリカ人学生を学ばせるため），アメリカの諸大学は 1980 年代に海外キャンパスを設立した。

　他方，オックスフォード大学とケンブリッジ大学を除けば，イギリスの大学は公的志向が強かった。しかしながら，サッチャー政権下（1979-1990），イギリスの諸大学に裕福な私費留学生が押し寄せるようになった。オーストラリアもまた私費留学生がもたらす経済効果に気づき，1989 年に「授業料全額支出」学生制度を始めた。アメリカ合衆国以外の英語圏諸国に見られるように国際学生の増加は「国際英語」の認識を高めた。特にイギリスやオーストラリアの英語試験業者は 1989 年に IELTS（国際英語力試験システム）を導入した（IELTS n. d.: web）。

5-4. 近年の国際学生移動

　1991 年にソビエト連邦が崩壊した時，国際化の意味が変化していった。アメリカ合衆国は超大国として残ったが，EU もまた拡大し，勢力が増した。複数の国々による共同政策が設立されるようになった。ヨーロッパにおける学生移動，特に 3-12 か月の短期間の移動を増加させるため，1987 年にエラスムス計画（ERASMUS）が導入された。同計画の初期の段階では，年間 3000 人の留学生の移動が増加した（文部科学省 n.d.: web）。

　ERASMUS 計画は 1995 年にソクラテスと呼ばれる新プログラムを実施し，年間 10 万人もの留学生を生み出すようになった。同時に，レオナルド・ダビンチと呼ばれる国際的な職業訓練交流プログラムも設立された（European Commission 2010a: web, European Commission 2010b: web）。1999 年のボローニア宣言の直後，2000 年に単位互換と比較可能な学位授与を含んだソクラテスⅡが導入された（吉川 2003：82）。

international students. To receive more international students (and to educate American students), American universities established oversea campuses in 1980s.

On the other hand, except Oxford and Cambridge, universities in the UK ware public oriented. However, under Thatcher government (1979–1990), wealthy private international students started flowing to universities in the UK. Australia also discovered the economic benefits brought by private international students, and started their "full–fee" student system in 1989. As English countries other than the USA saw increased numbers of international students, the recognition of "international English" also increased. Some English language test providers, especially in the UK and Australia, established the IELTS (International English Language Testing System) in 1989 (IELTS n.d.: web).

5-4. Contemporary International Student Mobility

When the Soviet Union dissolved in 1991 the meaning of internationalization underwent some changes. The USA remained as a super–power, but the EU expanded and increased its power as well. Cooperative policies of a plurality of countries were established. To increase student mobility in Europe, a relatively short–term (3 to 12 month) student mobility program called ERASMUS (European Region Action Scheme for the Mobility of University Students) was established in 1987. By the end of its first stage, it had increased student mobility by 3000 international students per year (MEXT n.d.: web).

The ERASMUS program also merged with a new educational program called Socrates, which started in 1995, and this collaboration resulted in adding 100,000 international students per year. At the same time, an international vocational exchange program called Leonardo da Vinci was established (European Commission 2010a: web, European Commission 2010b: web). Just after the Bologna Declaration of 1999, Socrates II, which concerns credit transfers and comparative diploma supplements, started in 2000 (Yoshikawa 2003: 82).

中国の経済力の増強もまた国際教育市場に影響を及ぼしている。たとえば，1992 年に設立されたアメリカ国際教育基金（AIEF）は様々な留学生をターゲットとしているが，現在の主要なソースは中国である（AIEF n.d.: web）。教育の質保障が国際的な学生移動で重要なため，オーストラリアは 2001 年にオーストラリア大学品質機関を設立した（米澤と木村 2004：S-4）。

　情報技術は英語の影響を広めた他の要因である。英語が事実上のリンガフランカになったため，英語で受講できる大学の人気が高まった。時には，非英語圏の国々であっても英語プログラムが作られた。留学生の数を増やすために，フランスやスイス，ドイツ，韓国，日本などの非英語圏の国々の多くの大学にて英語プログラムが見られるようになった。たとえば，キャンパス・フランスによると，2010 年にフランスでは 586 の英語で教えられているプログラムがあった（Campus France 2010: web）。

　UNESCO によると（n.d.b: web），アメリカ合衆国が最も留学生の受け入れ数が多く，次にイギリスが多い。フランスは 3 番目に留学生の受け入れ数が多いが，オーストラリアが着実に留学生の数を増やしている。主要国の留学生受入数は以下のとおりである。

オーストラリア 230,635（2008），オーストリア 53,396（2008），ベルギー 29,844（2008），カナダ 68,520（2006），チェコ 27,958（2008），中国 51,038（2008），キューバ 30,961（2009），デンマーク 12,695（2007），エジプト 35,031（2007），フィンランド 11,303（2008），フランス 243,236（2008），ドイツ 189,347（2008），ギリシア 21,160（2007），ハンガリー 15,459（2008），インド 12,374（2006），アイルランド 12,794（2008），イタリア 57,271（2007），日本 126,568（2008），ヨルダン 26,637（2008），カザフ 10,458（2009），キルギス 25,603（2008），レバノン 22,674（2007），マカオ 12,648（2008），マレーシア 30,581（2007），オランダ 30,052（2008），ニュージーランド 31,565（2008），ノルウェー 16,104（2008），ポーランド 13,021（2007），ポルトガル 17,950（2007），ルーマニア 13,857（2008），ロシア 60,288（2007），セルビア 11,259（2008），スペイン 37,726（2008），タイ 19,361（2009），トルコ 20,219（2008），イギリス 34,1791（2008），ウクライナ 32,573（2008），アメリカ合衆国 624,474（2008），サウジアラビア 15,759（2008），南アフリカ 63,964（2008），韓国 40,322（2008），スウェーデン 22,653（2008），スイス 31,706（2008）

As China's economic power grows, it also influences the international education market. For example, though the American International Education Foundation (AIEF), established in 1992, targets a variety of international students, the major source is now China (AIEF n.d.: web). As accreditation is important for international student mobility, Australia established the Australian Universities Quality Agency in 2001 (Yonezawa and Kimura 2004: S-4).

Information technology is another factor that is strengthening English influences. As English became a de facto lingua franca, universities with English enrolment became popular. In some cases, non-native English speaking countries have established English programs. To increase the number of international students, English-based programs are becoming popular throughout many universities and colleges in non-native English countries, including France, Switzerland, Germany, South Korea and Japan. According to Campus France, for example, 586 programs taught in English are available in 2010 in France (Campus France 2010: web)

According to UNESCO (n.d.b: web), the USA is the largest international receiver of students, and the UK follows. France is the third largest receiver, but Australia is increasing its international student population at a steady clip. The numbers of international students in major countries are as follows.

Australia 230,635 (2008), Austria 53,396 (2008), Belgium 29,844 (2008), Canada 68,520 (2006), Chez Republic 27,958 (2008), China 51,038 (2008), Cuba 30,961 (2009), Denmark 12,695 (2007), Egypt 35,031 (2007), Finland 11,303 (2008), France 243,236 (2008), Germany 189,347 (2008), Greece 21,160 (2007), Hungary 15,459 (2008), India 12,374 (2006), Ireland 12,794 (2008), Italy 57,271 (2007), Japan 126,568 (2008), Jordan 26,637 (2008), Kazakhstan 10,458 (2009), Kyrgyzstan 25,603 (2008), Lebanon 22,674 (2007), Macau 12,648 (2008), Malaysia 30,581 (2007), Netherlands 30,052 (2008), New Zealand 31,565 (2008), Norway 16,104 (2008), Poland 13,021 (2007), Portugal 17,950 (2007), Romania 13,857 (2008), Russia 60,288 (2007), Serbia 11,259 (2008), Spain 37,726 (2008), Thailand 19,361 (2009), Turkey 20,219 (2008), UK 34,1791 (2008), Ukraine 32,573 (2008), USA 624,474 (2008), Saudi Arabia 15,759 (2008), South Africa 63,964 (2008), South Korea 40,322 (2008), Sweden 22,653 (2008), Switzerland 31,706 (2008)

Source: UNESCO (n.d.b) web

出典：UNESCO（n.d.b）web

　UNESCO によると（n.d.b: web），中国はアメリカ合衆国やイギリス，オーストラリア，日本にとって最大の供給源である。アメリカ合衆国，イギリス，フランス，オーストラリア，ドイツ，日本における留学生の主要供給源は以下のとおりである。

アメリカ合衆国合計 624,474（2008）：中国 110,246，インド 94,664，韓国 69,198，日本 34,010，カナダ 29,082，メキシコ 14,853，トルコ 12,047
イギリス合計 341,791（2008）：中国 45,356，インド 25,901，アイルランド 15,261，アメリカ合衆国 13,895，フランス 12,685，ナイジェリア 11,783，マレーシア 11,727
フランス合計 243,236（2008）：モロッコ 26,998，中国 20,852，アルジェリア 18,780，チュニジア 10,812，セネガル 9,298
オーストラリア合計 230,635（2008）：中国 57,596，インド 26,520，マレーシア 18,576，香港 13,334，インドネシア 10,242
ドイツ合計 189,347（2008）：ポーランド 10,797，ロシア 9,795，ブルガリア 9,794，トルコ 8,899，ウクライナ 6,436
日本合計 126,568（2008）：中国 77,916，韓国 23,290，ベトナム 2,541，マレーシア 2,012，タイ 1,975
出典：UNESCO（n.d.b）web

　高等教育機関にとって，学位コースが最も重要である。しかしながら，学位プログラムは投資に時間がかかるため，私費留学生にとってリスクが高い。必要な履修の期間を短くするため，デュアル・ディグリー・プログラムやツイニング・プログラムが開発された。しかしながら，国際教育の商業化のため，初級レベルのプログラムもまた重要である。この視点から，留学生のための短期語学プログラムの人気が高まった。いくつかの短期プログラムには，視察旅行や文化体験が組み込まれ，これらのプログラムは「教育観光」とも呼ばれている。

第 5 章のおわりに

　歴史的に，学生の移動は常に変化してきた。古代や中世では，宗教的な団体がコスモポリタンな教育機関を設立してきた。第一次世界大戦後，留学は平和のために政治的に重要になった。IIE やブリティシュ・カウンシル等の組織が

According to UNESCO (n.d.b: web), China is the largest source for the USA, UK, Australia and Japan. The major sources of international students in the USA, the UK, France, Australia, Germany and Japan are as follows.

USA total 624,474 (2008): from China 110,246, India 94,664, South Korea 69,198, Japan 34,010, Canada 29,082, Mexico 14,853, Turkey 12,047
UK total 341,791 (2008): from China 45,356, India 25,901, Ireland 15,261, USA 13,895, France 12,685, Nigeria 11,783, Malaysia 11,727
France total 243,236 (2008): from Morocco 26,998, China 20,852, Algeria 18,780, Tunisia 10,812, Senegal 9,298
Australia total 230,635 (2008): from China 57,596, India 26,520, Malaysia 18,576, Hong Kong 13,334, Indonesia 10,242
Germany total 189,347 (2008): from Poland 10,797, Russia 9,795, Bulgaria 9,794, Turkey 8,899, Ukraine 6,436
Japan total 126,568 (2008): from China 77,916, South Korea 23,290, Vietnam 2,541, Malaysia 2,012, Thailand 1,975
Source: UNESCO (n.d.b) web

For higher educational institutions, degree programs are the most important attraction. However, degree programs require a longer investment of time, and can be risky undertakings for private students. To reduce the days of enrollment needed, dual degree programs and twinning programs have been established. For commercialized international education, however, programs at the entrance level are important, as well. In this regard, short language learning programs for international students have become popular. Some short programs offer interesting excursions and cultural activities, and these programs are also referred to as "educational tourism."

Conclusion of Chapter 5

Historically, student mobility has always changed. During the Ancient and Medieval ages, religious organizations often established cosmopolitan educational institutions. After the First World War, study abroad has become an important political issue for

作られた。留学生は経済的にも重要である。イギリスやオーストラリア等の
国々は，私費留学生からの経済的な収益を発見するようになった。

参考文献

AEI（2009a），*Transnational education in the higher education sector*, Canberra, AEI
AEI（2009b），*Export Income to Australia from Education Services in 2008*, Canberra, AEI
AIEF（n.d.），*About AIEF*, http://www.aief-usa.org/aboutief/whoweare.htm，2010 年 8 月 31 日閲覧

British Council（n.d.），*1930s and 1940s*, http://www.britishcouncil.org/history-when-1930s-1940s.
　　htm，2010 年 8 月 31 日閲覧
Campus France（2010），*Programs Taught in English*, http://www.campusfrance.org/fria/taughtie/
　　index.html#app=f692&e8c9-si=0，2010 年 8 月 31 日閲覧
English Australia（2009），*Major ELICOS Regional Markets in 2008*, Sydney, English Australia
江藤裕之（2006）「学問の自由と大学人の危機」『長野県看護大学紀要』8，99-107 頁

ETS（n.d.），*About ETS*, http://www.ets.org/about/who/，2010 年 8 月 31 日閲覧
European Commission（2010a），*The Erasmus Programme*, http://ec.europa.eu/education/lifelong-
　　learning-programme/doc80_en.htm，2010 年 8 月 31 日閲覧
European Commission（2010b），*Leonardo da Vinci Programme*, http://ec.europa.eu/education/
　　lifelong-learning-programme/doc82_en.htm，2010 年 8 月 31 日閲覧
IIE（1920），*Institute of International Education First Annual Report*, New York, IIE
IIE（n.d.a），*A Brief History of IIE*, http://www.iie.org/en/Who-We-Are/History，2010 年 8 月 31 日
　　閲覧
IIE（n.d.b），*Atlas of Student Mobility*, http://atlas.iienetwork.org/，2010 年 8 月 31 日閲覧
IELTS（n.d.），*History of IELTS*, http://www.ielts.org/researchers/history_of_ielts.aspx，2010 年 8 月
　　31 日閲覧
文部科学省（n.d.），ERASMUS 計画，http://www.mext.go.jp/b_menu/shingi/chukyo/chukyo4/007/
　　gijiroku/030101/2-7.htm，2010 年 8 月 31 日閲覧
宮永孝（2001）「日本洋学史：日本人と南蛮語学」『社会史林』48(1)，81-180 頁

NAFSA（n.d.），*The History of NAFSA*, http://www.nafsa.org/about.sec/history/，2010 年 8 月 31 日
　　閲覧
坂本千春，池谷文夫（2010）「リュケイオンにおける教育とアテナイ社会」『茨城大学教育学

peace. IIE, the British Council, and other organizations were established. International students are also important economically. The UK, Australia, and other countries discovered the economic benefits brought by private international students.

References

AEI (2009a), *Transnational education in the higher education sector*, Canberra, AEI

AEI (2009b), *Export Income to Australia from Education Services in 2008*, Canberra, AEI

AIEF (n.d.), *About AIEF*, http://www.aief-usa.org/aboutief/whoweare.htm, Accessed August 31, 2010

British Council (n.d.), *1930s and 1940s*, http://www.britishcouncil.org/history-when-1930s-1940s. htm, Accessed August 31, 2010

Campus France (2010), *Programs Taught in English*, http://www.campusfrance.org/fria/taughtie/ index.html#app=f692&e8c9-si=0, Accessed August 31, 2010

English Australia (2009), *Major ELICOS Regional Markets in 2008*, Sydney, English Australia

ETO, Hiroyuki (2006), "Academic Freedom and a Threat to Scholars and Students" *Bulletin / Nagano College of Nursing*, Vol. 8, pp. 99-107

ETS (n.d.), *About ETS*, http://www.ets.org/about/who/, Accessed August 31, 2010

European Commission (2010a), *The Erasmus Programme*, http://ec.europa.eu/education/lifelong-learning-programme/doc80_en.htm, Accessed August 31, 2010

European Commission (2010b), *Leonardo da Vinci Programme*, http://ec.europa.eu/education/ lifelong-learning-programme/doc82_en.htm, Accessed August 31, 2010

IIE (1920), *Institute of International Education First Annual Report*, New York, IIE

IIE (n.d.a), *A Brief History of IIE*, http://www.iie.org/en/Who-We-Are/History, Accessed August 31, 2010

IIE (n.d.b), *Atlas of Student Mobility*, http://atlas.iienetwork.org/, Accessed August 31, 2010

IELTS (n.d.), *History of IELTS*, http://www.ielts.org/researchers/history_of_ielts.aspx, Accessed August 31, 2010

MEXT (n.d.), *ERASMUS Keikaku*, http://www.mext.go.jp/b_menu/shingi/chukyo/chukyo4/007/ gijiroku/030101/2-7.htm, Accessed August 31, 2010

MIYANAGA, Takashi (2001), "Nihon Yougakushi - Nihonjin to Nanban Gogaku", *Hosei journal of sociology and social sciences*, Vol. 48, No. 1, pp. 81-180

NAFSA (n.d.), *The History of NAFSA*, http://www.nafsa.org/about.sec/history/, Accessed August 31, 2010

SAKAMOTO, Chiharu and IKETANI, Fumio (2010), "Education of the Lyceum and Athens

部紀要』59，1-20 頁

Tourism Australia（2007），*Study Tourism Report*, Canberra, Tourism Australia

UNESCO（n. d. a），*Organization's History*，http: //www. unesco. org/new/en/unesco/about-us/
who-we-are/history/，2010 年 8 月 31 日閲覧

UNESCO（n.d.b），*International Flows of Mobile Students at Tertiary Level* http://stats.uis.unesco.
org/unesco/TableViewer/tableView.aspx，2010 年 8 月 31 日閲覧

US Department of State（n.d.），*About Fulbright Program*, http://fulbright.state.gov/fulbright/about,
2010 年 8 月 31 日閲覧

米澤彰純，木村出（2004）『高等教育グローバル市場の発展』JBICI working paper, no. 18,
JBIC Institute

吉川裕美子（2003）「ヨーロッパ統合と高等教育政策」『学位研究』17，71-90 頁

Society", *Ibaraki Daigaku Kyouiku Gakubu Kiyou*, Vol. 59, pp. 1–20

Tourism Australia (2007), *Study Tourism Report*, Canberra, Tourism Australia

UNESCO (n. d. a), *Organization's History*, http: //www. unesco. org/new/en/unesco/about–us/ who–we–are/history/, Accessed August 31, 2010

UNESCO (n.d.b), *International Flows of Mobile Students at Tertiary Level* http://stats.uis.unesco. org/unesco/TableViewer/tableView.aspx, Accessed August 31, 2010

US Department of State (n.d.), *About Fulbright Program*, http://fulbright.state.gov/fulbright/about, Accessed August 31, 2010

YONEZAWA, Akiyoshi and KIMURA, Izuru (2004), *Koutou Kyouiku Global Shijou no Hatten*, *JBICI Working Paper No. 18*, JBIC Institute

YOSHIKAWA, Yumiko (2003), "Changes of Policy for Higher Education in the Process of European Integration", *Research in Academic Degrees*, Vol. 17, pp. 71–90

第 6 章

日本における国際学生

第6章のはじめに

日本は学生の送り出しの長い歴史を持っているが，留学生の受け入れの歴史は比較的短い。短い歴史ではあるが，日本における留学生の移動は大きく変わってきた。元々日本は留学生受け入れの主要国ではなかった。日本政府が1896年に清朝から中国人学生を公式に受け入れたとき，留学生受け入れのためのシステムはまだ発展の初期の段階だった。しかしながら，政府開発援助（ODA）を用い，1954年以降は国際的に研修者を受け入れている。

日本で学ぶ海外の学生は質の面から判定されてきたが，留学生の人数もまた近年では重要になっている。1983年の留学生10万人受け入れ計画や2008年の留学生30万人受け入れ計画の下，日本政府は政治的，経済的，文化的な理由から留学生数の増加を試みている。

本章における海外留学の定義は国際学生移動とほぼ同義である。たとえば，北海道から本州に来た学生は本章では海外留学生ではない。他方，台湾から本州に来た学生は少し複雑である。台湾が日本の領土であった時は，台湾人学生で，本州で学ぶ者は本章では海外留学生に含まれない。台湾が日本から別れた後に本州に来た台湾人学生は海外留学生として扱う。

Chapter 6

International Students in Japan

Introduction of Chapter 6

Though Japan also has a long history as a student sender, its history as an international student receiver is relatively short. However, within this short history, international student mobility in Japan has changed significantly. Japan was not a major international student receiver originally. When the Japanese government received Chinese students from the Sin dynasty officially in 1896, the system for the acceptance of international students was still in an incipient stage of development. However, using Official Development Assistance (ODA), Japan has now been accepting international trainees since 1954.

Though students from overseas studying in Japan have customarily been determined by quality, the actual quantity of international students is more recently also becoming important. Under the "Plan to Accept 100,000 International Students" formulated in 1983 and the subsequent "Plan to Accept 300,000 International Students" from 2008, the Japanese government has been trying to increase the number of international students for political, economic and cultural reasons.

The definition of "study abroad" in this chapter is almost the same as that of "international student mobility." For example, a student coming from Hokkaido (the northernmost major island in Japan) to Honshu (Japan's main island) would not be considered "study abroad" in this chapter. On the other hand, a student coming from Taiwan to Honshu is a bit complicated. When Taiwan was a Japanese territory, Taiwanese students who were in Honshu at the time are not categorized as

本章における国際学生の定義はシンプルである。ある国の国境を越えた学生は国際学生として扱う。たとえば北京から東京に来た中国人学生は国際学生である。日本の横浜出身で東京に来た中国系の学生は国際学生に含まない。しかしながら，ハワイから東京に来た日系人の学生は本章では国際学生として扱う。

6-1.　日本における教育の国際化に関する小史

　中国の隋（581-618）や唐（618-907）の時代から，日本は学生の送り出し国，または教師の受け入れ国であった。中国の諸王朝に国家プロジェクトとして学生を送り出す前から，公式・非公式に日本人は朝鮮半島や中国に先進の知識を学びに行っていた。日本から唐への公式訪問は894年に終わったが，引き続き日本人学生は私的に朝鮮半島や中国へ行った。多くの場合，平安時代（8〜12世紀）の終わりまで日本人学生は貴族や僧侶であった。

　古代の日本政府や幾人かの貴族は，中国からの先進の知識をエリートが学べる学校を開いた。仏教寺院もまた教育機関として機能し，次第に一般的にも開かれていった。鎌倉時代（12〜14世紀）や室町時代（14〜16世紀）は事実上武士が支配層になり，日本人僧侶は引き続き朝鮮半島や中国へ学びに行った。幾人かの大名は世俗的な学校を開設した。

　16〜17世紀のスペインやポルトガルとの接触の後，ヨーロッパ諸国からの火器の技術の受け入れにより，日本は地域的な軍事大国になった。スペインや

118　　第6章　日本における国際学生

international students in this chapter. Taiwanese students who were in Honshu after Taiwan separated from Japan are treated as international students, though.

The definition of "international student" in this chapter is simple. A student who crosses a particular country's border is considered an international student in this chapter. For example, a Chinese student coming from Beijing to Tokyo is an international student. An ethnic Chinese student from Yokohama in Japan who comes to Tokyo does not count as an international student. However, an ethnic Japanese student who comes to Tokyo from Hawaii is treated as an international student in this chapter.

6-1. A Short History of Educational Internationalization in Japan

Following the era of the Sui (581-618) and Tang (618-907) Dynasties of China, Japan was a student sender or professor receiver. Before these national projects that sent students to study under Chinese dynasties started, the ancient Japanese people already visited Korea and China to acquire advanced knowledge both officially and unofficially. Despite the close of official Tang visits from Japan in 894, Japanese students continued to visit Korea and China privately. In most cases, the Japanese students were aristocrats or monks, until the end of Heian Period (8th - 12th centuries).

The ancient Japanese government and some aristocrats opened schools where the elite could study advanced knowledge from China. Buddhist temples also served as educational institutions, and gradually opened to the public. Though samurai became de facto rulers following the Kamakura Period (12th - 14th centuries) and the Muromachi Period (14th - 16th centuries), Japanese monks continued to visit Korea and China to continue their studies. Some samurai lords also established secular schools.

After contact was initiated with Spain and Portugal in the 16th and 17th centuries, Japan became a regional military power because of the imported technology of

ポルトガルからの宣教師たちは周防（山口県）に 1551 年，豊後（大分県）に
1561 年にミッション・スクールを創設した。1580 年には当時最も勢力のあっ
た大名である織田信長の拠点があった安土に公的なミッション・スクールが設
立された。日本人学生はキリスト教だけでなく，西洋の科学も学んだ（宮永
2001：161）。しかしながら，日本は留学生受け入れの主要国にはならず，引き
続き海外からの知識を学んだ。

　鎖国下の江戸時代（1603-1868）であっても，日本人の学者は長崎でオランダ
人から西洋の技術を学ぶことができた。1720 年に外国書の規制が緩和され，
江戸幕府や諸大名が公的な学校を設立するようになった。1855 年には西洋研
究のための公的な学校もまた江戸に設立されている（宮永 2002：81）。鎖国政
策にもかかわらず，江戸時代の識字率と学術水準は高かった。興味深いことに，
鳴滝塾や順天堂，松下村塾，慶應義塾など社会階層を問わない私塾が身分制度
のある江戸時代に設立された。世界の先進的な知識を得るため，これらの私塾
には国内各地から盛んに学生が移動した。

　政治的な状況や交通技術もまた日本の学生移動に影響した。アメリカ合衆国
や他の西洋列強との接触は江戸幕府を開国させた。蒸気船による旅は従来の移
動手段よりも早く，安全になり，日本からの人的な移動を促進させた。江戸時
代末期，1862 年に江戸幕府はオランダへ公式に学生を送り出した。江戸幕府
は 1865 年にロシアへ，1866 年にイギリスへ，1867 年にフランスへ日本人学生
を送っている（宮永 1989：134）。さらに，江戸幕府の意に反して，いくつかの
大名も同様に若者を海外で学ばせている。例として 1863 年に山口からイギリ
スに送られた 5 人の若い学生達である「長州ファイブ」が挙げられる。彼らは
江戸の支配を引き継いだ明治政府を設立するのに大いに貢献した。

firearms from European countries. Missionaries from Spain and Portugal established a mission school in Suo (Yamaguchi prefecture) in 1551 and in Bungo (Oita prefecture) in 1561. An official mission school was established in 1580 in Azuchi, which was a capital city of Lord Oda Nobunaga, who was the predominant samurai at that time. Japanese students could study not only Christianity, but also Western sciences (Miyanaga 2001: 161). However, Japan did not become a significant international student receiver and continued learning from overseas sources.

Even during the isolated Edo Period (1603-1868), Japanese scholars could learn Western technologies from Dutch people in Nagasaki. In 1720, imported books were deregulated, and official schools were gradually established by the Edo government and various lords. An official school for Western Studies was also established in Edo in 1855 (Miyanaga 2002: 81). Despite the policy of isolation, literacy rates and academic standards were relatively high during the Edo Period. Curiously, irrespective of social class, private schools such as Narutakijuku, Juntendo, Shokasonjuku and Keiogijuku were also established during the hierarchical Edo Period. To gain advanced knowledge of the world, vivacious internal student mobility to these private schools was seen.

The political situation and transport technology also affected Japanese student mobility. Encounters with the US and other Western powers encouraged the Edo government to open its doors. As travel by steamship was faster and safer than previous modes of transport, it enabled greater human mobility from Japan. At the end of the Edo Period, the government officially sent Japanese students to the Netherlands in 1862. The Edo government also sent Japanese students to Russia in 1865, to the UK in 1866 and to France in 1867 (Miyanaga 1989: 134). In addition, against the wishes of the Edo government, some feudal lords sent their younger people to study overseas as well. One such example of this was the "Choshu Five," five younger students sent from Yamaguchi to the UK in 1863. This group contributed to the building of the Meiji government, which succeeded the Edo rulers.

6-2. 明治維新と西洋化

　明治政府は 1871 年に文部省を設立した。明治政府は 1872 年に国の教育制度の改革を行い（学制），1873 年には公的な高等教育制度が分類された。学問別の高等教育機関に加え，1886 年には後に東京大学となる最初の帝国大学が設立された。留学に加え，明治初期においてこれらの高等教育機関では海外からの客員教授が重要であった（竹中 2006：98）。

　明治初期の間，日本の高等教育機関は公的に西洋からの教授を招聘していた。日本は西洋からの先進的な知識を必要としており，これらの外国人教授たちは，初期の頃，英語やフランス語，ドイツ語などヨーロッパの諸言語を用いて日本のエリートを教育した。ラフカディオ・ハーンやエドワード・モース，ウィリアム・クラーク，エルヴィン・フォン・ベルツ，ギュスターヴ・エミール・ボアソナードなど，幾人かの外国人教授たちは今なお日本の教育者の間で良く知られている。これらの外国人教授の重要性は，日本人教授の育成に伴い変わっていった。しかしながら，日本におけるヨーロッパ言語の教育は引き続き重要であった。

　これらの公的な高等教育機関はエリートのために作られたが，江戸時代と同様に，私立の学校は広く開かれていた。東京だけでも，1872 年に 1127 校の私学があり，そのいくつかはヨーロッパ言語で授業が行われていた（宮永 1999：205）。しかしながら，これらの私学の水準はまちまちであった。多くはヨーロッパの文献の翻訳に集中しており，口語のコミュニケーションは低い水準であった。しかしながら，これらの私学のうち，高い学術水準を達成するものもあった。1918 年の大学令（1919 年に施行）により，文部省は私立大学を認可した。次第に私立大学の数は増加し，第二次世界大戦後には私学の数が優勢になった（堀 2007：227-228）。

　やがて，日清戦争後に日本が軍事的，技術的に地域大国になったことにより，

6-2. Meiji Restoration and Westernization

In 1871, the Ministry of Education (Monbusho) was established by the Meiji government. The Meiji government started to reform the national educational system (Gakusei) in 1872, and the official higher education system was categorized in 1873. In addition to discipline-based higher education institutions, the first Imperial University, which later became the University of Tokyo, was established in 1886. In addition to study abroad, visiting scholars from overseas were still important in these higher education institutions of the early Meiji Period (Takenaka 2006: 98).

During the early Meiji Period, some Japanese higher education institutions invited professors from Western countries on an official basis. Japan still needed considerable advanced knowledge from Western countries, and these international professors educated Japanese elites using European languages such as English, French and German at first. Some of these professors and lecturers, such as Lafcadio Hearn, Edward Morse, William Clark, Erwin von Bälz, Gustave Émile Boissonade, are still well-known among Japanese educators. The importance of these international professors changed gradually as Japanese professors grew more able themselves. However, European language education in Japan continued to be important.

Though these official higher education institutions were established for the elite, private schools also opened for everyone as in the Edo Period. In Tokyo alone, there were 1127 private schools in 1872, and some of them taught in European languages as well (Miyanaga 1999: 205). However, the standard of these private schools varied. Many of them concentrated on translating European literature, and were substandard at colloquial communication. Some of these private schools, however, also achieved high academic standards. The Ministry of Education permitted private universities under the University Law (Daigaku Rei) of 1918, which was enacted in 1919. The number of private universities increased gradually and their numbers became dominant after WWII (Hori 2007: 227-228).

Meanwhile, Japan became a student receiver following the Sino-Japan war, when

日本は学生の受け入れ国になった。続く日露戦争の勝利もまた政治的に重要な転機であった。当時の日本人学生と同様に，明治後期や大正時代（1912-1926）には中国や朝鮮半島，その他のアジア地域の学生が日本語を用いて日本で学ぶようになった。1925 年には 2095 人の中国人学生と 1914 人の朝鮮半島からの学生が日本で学んでいた（周 2007：24）。さらに，大正時代と昭和（1926-1989）初期の間，西洋諸国の植民地と同様に，日本帝国政府は朝鮮半島や台湾に日本語基準の教育機関を設立した。日本の領土が拡大するにつれ，日本列島以外の日本語基準の教育機関が拡散していった。

6-3. 日本における国際的な高等教育の普及

　第二次世界大戦後，アメリカ合衆国と連合国の占領は日本の教育制度を変えた。教育基本法が 1947 年に施行され，同 1947 年の学校教育法によって新制大学が設立された（堀 2007：230）。日本における高等教育はもはやエリートだけのものではなく，一般の日本人学生のため日本語ベースのカリキュラムが優勢になった。新制大学は今日でも北海道から沖縄まで設立され続けている。

　冷戦時代，アメリカ政府の協力により，日本は経済成長に集中できた。軍事品に代わり，日本は高品質な日用品を生産した。1950-60 年代に日本経済は成長し，高度な教育を受けた日本人の数もまた増加した。石油危機にもかかわらず，教育を受けた若い労働力により，1970-80 年代に日本は経済大国になった。いくつかの発展途上国は日本の経済的なサクセス・ストーリーを学ぶため，地元のエリートを日本の大学へ送った。

　さらに，第二次世界大戦後の新興国の独立は国際政治の状況を変えた。新たに独立した国々は建国のための人材を必要としており，旧宗主国は主要な留学

Japan became a regional power both militarily and technologically. The following victory in the Russo-Japan war was also an important political milestone. As did Japanese domestic students at that time, students from China, Korea, and other Asian regions learned in Japan using the Japanese language during the late Meiji and Taisho (1912-1926) Periods. In 1925, 2095 Chinese students and 1914 Korean students were studying in Japan (Zhou 2007: 24). In addition, during the Taisho and early Showa (1926-1989) Periods, the Japanese imperial government established Japanese-based educational institutions in Korea and Taiwan, in a manner similar to that seen in colonies of Western countries. As long as Japanese territory expanded, Japanese-based educational institutions outside Japanese islands continued to spread.

6-3. Popularization of International Higher Education in Japan

After World War II, the occupation by the USA and allied countries changed the Japanese educational system. The Basic Law on Education (Kyoiku Kihon Hou) of 1947 was enacted, and newer universities were established under the School Education Law (Gakko Kyoiku Hou) of 1947 (Hori 2007: 230). Higher education was no longer only for the elite in Japan, and Japanese-based curricula become dominant for ordinary Japanese students. Newer universities and colleges are still being established from Hokkaido to Okinawa today.

During the era of the Cold War, by cooperating with the US government, Japan could concentrate on its economic development. Instead of military products, Japan produced high quality manufactured commodities. During the 1950s and 60s, the Japanese economy grew, and the numbers of highly educated Japanese people also increased. Despite the oil crises, using an educated younger workforce, Japan became an economic superpower in 1970s and 80s. Some developing countries tried to learn from Japan's economic success story, and sent their local elite to Japanese universities.

In addition, the independence of newer countries after WWII changed the international political situation. Newer independent countries needed human resources

生の受け入れ国となった。さらに，日本と旧西ドイツは好景気を迎え，国策として留学生を受け入れるようになった。同時に，日本は 1951 年からフルブライト奨学金による研究者や大学院生のアメリカ合衆国への送り出しを行っている（文部科学省 2008：293）。

　初期の頃，政府開発援助（ODA）は留学生受け入れのため重要であった。第二次世界大戦が終わったころ，日本は ODA の受け入れ国だった。しかしながら，1950 年のコロンボ・プランの受け入れ後，日本は寄付者になった。ODA を用い，日本は 1954 年から国際的に研修生を受け入れている。さらに，JICA（国際協力機構）が 1974 年に設立された（JICA n.d.a: web）。JICA の協力の下，JICE（日本国際協力センター）が 1977 年に設立され，JDS プログラム（人財育成奨学計画）が行われるようになった（JICE n.d.: web）。第二次世界大戦の賠償金の代わりに，政治的な視点から，日本政府は特にアジア諸国からの国際学生に資金援助を行っており，日本の諸大学は教育機会を提供している。

　日本が経済大国になった時，文化交流もまた重要になった。1972 年に設立された国際交流基金（JF）は 2009 年時点で 22ヵ所の海外センターを開設した（Japan Foundation n.d.: web）。1980 年代末の日本のバブル経済の少し前，1983 年に日本政府は留学生 10 万人受け入れ計画を導入した（図 6-1）。日本政府は他の先進国と同程度の留学生数を目指した。1957 年に設立された旧日本国際教育協会（AIEJ，現日本国際教育支援協会：JEES）と国際交流基金は 1984 年に留学生のための日本語能力試験（JLPT）を開始した。現在，多くの日本の大学は日本語能力試験を求めている（JLPT n.d.: web）。

126　　第 6 章　日本における国際学生

to build up their nations, and former colonial powers became large international student accepters. Furthermore, Japan and the former West Germany, both of which had booming economies, began to accept international students as a matter of national policy. At the same time, Japan was sending researchers and graduate students to the USA under the Fulbright Program, and had been since 1951 (MEXT 2008: 293).

At first, ODA (Official Development Assistance) played an important role in international student acceptance. At the time WWII ended, Japan was an ODA receiver. However, Japan became a donor after the acceptance of the Colombo Plan of 1950. Using ODA, Japan has been accepting international trainees since 1954. In addition, JICA (Japan International Cooperation Agency) was established in 1974 (JICA n.d.a: web). In cooperation with JICA, JICE (Japan International Cooperation Center) was established in 1977, and is supporting the JDS (Japanese Grant Aid for Human Resource Development Scholarship) program (JICE n. d.: web). From a political perspective, instead of reparations for WWII, the Japanese government provides financial aid for international students from Asian countries in particular, and Japanese universities offer them learning opportunities.

When Japan became an economic superpower, cultural exchange also became important. The Japan Foundation (JF), established in 1972, opened overseas centers, and had 22 such centers as of 2009 (Japan Foundation n.d.: web). Just before the bubble economy of Japan in the late 1980s, the Japanese government initiated a plan to accept 100,000 international students (called the Ryugakusei 10 Mannin Keikaku) in 1983 (Fig. 6-1). The Japanese government tried to increase the number of international students to be on par with other developed countries. Cooperating with the former Association of International Education, Japan (AIEJ), established in 1957 (now Japan Educational Exchanges and Services: JEES), the JF started the Japanese Language Proficiency Test (JLPT) for international students in 1984. Many Japanese universities now require the JLPT (JLPT n.d.: web).

図 6-1　日本における留学生数

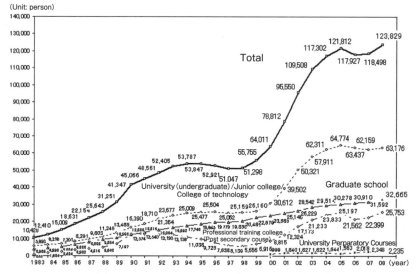

出典：JASSO (n.d.a) *Trends in Number of International Students by Institutional Type (as of each May 1)*, web

　留学生 10 万人受け入れ計画の導入にもかかわらず，留学生数の増加はたやすくなかった。理由の一つは大学の授業が日本語で行われていたことで，もう一つの理由は円高が学生にとって極端なコスト高になったことである。円高は日本におけるインバウンド観光にとってもマイナスのインパクトであったが，インバウンドの私費留学生にとっても同様に働いた。他方，円高は留学生や研修生を呼び寄せる場合もあった。日本での将来的な就職の可能性は私費留学生にとって強いインセンティブになった。日系企業の海外進出は留学生にとって仕事の創造をもたらす可能性があった。さらに，当時若い日本人が裕福になったことにより，学生ビザを有さない私費の研修生が非熟練労働者として日本で働くこともあった。日本政府は非熟練労働者としての外国人ゲストワーカーを受け入れていないため，私費の国際研修生は追加的な労働力として重要であった。

Figure 6-1 Number of International Students in Japan

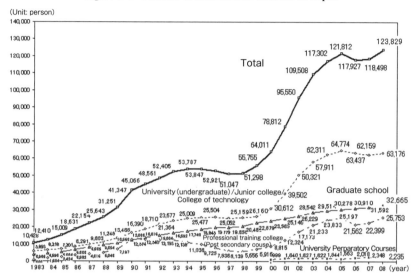

Source: JASSO (n.d.a) *Trends in Number of International Students by Institutional Type* (*as of each May 1*), web

Despite the introduction of the plan to accept 100,000 international students, increasing the numbers of inbound students was not easy. One reason was that university instruction was delivered in the Japanese language, and another was that the strong yen made costs prohibitive to some students. As a strong yen is a negative factor in the case of inbound tourism to Japan, it has a similar effect on private inbound students. On the other hand, a strong yen can also be a magnet for international students and international trainees from overseas. Future job opportunities in Japan were a strong incentive for private international students. The expansion of Japanese companies overseas offered great potential for job creation for international students. In addition, as younger Japanese became wealthier, private international trainees who did not have a student visa worked in Japan as unskilled laborers at that time. As the Japanese government did not allow foreign guest workers for unskilled labor, private international trainees provided an important additional workforce.

バブル経済期，国際化は日本人にとって流行の考えであった。円高を活用し，一般の日本人学生はアメリカ合衆国やヨーロッパ，オーストラリアで学ぶことが可能になった。日本における航空交通の規制緩和もまた海外旅行を安くした。大学生と時に高校生は親の資金援助により留学することができた。アメリカの大学の日本校が設立され，日本人学生が英語で学ぶようになった。より短い国際交流として，バブル経済の夜明けから，日本の大学と高校は世界各地に学生を送り出した。このトレンドにより，1992 年以降文部科学省は高校生の海外修学旅行の統計調査を行っている（文部科学省 2007：1-5）。いくつかの短期の学校交流プログラムは旅行代理店によってプロモートされ，商業化されたパッケージツアーのように日本語を話せるツアーガイドが随行した。

6-4. 日本におけるグローバリゼーションと英語基準プログラム

留学生の数を増やすためには，日本語学習のプロモーションが重要である。国際交流基金と同様に，JICA もまた 1998 年から発展途上国に日本センターを設立し，2009 年には 10 センターが運営されている（JICA n.d.b: web）。旧国際教育協会の業務を拡大し，2004 年に JASSO（日本学生支援機構）が設立され，入試から住居まで留学生のあらゆるサポートを行っている（JASSO 2008a：6）。

しかしながら，近年のグローバリゼーションと日本の若年人口の減少は日本で学びたい留学生のための英語基準のプログラムの設立を増加させている。政治と経済の理由から，日本政府は 2008 年に留学生 30 万人受け入れ計画を開始した。

2002 年に日本留学試験（EJU）が始まったのにもかかわらず，日本語を学んだ学生の数は限られている（JASSO n.d.a: web, JASSO n.d.b: web, JASSO n.d.c: web）。

130　　第 6 章　日本における国際学生

During the bubble economy, *kokusaika*, which is Japanese for internationalization, became a fashionable concept among Japanese people. Using the strong yen, ordinary Japanese students were able to study in the US, Europe, and Australia. The deregulation of air transportation in Japan made travel abroad cheaper as well. University students and sometimes high school students could study overseas with their parents' financial support. Branches of American universities also opened in Japan, and Japanese students studied at these in English. For shorter international exchanges, Japanese universities and high schools have been sending students around the world since the dawn of the bubble economy. Following this trend, MEXT has been providing statistics of outbound high school excursionists since 1992 (MEXT 2007: 1-5). Some short-term school exchange programs have been promoted by travel agencies, with Japanese speaking tour guides similar to those seen on commercial package tours.

6-4. Globalization and English-Based Programs in Japan

To increase the number of international students, the promotion of Japanese language studies is important. As with the JF, JICA also started to establish Japan Centers, especially in developing countries, since 1998, and 10 of these centers were operational as of 2009 (JICA n.d.b: web). JASSO was established in 2004 to expand the activities of the former AIEJ, and is now supporting international students in everything from their entrance examinations to their accommodations (JASSO 2008a: 6).

However, recent trends in globalization and the shrinking demographics of Japan's younger generation have served to accelerate the establishment of English-based programs for international students who would like to study in Japan. For political and economic reasons, the Japanese government launched a plan to accept 300,000 international students (called the Ryugakusei 30 Mannin Keikaku) in 2008.

Despite the start of the Examination for Japanese University Admission for International Students (EJU) in 2002, the number of international students who have

これは，日本の高等教育機関，特に大学院が英語で開講されている学位コース
の開設を行っている理由の一つである（図6-2，図6-3）。文部科学省によると，
日本の68大学が2007年の時点で英語開講の大学院の学位コースを提供してい
た（文部科学省 2008：22）。JASSOによると，1960年代の時点では，英語基準

図6-2　英語学位プログラムの設立年

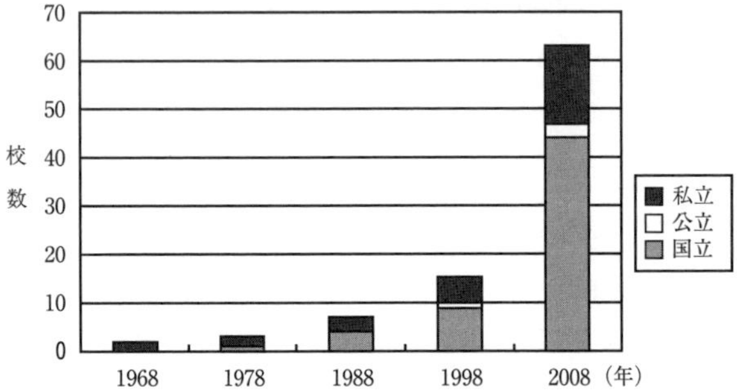

（単位：大学）

出典：Asamizu 2009, p. 184

図6-3　都道府県別英語学位コース大学数（2008年）

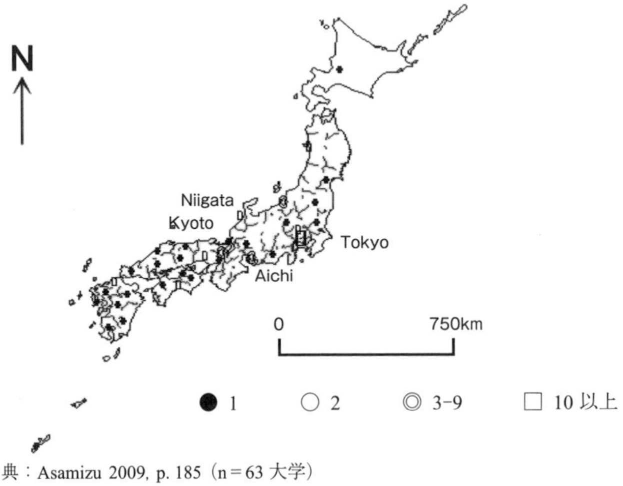

出典：Asamizu 2009, p. 185（n＝63大学）

learned Japanese is limited (JASSO n.d.a: web, JASSO n.d.b: web, JASSO n.d.c: web). This is one of the reasons Japanese educational institutions, especially at the graduate level, are currently trying to open special degree courses offered in English (Fig. 6-2, Fig. 6-3). According to MEXT, 68 universities in Japan had graduate degree courses

Figure 6-2 Establishment Year of Degree Program Offered in English

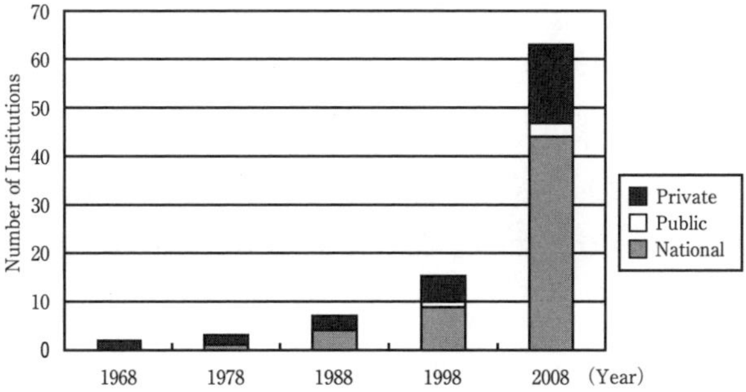

(Unit: Universities)
Source: Asamizu 2009, p. 184

Figure 6-3 Universities with English-based Degree Courses by Prefecture (2008)

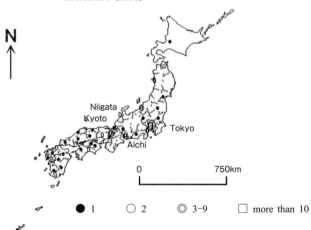

Source: Asamizu 2009, p. 185 (n = 63 Universities)

Chapter 6   International Students in Japan   133

の学位コースはわずか2大学だけであった（JASSO 2008b：factsheet）。

　非英語圏諸国における英語プログラムは効果があるが，解決策のすべてではない。非英語圏における英語プログラムが少ないうちは良いニッチ・マーケットである。しかし，英語プログラムが増えた時，競争が激しくなる。英語話者の従業員と教員を非英語圏で得ることは量の面からも質の面からも難しい。地元の独自性を英語プログラムに付加することは国際学生を引き寄せるために必要である。たとえば日本の大学の場合，海外からの英語話者の学生を受け入れているが，労働市場における英語のみ話せる人の需要は限られている。英語による入学と英語プログラムは重要であるが，現地語を学ぶサポートもまた重要である。

6-5. 日本における教育観光

　さらに，日本では留学生のための学位を有さないコースも特に学部の交換留学生向けに提供されている（図6-4，図6-5）。文部科学省によると，2008年の時点で，日本の65大学が比較的大きな短期留学生のための英語プログラムを有していた（文部科学省 2009a：40-41，文部科学省 2009b：web）。日本の大学とJICAや国際交流基金などの国際機関との共同プロジェクトも見られる。これらの機関は研修期間中，国際研修生に資金援助を行う。いくつかの日本の大学と国際的なパートナーはデュアル・ディグリー・プログラムやツイニング・プログラムを開設した。日本における留学生の学ぶ機会は今までになく大きくなっている。

　さらに，国際修学旅行や国際スタディ・ツアーを含む教育観光は日本の教育

134　　第6章　日本における国際学生

offers in English in 2007 (MEXT 2008: 22). According to JASSO, by contrast, only 2 universities opened English based degree programs in the 1960s (JASSO 2008b: factsheet).

While English-based programs in non-native English speaking countries are effective, they are not a total solution. As long as there are relatively few English-based programs in non-native English countries, it will be good niche marketing. However, as these English-based programs spread, the competition for students will become increasingly fierce. English speaking employees and teachers in non-English speaking countries are also a major issue, particularly from the perspectives of quantity and quality. English programs with local uniqueness are needed to attract international students. Japanese universities, for example, are accepting English-speaking students from overseas, though the job market for a monolingual English speaker in Japan is still limited. Entrance systems and programs offered in English are important, but support in learning the local language is also needed.

6-5. Japan's Educational Tourism

In addition, non-degree English courses for international students are also being offered in Japan, especially for undergraduate exchange students (Fig. 6-4, Fig. 6-5). According to MEXT, 65 universities in Japan offered relatively large English-based programs for short-term exchange students in 2008 (MEXT 2009a: 40-41, MEXT 2009b: web). Some collaborative projects between Japanese universities and international organizations such as JICA and JF can also be found. These organizations offer financial aid to international trainees during the training programs described above. Some Japanese universities and their international partners have also established dual degree programs or twinning programs. Learning opportunities for international students in Japan have never been greater.

Furthermore, educational tourism, including international excursions and study

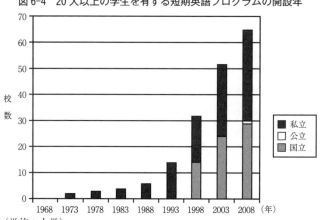

図6-4　20人以上の学生を有する短期英語プログラムの開設年
(単位：大学)
出典：文部科学省 2009a, pp. 40-41

機関にとって重要である。文部科学省は日本の高校を短期間訪問したい国際学生を受け入れるため，2005年にフレンドシップ・ジャパン・プランを開始した（文部科学省 2008：286）。インバウンドの教育観光はイギリスやオーストラリア，ニュージーランドなど，いくつかの英語諸国ではすでに普及している。日本政府といくつかの教育機関は，異文化理解と経済的な収入の視点から，インバウンド教育旅行の重要性に気付いている。

　いくつかのケースでは，旅行業者による教育旅行はスペシャル・インタレスト・ツーリズムのニッチであるとみなされる。2003年のビジット・ジャパン・キャンペーン（またはYokoso Japan）の開始から，日本政府は外国人観光客の受け入れに力を入れてきた。2008年には観光庁が設立され，様々な言語で日本に関する情報を広めている。日本における近年の文化理解ツアーは京都の伝統文化だけでなく，東京のポップ・カルチャーも紹介している。アニメやゲームなどの日本のポップ・カルチャーは多くの海外からの訪問者を引き付け，これらに焦点を置いたツアーも広まっている。日本ではもはやインバウンド観光

Figure 6-4 Establishment Year of Short English Programs which have more than 20 Students per Year

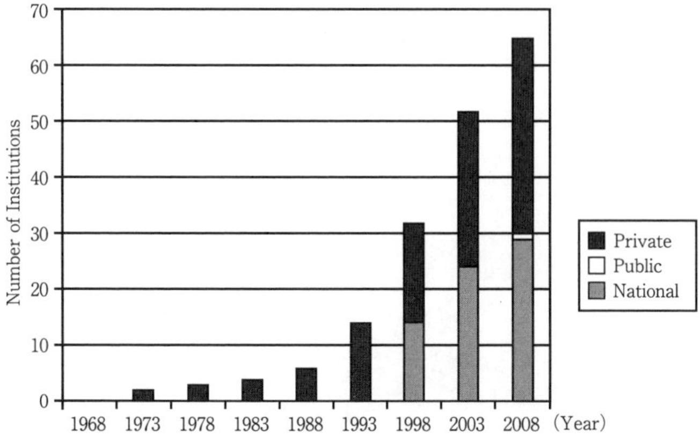

(Unit: Universities)
Source: MEXT 2009a, pp. 40-41

tours, are becoming important tools for Japanese educational institutions. MEXT launched the Friendship Japan Plan (Furendoshippu Japan Puran in Japanese) in 2005 to welcome international students who would like to briefly visit Japanese high schools (MEXT 2008: 286). Inbound educational tourism is already popular in some English speaking countries such as the UK, Australia and New Zealand. The Japanese government and some educational institutions have realized the importance of inbound educational tourism in achieving cross-cultural understanding and economic gains.

In some cases, educational tourism organized by travel agents can be thought of as a niche of special interest tourism. Since the Visit Japan Campaign (also called Yokoso Japan) was launched in 2003, the Japanese government has been working hard to make inbound tourists feel welcome. The Tourism Agency of Japan (Kankouchou), established in 2008, is also disseminating tourism information about Japan in several languages. Cultural understanding tours in Japan have recently gone beyond introducing traditional culture in Kyoto to introducing pop culture in Tokyo. Japanese pop culture mainstays such as anime and video games attract many international

図6-5 20人以上の学生を有する短期英語プログラム大学数（都道府県別・2008年）

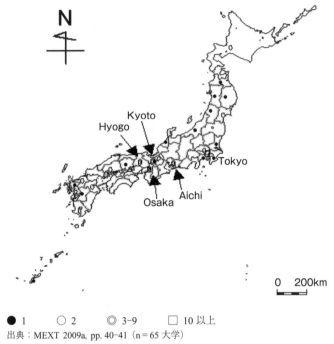

● 1　　○ 2　　◎ 3-9　　□ 10以上
出典：MEXT 2009a, pp. 40-41（n = 65大学）

は都市部だけの問題ではない。エコツーリズムやグリーン・ツーリズムで国際訪問者に教育的な経験を提供するものも日本にて可能性がある。ポストモダンの時代，ソフトパワーの文化的アトラクションは重要性が増している。生涯学習の視点から，教育観光は日本について紹介する素晴らしい方法である。

短期の体験プログラムのため，リンガ・フランカでの教育は，現地語が十分には分からない国際学生を引き付ける重要な方法である。より広いニッチ・マーケットを開拓するため，国際学生のための多言語プログラムの形成は，特に短期の交換コースにて可能であろう。しかしながら，アメリカ合衆国やカナ

Figure 6-5 Number of Universities Offered Short English Programs which has more than 20 Students per Year by Prefecture (2008)

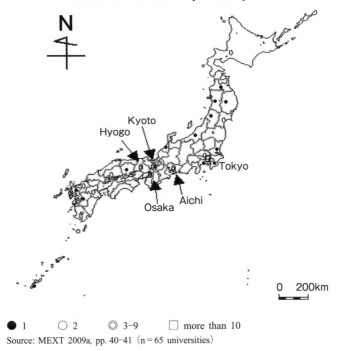

● 1 ○ 2 ◎ 3-9 □ more than 10
Source: MEXT 2009a, pp. 40-41 (n = 65 universities)

visitors, and tours that focus on these have been springing up. Inbound tourism is not just an urban issue anymore in Japan. Ecotourism and green tourism that provide educational experiences for international visitors also show great potential in Japan. In the post-modern era, "soft power" cultural attractions are increasingly important. As one aspect of lifelong education, educational tourism is a great way to teach others about Japan.

For short-term experience programs, education in a lingua franca is an important way to attract international students, as many of them do not understand the local language sufficiently to study with it. To explore wider niche markets, the creation of plural language programs for international students may be possible especially for

ダ，オーストラリアのような移民の多い国と違い，多言語の人材と運営コストもまた実施のための大きな問題である。

英語に続き，いくつかの日本の教育機関は短期交換学生のために英語や韓国語を用いているが，それ以外の言語は人材不足のため発展途上である。短期の教育プログラムを拡大するため，教育機関と他のグループ，たとえば旅行会社や通訳協会，国際NGOなどとの協力が重要である。さらに，現在の学生もまた，将来的には教員やオペレーター，マネジャーになるだろう。

第6章のおわりに

国際学生移動はインバウンドとアウトバウンドに分けられる。日本では，これらのカテゴリーのトレンドは歴史的に変わってきた。日本は教育的な人的送り出し国としての歴史が長く，さらに海外から教授の受け入れを行ってきた。日本は留学生の受け入れ国としての歴史は短い。はじめに述べたように，日本における国際学生の移動は大きく変わっている。

明治時代，国際学生の受け入れ自体が重要であった。しかしながら，バブル時代，国際学生の量もまた重要になった。日本へ来る国際学生は日本の先端技術や伝統文化を学ぶために来日した。近年では，人口減により，経営的に苦しんでいる日本の大学のため，留学生の数は経済的に重要視されている。

国際学生のための教育内容もまた変わってきた。短期交換学生を除き，専門科目を学んで卒業するために，留学生は日本語を修得する必要があった。しかしながら，近年の日本の大学によって提供されている英語基準の学位プログラムは日本語能力を求めない。文部科学省やJASSOなどの教育組織は質と量の

140　　第6章　日本における国際学生

short-term exchange courses. However, aside from immigrant-rich countries such as the USA, Canada and Australia, multilingual human resources and operating costs will present significant problems in practice.

Following the English language, some educational institutions in Japan are using Chinese and Korean languages for short-term exchange students; however, other language programs are still under development because of limited human resources in each institution. To expand short-term educational programs, collaboration between educational institutions and other groups, such as travel agents, interpreting societies and international NGOs (Non Governmental Organization), will be important. To help things along, current students also may become instructors, operators and/or managers in the future.

Conclusion of Chapter 6

International student mobility can be categorized as inbound or outbound. In Japan, the trends in these categories have changed historically. Japan has a long history as an educational human sender, and has received professors from overseas. The history of Japan as an international student receiver, however, is relatively short. That being said, international student mobility in Japan has been changing significantly.

During the Meiji Period, acceptance of international students itself was important. During the bubble economy, however, the quantity of international students also became important. International students visited Japan to study advanced technology or traditional Japanese culture. More recently, because of depopulation trends, the quantity of international students has become an increasingly important economic consideration for financially struggling Japanese universities.

The contents of education for international students also changed. Except for short-term exchange students, international students needed to master the Japanese language to study major subjects and to graduate. However, current English-based degree programs offered by Japanese universities do not require Japanese language

面から様々な国際学生について調べている。

　さらに，日本における短期国際プログラムもまた変化の可能性に面している。バブル経済期，国際化はファッションであり，多くの日本の大学は日本人学生を海外に送り，異文化理解のために国際学生を受け入れてきた。しかしながら，いくつかの国でインバウンド教育観光が商業化し，いくつかの日本の大学もまた短期プログラムの経済効果について理解している。ポピュラー文化を含んだ文化的な吸引力は教育観光客を引き付けるために必要である。

　しかしながら，量の拡大はグローバルな競争に生き残るための唯一の方法ではない。興味深いことに，人口減少にもかかわらず，日本の大学は増え続けている。世界の全ての大学が巨大な研究大学になる必要は無い。いくつかは独自性のある教育を提供する小規模な教育機関であることも可能であろう。もし教育機関が地域のマーケットと比べて大きすぎなければ，十分な質を有したローカルな独自性は持続可能なベースで国際学生を十分引き付けられるだろう。

参考文献

ASAMIZU, Munehiko (2009), "Some Challenges of Japan's Geographical Education in English", *Abstract and Proceedings: International Geographical Union (IGU)*, Commission of Geographical Education Tsukuba Conference 2009, pp. 182–187

堀雅晴 (2007)「私立大学における大学ガバナンスと私学法制をめぐる歴史的検証」『立命館法學』316, 220–289 頁

国際交流基金 (n.d.)「国際交流基金について」, http://www.jpf.go.jp/j/about/index.html, 2009年10月8日閲覧

JASSO (2008a), *JASSO Outline 2008–2009*, Tokyo, JASSO

JASSO (2008b) *UNIVERSITY DEGREE COURSES OFFERED IN ENGLISH* (factsheet), Tokyo, JASSO

JASSO (n.d.a), Trends in Number of International Students by Institutional Type (as of each May 1),

ability. Educational organizations such as MEXT and JASSO are studying variations in international students from the perspectives of quality and quantity.

In addition, short–term international programs in Japan also face many possibilities for change. During the bubble economy, internationalization was a kind of fashion, and many Japanese universities sent Japanese students overseas and received international students in Japan for the purpose of cross–cultural understanding. However, as some countries have commercialized inbound educational tourism, some Japanese universities have now recognized the economic benefits of short–term programs. Desirable cultural magnets, include popular culture, will be needed to attract educational tourists.

It should be noted, though, that expansion in quantity is not the only way to survive intense global competition. Quite curiously, the number of universities in Japan is still increasing in spite of Japan's depopulation. Not every university in the world needs to be a large research university. Some can remain as small educational institutions that offer a uniquely targeted education. If the educational institution is not too large when compared to the regional market, local uniqueness with sufficient quality should be good enough to attract international students on a sustainable basis.

References

ASAMIZU, Munehiko (2009), "Some Challenges of Japan's Geographical Education in English", *Abstract and Proceedings: International Geographical Union (IGU)*, Commission of Geographical Education Tsukuba Conference 2009, pp. 182–187

HORI, Masaharu (2007), "Shiritsu Daigaku ni okeru Daigaku Governance to Shigaku Housei wo meguru Rekishiteki Kenshou", *Ritsumeikan Hougaku*, Vol. 316, pp. 220–289

Japan Foundation (n.d.), *Kokusai Koryu Kikin ni Tsuite*, http://www.jpf.go.jp/j/about/index.html, Accessed 8 October, 2009

JASSO (2008a), *JASSO Outline 2008–2009*, Tokyo, JASSO

JASSO (2008b) *UNIVERSITY DEGREE COURSES OFFERED IN ENGLISH* (factsheet), Tokyo, JASSO

JASSO (n.d.a), Trends in Number of International Students by Institutional Type (as of each May 1), http://www.jasso.go.jp/statistics/intl_student/documents/data08_02_e.pdf, 2010 年 3 月 18 日閲覧

JASSO (n.d.b), "Short-term Study Programs" http://www.jasso.go.jp/study_j/documents/short_term.xls, 2009 年 6 月 26 日閲覧

JASSO (n.d.c), *What is EJU?*, http://www.jasso.go.jp/eju/whats_eju_e.html, 2009 年 10 月 8 日閲覧

JICA (n.d.a), *History*, http://www.jica.go.jp/english/about/history/, 2009 年 10 月 8 日閲覧

JICA (n.d.b), *About the Japan Center*, http://japancenter.jica.go.jp/japancenter_e.html, 2009 年 10 月 8 日閲覧

JICE (n.d.), *Overseas Student Program*, http://sv2.jice.org/e/jigyou/ryuugakusei.htm, 2009 年 10 月 8 日閲覧

JLPT (n.d.), *What is the JLPT?*, http://www.jlpt.jp/e/about/index.html, 2009 年 10 月 8 日閲覧

文部科学省（2007）『平成 18 年度高等学校における国際教育等の状況について』文部科学省

文部科学省（2008）『文部科学白書』文部科学省

文部科学省（2009a）『平成 21 年度版我が国の留学生制度の概要』文部科学省

文部科学省（2009b）『留学生に対する日本語教育の現状』, http://www.kantei.go.jp/jp/singi/jinzai/jitsumu/dai5/siryou2_2.pdf, 2010 年 3 月 18 日閲覧

宮永孝（1989）「幕府イギリス留学生［上］」『社会労働研究』36(3), 133-193 頁

宮永孝（1999）「幕末・明治の英学」『社会志林』46(2), 173-228 頁

宮永孝（2001）「日本洋学史：日本人と南蛮語学」『社会志林』48(1), 81-180 頁

宮永孝（2002）「日本洋学史：蘭学事始」『社会志林』49(2), 62-124 頁

竹中暉雄（2006）「『学制』に関する諸問題」『桃山学院大学人間科学』32, 84-144 頁

周一川（2007）「近代日本に留学した中国人の総数をめぐって」『中国研究月報』61(2), 21-28 頁

http://www.jasso.go.jp/statistics/intl_student/documents/data08_02_e.pdf, Accessed March 18, 2010

JASSO (n.d.b), "Short-term Study Programs" http://www.jasso.go.jp/study_j/documents/short_term. xls, Accessed June 26, 2009

JASSO (n.d.c), *What is EJU?*, http://www.jasso.go.jp/eju/whats_eju_e.html, Accessed 8 October, 2009

JICA (n.d.a), *History*, http://www.jica.go.jp/english/about/history/, Accessed 8 October, 2009

JICA (n.d.b), *About the Japan Center*, http://japancenter.jica.go.jp/japancenter_e.html, Accessed 8 October, 2009

JICE (n.d.), *Overseas Student Program*, http://sv2.jice.org/e/jigyou/ryuugakusei.htm, Accessed 8 October, 2009

JLPT (n.d.), *What is the JLPT?*, http://www.jlpt.jp/e/about/index.html, Accessed 8 October, 2009

MEXT (2007), *Heisei 18 Nendo Koutougakko ni Okeru Kokusaikyouiku Nado no Joukyou ni Tsuite*, Tokyo, MEXT

MEXT (2008), *Monbukagaku Hakusho*, Tokyo, MEXT

MEXT (2009a), *Heisei 21 Nendoban Wagakuni no Ryugakusei Seido no Gaiyou*, Tokyo, MEXT

MEXT (2009b), *Ryugakusei ni Taisuru Nihongo Kyouiku no Genjou*, http://www.kantei.go. jp/jp/singi/jinzai/jitsumu/dai5/siryou2_2.pdf, Accessed March 18, 2010

MIYANAGA, Takashi (1989), "Bakufu Igiris Ryugakusei - jou", *Society and labour*, Vol. 36, No. 3, pp. 133-193

MIYANAGA, Takashi (1999), "Bakumatsu Meiji no Eigaku", *Hosei journal of sociology and social sciences*, Vol. 46, No. 2, pp. 173-228

MIYANAGA, Takashi (2001), "Nihon Yougakushi - Nihonjin to Nanban Gogaku", *Hosei journal of sociology and social sciences*, Vol. 48, No. 1, pp. 81-180

MIYANAGA, Takashi (2002), "Nihon Yougakushi - Rangaku Kotohajime", *Hosei journal of sociology and social sciences*, Vol. 49, No. 2, pp. 62-124

TAKENAKA, Teruo (2006), "Some Comments on the Educational Philosophy of Gakusei (The First Educational System Ordinance in Modern Japan, 1872)", *Momoyama Gakuin Daigaku Ningen Kagaku*, Vol. 32, pp. 84-144

ZHOU, Yichuan (2007), "Kindai Nihon ni Ryugaku shita Chugokujin no Sousu wo megutte", *Chugoku Kenkyu Geppo*, Vol. 61, No. 2, pp. 21-28

第7章

地球規模の移動と日本における国際観光

第7章のはじめに

UNWTO（国際連合世界観光機関）は普段住んでいるところ以外の目的地に1泊以上滞在する訪問者を観光客としている。さらに，観光客は訪問者のうち，1年未満滞在する人を指す。この定義によると，2008年の時点で国際観光客は9億2200万人いた（UNWTO 2009：2）。UNWTO（2009：2）によると，国際観光客は1950年の時点では2500万人であったが，2000年には6億8400万人に増加した。

他方，国や地方の組織や機関によってさまざまな観光の定義がある。たとえば，日本の場合，「ツーリスト」は「観光客」と訳されるが，日帰り訪問者を含む場合もあり，「楽しむための旅人」や「楽しむための訪問者」を指す場合もある（Asamizu 2008：37-39）。

国や地方における観光の定義もまた歴史的に変わってきた。日本の旧運輸省における「観光」政策は団体のパッケージツアーを旅の主な形態としていた。しかしながら，近年では，観光活動が多様化し，日本の多くの政府機関が観光政策に関わっている。

運輸省を再編した国土交通省は日本における観光政策の主要な決定機関であるが，経済産業省はコンベンション，文部科学省は修学旅行やヘリテージ・ツーリズム，農林水産省はグリーンツーリズムを通じた地方活性化，環境省はエコツーリズムに関わっている。外来語の「ツーリズム」は英語の「tourism」

Chapter 7

Global Mobility and Japan's International Tourism

Introduction of Chapter 7

UNWTO (United Nations World Tourism Organization) defines tourists as visitors that stay at a destination other than their usual environment for more than one night. Visitors are also defined as tourists if they stay at a destination for less than one year. Under these definitions, international tourist arrivals reached 922 million in 2008 (UNWTO 2009: 2). According to UNWTO (2009: 2), international tourist arrivals have continued to grow from 25 million in 1950 to 684 million in 2000.

On the other hand, a variety of other definitions of tourism used by national and regional tourist boards and government agencies. For example, in Japan, "tourists" are translated as "*kankoukyaku*" ("*kankou*" means tourism and "*kyaku*" means visitors or customers) and these may include same-day visitors; though they are more usually classified as "pleasure travelers" or "pleasure visitors" (Asamizu 2008: 37-39).

National and regional definitions of tourism have also changed historically. The former Ministry of Transport oversaw the "*kankou*" policies of Japan when mass tourism, typified by group package tours, was the dominant form of travel. More recently, however, as tourism activities have diversified a variety of government ministries have become involved in managing tourism policy in Japan.

The Ministry of Land, Infrastructure, Transport and Tourism (MLIT), restructured from the Ministry of Transport, is still major player in the formation and execution of Japanese tourism policy, however, for example, the Ministry of Economy, Trade and Industry (METI) supports conventions, the Ministry of Education, Culture,

147

から来ているが，これらの省庁はこれらの活動を表すために英語の "tourism" を音写した「ツーリズム」という単語を用いている（Asamizu 2008：39-41）。

7-1. 日本における人的移動小史

　歴史的に，日本は海に囲まれているため，国際的な人的移動は地理的に限られていた。この地理的な孤立にもかかわらず，日本における人的移動は長い歴史を持っている。日本の古代国家が統一される前（6世紀），日本列島のいくつかの地方政権は朝鮮半島や中国に使節を送り，さらに教育のため若くて能力のある日本人を派遣した。江戸幕府（1603-1867）が鎖国する前，日本人商人は東南アジア一帯で交易を行っていた。江戸幕府の鎖国にもかかわらず，中国，朝鮮，オランダは日本と政治的，教育的，交易的な関係を続けていた。

　日本は国内観光の長い歴史もまた持っている。明治政府（1868-1912）の文明開化が起こる前，日本人は徒歩や馬，船で旅を楽しんだ。江戸時代，封建制の徳川幕府はイギリスの中世と同様に，旅の目的を制限した。巡礼と湯治は江戸時代の日本の庶民にとって人気があった。巡礼は元々は宗教的な活動であるが，カンタベリー巡礼と同様に，お伊勢参りでも大規模で豪華な宿泊施設やガイド付きツアーが発達した。同様に，湯治も本来治癒が目的であったが，いくつかの日本の温泉はイギリスのバースのように大規模な温泉保養地になった。

148　第7章　地球規模の移動と日本における国際観光

Sports Science and Technology (MEXT) promotes educational excursions and heritage tourism, the Ministry of Agriculture, Forestry and Fisheries (MAFF) funds rural revitalization through "green tourism" and the Ministry of the Environment subsidizes environmentally friendly "ecotourism" in Japan. The loan-word "turizumu", a phonetic transcription of the English "tourism", is used to refer to the activities promoted by these ministries (Asamizu 2008: 39-41).

7-1. A Short History of Human Mobility in Japan

Historically, as Japan is surrounded by sea, international human mobility was geographically limited. Despite this geographical isolation, Japan's international human mobility has a long history. Before the formation of ancient unified national Japanese (6C), several regional powers within the Japanese archipelago sent envoys to Korea and China, governments also sent younger, talented Japanese to Korea and China to be educated. Before the Edo Government (1603-1867) closed the country, Japanese merchants traded goods widely in Southeast Asia. Despite the isolation policy of Edo government, China, Korea and Dutch continued to have political, educational and trade relations with Japan.

Japan has a long history of domestic tourism, too. Before modernization of Japan initiated by the enlightenment policy of the Meiji Government (1868-1912), Japanese people enjoyed travel on foot, by horse and by ship. During the Edo period, the feudal Tokugawa government placed limitations upon the purpose of travel in a similar way to that of rulers in the British Medieval period. Pilgrimage and travel to hot springs became popular among ordinary Japanese citizens during the Edo Period. Pilgrimage was originally a religious activity; however, large-scale, gorgeous accommodations and guided tours were developed for Ise Shrine visitors like that provided to "pilgrims" visiting Canterbury Cathedral. Similarly, travel to hot springs (*onsen*) was seen to have a purely medicinial purpose; however, some hot springs in Japan evolved into large spa resorts like that of Bath.

明治時代，馬車や鉄道，蒸気船など，輸入された交通技術によって旅が楽に
なった。そのうち，鉄道は国中に急速に普及し，各地の特産を含めた携帯食で
ある駅弁など，旅行者向けのサービスも発達した。

　教育者や外交官，商人を除き，日本における国際旅行の歴史は比較的短い。
江戸末期から，西洋の外交官や商人のためホテルやリゾート施設が日本に作ら
れた。明治政府による近代化の努力にもかかわらず，日本の経済力は比較的弱
かった。日本におけるホテルやリゾート施設は西洋からの訪問者向けであり，
多くの日本人にとって高価なものであった。

　1964 年の東京オリンピックにおけるホテルブームまで，ホテルに滞在する
ことは一種の社会的ステータス・シンボルであり，多くの日本人は旅館に泊
まった。明治と大正（1912-1926）時代，娯楽のための国際観光もまた高価なも
のであった。日本の植民地を除き，当時の日本の観光は圧倒的にインバウンド
志向であった。

7-2. アウトバウンド観光国としての日本
　日本は現在では主要なアウトバウンド観光国の一つとして知られている。外
務省によると，2009 年の時点で，日本人の海外旅行者が 1544 万 6000 人だっ
たのに対し，国際訪問者は 758 万 1000 人だった（外務省 n.d.: web）。

　第二次世界大戦直後，日本はインバウンド観光国であった。第二次世界大戦
での敗戦に続き，日本政府は外貨不足のため，旅行の目的を制限した。インバ
ウンド観光は歓迎されたが，日本人による娯楽のための海外旅行は 1940-50 年

150　　第 7 章　地球規模の移動と日本における国際観光

During Meiji period, imported transportation technologies such as coaches, railways and steam ships made travel easier. The railway system above all, saw rapid nationwide development and was accompanied by the provision of services for tourists such as the portable lunch box, with local specialties called "station lunches" or "*ekiben*".

With the exception of travel by educators, diplomats and merchants, international travel has a relatively short history in Japan. Since the end of Edo period, hotels and resort facilities for Western diplomats and merchants were established in Japan. Despite the modernization efforts by the Meiji Government, Japanese economic power was still relatively weak. Hotels and resort facilities in Japan became a commodity designed for and consumed by Westerner visitors remaining too expensive for the majority of Japanese people.

Until the hotel boom resulting from the Tokyo Olympic Games of 1964, stay at hotels was a kind of social status symbol enjoyed only by the while the traditional Japanese inn (*ryokan*) remained popular among most Japanese. International pleasure tourism was also expensive for ordinary Japanese people during Meiji and Taisho (1912-1926) periods. With the exception travel to regions colonized by the Japanese government, tourism in Japan was overwhelming orientated towards inbound travel at that time.

7-2. Japan as an Outbound Tourism Country

Japan is now known as one of the major outbound tourism countries. According to the Ministry of Foreign Affairs (MOFA), there were 15,446 thousand Japanese overseas departures and 7,581 thousand international arrivals to Japan in 2009 (MOFA n.d.: web).

At the end of WWII, Japan was still an inbound tourism destination. Following the defeat of Japan in the Second World War, the Japanese government regulated the purpose of travel due to the shortage of foreign currency. Inbound tourism was

代は禁止された。しかしながら，日本の経済力が 1960 年代に強くなり，日本政府は国際観光政策を変えた。1964 年の東京オリンピックの前年，観光基本法が制定され，日本人のアウトバウンド観光が再開された。

　1970-80 年代の日本の経済力のさらなる発展に付随し，円が強くなった。さらに，第二次世界大戦後に商業的な航空交通システムが発達し，航空運賃が安くなったことにより，日本人は海外旅行のための利便性と経済的な機会を持つことができた。1970 年代以降，日本の航空会社は国内・国際の日本人旅行者のためにホテルチェーンを開発した（Sugita 2007：161-163）。

　1980 年代，日本の経済力が強くなり，日本とアメリカ合衆国の間で貿易摩擦が起こった。貿易戦争の危機回避のため，貿易不均衡解消策として，工業製品の不均衡の代わりに，日本政府により政治的に旅行者の流れを促す観光政策がとられた。日本政府は 1987 年にアウトバウンド観光を促すテンミリオン計画を実施した。1980 年代の日本人観光客は団体志向であり，海外からたくさんの土産品を購入した。この政策と同時に，日本の観光産業もグアムやハワイ，アメリカ西海岸，オーストラリアのクイーンズランド州などで日本人向けの開発を行った。

　1980 年代末のバブル経済期の他の重要な観光政策として 1987 年のリゾート法がある。輸出関連の工場へ対する投資を減らすため，日本政府はリゾート開発の規制緩和を行った。同法が施行される前，国立公園は開発を厳しく制限されていた。しかし，リゾート法の施行によりゴルフ場やスキー場，テーマパーク，ビーチリゾート，マリーナの開発が規制緩和された。

　リゾート法の別の目的は，農村部の活性化である。戦後の産業化により，農

welcomed, but Japanese people could not travel abroad for pleasure during the 1940s and 50s. However, as Japanese economic power increased during the 1960s; the Japanese government changed its international tourism policies. Just one year before the Tokyo Olympic Games of 1964, the "Basic Law of Tourism" (*Kankou Kihon Hou*) was enacted and outbound tourism by Japanese people restarted.

Concomitant with the further increase in Japanese economic power in the 1970s and 80s, the Yen became stronger, too. In addition, as the commercial air transportation system saw extensive development after WWII, and as air fares became cheaper, Japanese tourists were supplied with convenient, economical opportunities for overseas travel. Since the 1970s, Japanese air companies went on to develop hotel chains targeted at domestic and international Japanese travelers (Sugita 2007: 161-163).

In the 1980s Japanese economic power increased to the extent that it created trade friction between Japan and the US. Faced with the prospect of trade war, controlling the flow of international tourism became political issue; the Japanese government enacted tourism policies designed to offset the imbalance of trade in manufactured goods. The Japanese government implemented an outbound tourism campaign named the "Ten million program" (*Ten Mirion Keikaku*) in 1987. Japanese tourists in the 1980s were especially group-oriented and bought a lot of souvenirs from overseas. In tandem with these policies, the Japanese tourism service industry also developed a large number of tourism facilities in Guam, Hawaii, the West Coast of the US and Queensland of Australia targeted at Japanese tourists.

Another important tourism policy during the bubble economy of the late 1980s was the "Resort Law" (*Rezouto Hou*) enacted in 1987. To reduce the investment in factories related to export, the Japanese government deregulated resort development. Before this law was enacted, national parks were subject to stringent development restrictions. With the enactment of the Resort Law however, the development of golf courses, ski resorts, theme parks, beach resorts and marinas was derestricted.

Another purpose of the Resort Law was the revitalization of rural areas. As a

村部での人口減は日本では重要な問題になっていた。農村部にリゾート施設を作ることは地方の雇用を生む良い機会であった。地方の希薄な人口にもかかわらず，都会の富裕層のため，大規模で豪華なリゾート施設が北海道から沖縄まで作られた。農村部におけるこれらの巨大なリゾートの開発のため，日本政府と大規模な開発業者は共同開発を行った。これらの共同開発は第三セクター開発として知られている。

7-3. バブル後の観光のトレンド

バブル経済の終焉は，国内・国際の両方から，日本の観光にとって大きな転機になった。リゾート法によって作られた大規模で豪華なリゾート施設の多くは経営破たんした。失敗の原因の一つは単純にこれらの施設を支えていた富裕層が減ったことだが，他の理由として，日本人の観光形態のトレンドが変わったことも挙げられる。第二次世界大戦後からバブル経済が終わる1990年代の初頭まで，従業員のための福利厚生プログラムとして，日本の企業の多くはガイド付き団体ツアーを行っていた。しかしながら，1990年代半ばには，この傾向が変わっている。現在では個人の観光客がスペシャル・インタレスト・ツアー／ツーリズム（SIT）やエコツーリズム，グリーンツーリズムなど，様々な形態の観光を行っている。

先述のように，バブル経済期の多くの日本人観光客は団体旅行に参加しており，多くの会社は従業員を巨大な浴槽やレストラン，その他の娯楽施設を備えた大規模な温泉リゾートに連れて行くために添乗員付きバスを用意した。「一生懸命働き，一生懸命遊ぶ」のがバブル経済期の多くの日本の都市住民にとって典型的な暮らしであった。

他方，日本における労働環境は変わってきている。終身雇用のフルタイム労働者は，特に若い世代で少なくなり，一年契約の労働者やパートタイム労働者

result of post-war industrialization, depopulation of rural areas has been an important issue in Japan. The creation of resort facilities in rural areas was seen as a good opportunity to promote regional employment. Despite the sparse local regional population, large-scale, gorgeous resort facilities were established from Hokkaido to Okinawa targeted at urban rich visitors. In order to develop large-scale these massive resort facilities in rural areas, joint ventures between Japanese government and large private developers were established. These joint ventures became known as "third sector" (*dai-san sekuta*) developments.

7-3. Post Bubble Tourism Trends

The end of the bubble economy was an important turning point for Japanese tourism, both domestically and internationally. Many of the large-scale gorgeous resort facilities established by the Resort Law became bankrupt. One reason for their failure was simply the decline in the number of people rich enough to afford to visit them, but another fact was a change in the trend of Japanese tourism. During the period between the end of WWII to the end of the bubble economy in the early 1990s, many Japanese companies organized group guided tours as part of social welfare programs for their employees. By the mid 1990's however, this trend was changing. Individual tourists now became involved in various types of travel activities such as Special Interest Tour/Tourism (SIT), Ecotourism and Green tourism.

As previously mentioned, many Japanese tourists took part in group tours during the bubble economy and many companies provided buses with attendant tour-guides to take employees to large-scale hot spring resorts equipped with large baths, restaurants and other entertainment facilities. A culture of "work hard, play hard" typified the way of life of many urban Japanese people during the period of the bubble economy.

On the other hand, working conditions in Japan are changing. The proportion of tenured full-time workers, especially in the younger generations, has been declining

の人口が増えている。終身雇用の労働者向けの団体旅行もまた少なくなってきている。終身雇用のポストが少なくなったため，従業員の労働時間は長く，仕事は厳しく，労働環境はより競争的になった。終身雇用の会社従業員，特に都会の社員にとって，彼らが持っていないもので，価値のあるものは，平和と静けさである。そのため，大規模な温泉リゾートに代わり，自然豊かな露天風呂がある小さな温泉宿が日本の上級社員とその家族にとって人気になってきた。

　日本において，農村部での過疎化は大きな問題である。日本の農家は安い輸入農産物のため，経済的に厳しい。日本政府，特に農林水産省は 1995 年に施行されたグリーンツーリズム法によって農村に新たな産業が生まれることを試みている。この法律は創造のための経済的刺激や農家民泊のプロモーション，農産物加工，観光客のための農業体験などをもたらしている。

　バブル期にもたらされた大規模リゾート開発と比べると，リフォームや農家民泊の創設は大きなコストがかからない。さらに，Mock と Metalkova-Markova（2007：40-41）によると，都市の住人は典型的な農業体験に興味を持っている。日本の大多数の人口は都市化されているため，グリーンツーリズムは大いに発展の可能性がある。農林水産省は 2003 年の「オーライ！ニッポン」（都市と農山漁村コミュニティの交流と共生）など，観光に関連する新たなプログラムに支援している（Asamizu 2007：142-143）。環境省も 2008 年施行のエコツーリズム推進法により，自然でのレジャー活動をサポートしている。

　日本人のアウトバウンド観光は団体志向であったが，近年では先述の国内旅行に見られるように，個人による自由な独立旅行の傾向が見られる。たとえば，韓国はかつて日本の会社にとって人気のある団体旅行先であった。しかしなが

and the proportion of one-year contract workers and part-time workers has been increasing. The number of group tours organized for tenured workers also decreased. As the number of tenured positions decreased, employees' working hours became longer, work more strenuous and the working environment became more competitive. For tenured company employees, especially in urban areas, the environment that they lack, and most value, is that of peace and quiet. Thus, instead of large-scale hot spring resorts, small traditional hot spring inn with outdoor baths (*roten-buro*) in natural environments becomes popular among Japanese executives and their families.

The depopulation of rural areas is also still serious problem in Japan. Japanese farmers are facing a harsh financial situation due to the import of cheap agricultural products. The Japanese government, especially the Ministry of Agriculture, Forestry and Fisheries (MAFF), is promoting the creation of new industries in agricultural villages and via the "Green Tourism Law" (*Gureen Turizumu Hou*) enacted in 1995. This law provides financial stimulation for the creation and promotion of farmhouse inns, cooked agricultural products, and agricultural experiences for tourists.

Compared with the large-scale resort development carried out during the bubble period, the reform and creation of farmhouse inns involves less cost. In addition, according to Mock and Metalkova-Markova (2007: 40-41), typical agricultural activities appear unique novel and interesting to urban city dwellers. As the vast majority of the population of Japan is urbanized, green tourism has great growth-potential. MAFF is also supporting newer programs related to tourism such as, the "project for interchange and coexistence between urban and rural communities", (termed "*Orai-Nippon*") started in 2003 (Asamizu 2007: 142-143). The Ministry of the Environment is also supporting leisure activities in nature via the "Ecotourism Promotion Law" (*Eko Turizumu Suishin Hou*) enacted in 2008.

Japanese outbound tourists tended to travel in groups, but recently as we saw the case of domestic travel, the trend has been towards individualization: participation in 'Free Independent Travel'. For example, Korea used to be a popular group tourism

ら，韓国は人気の高い観光地であるものの，今ではグルメなレストラン，伝統的な美容，ポピュラー文化，医療など，様々な分野で，特に女性の間で，自由な個人の観光客の訪問地として知られている。Schumann（2007：196-197）によると，日本の家族マーケットで，特に年配の母親と娘の場合，グアムの観光産業にとって非常に大きな可能性がある。梅田（2008：40-43）によると，バリでは日本人の間で引率バスツアーのあるマス・マーケットのリゾートの人気が高かったが，近年ではトレンドが変わり，女性の個人観光客は贅沢なアジアン・スパを有した静かな田舎のヴィラを好むとしている。

7-4. 日本におけるインバウンド観光政策

バブル経済後，国内観光政策と同様に，日本政府は新しい国際観光政策を実施した。先述のように，日本におけるインバウンド観光は比較的小さかった。バブル経済の崩壊にもかかわらず，円高は 1980 年代初頭よりも著しかった（Schumann 2007：183-184）。観光に関する規制もまだ存在しており，東京在住者にとって近隣諸国へのアウトバウンド旅行は北海道や沖縄へ行くよりも安かった。バブル後の不景気になると，インバウンドとアウトバウンドの不均衡は，日本政府にとってもはや望ましいものではなかった。

インバウンド観光を新たに活性化させる一環として，日本政府はコンベンションの重要性を認識し，1994 年にコンベンション法が施行された。円高であっても，コンベンション客は会社からの経済援助があるため，コンベンション誘致には大きな可能性があった。さらに，日本における観光客数には大きな季節変動があった。しかしながら，娯楽目的の観光客とコンベンション客の季節的なパターンは異なっているため，コンベンション客のマーケットはニッチ・マーケットとして非常に有望であった。国土交通省だけでなく，経済産業省もコンベンションや博覧会のサポートを行った。

さらにインバウンド観光客数を増やすため，日本政府は「ウエルカムプラン

destination for Japanese companies. Now however, Korea remains popular, but as a destination for free individual tourists, especially females, who are diversifying to enjoy gourmet restaurants, traditional aesthetics, popular culture and medical activities. According to Schumann (2007: 196-197), the Japanese family market, especially elder mothers and daughters, has great potential for the tourism industry in Guam. According to Umeda (2008: 40-43), mass-market resorts providing guided bus tours were popular among Japanese group tourists in Bali, however, the trend is now changing, with female individual tourists now preferring peace and quiet in a rural villa equipped with a luxurious Asian spa.

7-4. Japan's Inbound Tourism Policies

After the period of the bubble economy, as with domestic tourism policies, the Japanese government implemented new international tourism policies. It should also be noted that inbound tourism to Japan was relatively small. Despite the burst of bubble economy, the Yen was still stronger than in the early 1980s (Schumann 2007: 183-184). Regulations related to tourism still existed and outbound travel to neighboring countries was cheaper than travel to Hokkaido and Okinawa for Tokyo residents. In the depression following the bubble era, the imbalance between inbound and outbound tourism was no longer considered desirable by the Japanese government.

As part of this new drive to stimulate inbound tourism, the Japanese government realized the importance of conventions and the "Convention Law" (*Konbenshon Hou*) was enacted in 1994. Even in spite of a strong yen, great potential was seen in the promotion of conventions since their visitors are economically supported by companies. In addition, the number of tourists in Japan has a large seasonal diversity. However, the seasonal travel pattern of pleasure-tourists and convention-goers are different, so the conventions market was eyed as an extremely advantageous niche market. Not only MLIT but also METI supports conventions and exhibitions.

To increase the volume of inbound tourism further, the Japanese government

Chapter 7   Global Mobility and Japan's International Tourism   159

21」を 1996 年に実施した。しかしながら，これらのインバウンド観光政策にもかかわらず，2000 年代初頭のインバウンド観光客は少なかった。しかしながら，2003 年に日本政府は大規模なインバウンド推進プログラムである「ビジット・ジャパン・キャンペーン」（VJC または Yokoso Japan）を実施した。小泉首相がコマーシャルに登場したり観光国際会議に参加したりしたこともあり，このキャンペーンは以前のものよりは効果があった。しかしながら，日本人の近年の観光客のトレンドからすでに見てきたように，国際観光は個人化と多様化が進んでいる。日本がより多くの個人の国際観光客を受け入れるためには，インバウンド観光のための様々な視点からインフラやサービスの整備が必要である。

　歴史的に，日本のインバウンド観光のトレンドは主要都市周辺の団体ガイドツアーが主流であった。しかしながら，近年では，地方の町や村でもまた自由な個人観光客の訪問が見られる。大都市ではツアーガイド・通訳付きの団体旅行がインバウンド観光客の間で人気があった。リピーターとして自由な独立した国際観光客をたくさん受け入れるためには，異なった観光資源が必要である。たとえば，現在でも，いくつかのローカルな文化やサブカルチャーが日本のインバウンド観光で焦点になっている。しかしながら，これらの特別な関心の観光客が成長するのに対する主な阻害要因として，日本語以外の言語のアナウンスの不足が挙げられる。日本のインバウンド観光を推進するために，標識やパンフレット，通訳など，外国語サポートシステムやサービスの量的，質的な改善が，最低でも英語，韓国語，中国語で求められている。

　観光と教育を合わせた教育観光もまた大きな可能性を持っている。ルネッサンス期（14-16 世紀）のイギリスにおけるグランドツアーでは，教育目的の旅は観光と深く結びついていた。オーストラリア政府，特にオーストラリア政府観光局（TA）は学生のための学校訪問や訪問者のための短期教育プログラム

initiated "Welcome Plan 21" (*Uerukamu Puran 21*) in 1996. However, despite these inbound tourism policies, inbound visitors in the early 2000s were still small. In 2003, however, the Japanese government initiated a large inbound tourism promotion program called the "Visit Japan Campaign" (VJC or *Yokoso* Japan). Partly as a result of the efforts of Prime Minister Koizumi, who made advertisements and joined international tourism conferences, this campaign was more effective than previous policies. However, as we have seen in exemplified by the recent trend of Japanese tourists, international tourists are likewise individualized and diversified. In order for Japan to succeed in welcoming large numbers of individual international tourists, many of aspects of the infrastructure and services supporting inbound tourism will have to be developed.

The historical trend of Japan's inbound tourism was predominantly group guided tours around major cities. More recently however, regional towns and villages are witnessing the arrival of free independent travelers. Visits to large cities were popular with international tourists traveling in a group accompanied by a tour guides / interpreter. In order to welcome larger numbers of repeat free independent international tourists, different tourism resources will be needed. For example, even now, some local cultures and sub-cultures are becoming a focus for Japan's inbound tourism. However, a major stumbling block to the growth of such special interest, cultural tourism, geared towards free independent international travelers is the lack of announcements in languages other than Japanese. A far greater quantity and quality of foreign language support systems and services, such as signage, pamphlets, and interpreters, at least in English, Korean and Chinese, will be needed in order to promote Japan's inbound tourism.

The combination of tourism and education ‐ educational tourism ‐ has great potential too. Since the Renaissance era (14-16C) of the British Grand Tour, educational travel has been closely related to tourism. The Australian government, especially Tourism Australia (TA), vigorously promotes international, inbound "Study

などのインバウンド学習観光を対外的に精力的にプロモートしてきた。教育観光と海外教育プログラムは海外からの観光客をもたらし，オーストラリアにて一大マーケットになった。

　日本では，生徒・学生のための教育旅行が主要な教育活動として明治時代から行われている。バブル経済期には日本の学校からの海外修学旅行が盛んになり，1992年から日本政府は中，高生の海外修学旅行の統計を集めるようになった。他方，日本政府がインバウンドの教育観光マーケットの重要性に気付いたのはつい最近のことである。海外からの学校訪問者を受け入れるため，文部科学省（2008：286）は2005年にフレンドシップ・ジャパン・プランを導入した。

　日本における観光産業は1960年代よりも多様化しており，観光産業の様々な変化を反映するため，新たな観光の法である観光立国推進基本法が2007年に施行（2006年制定）された。さらに，2008年には観光庁が設立され，観光のプロモーションやより効果的な観光の創造を行っている。

　国際観光の規制緩和も日本では進みつつある。たとえば，中国は日本の観光産業にとって最大の可能性を持ったマーケットであると思われている。劉（2008：156-159）によると，2000年まで来日する中国からの訪問者はいくつかの都市からの団体観光客に限られていた。しかしながら，訪日旅行を行う中国人の居住地は次第に多様化し，個人化も進んだ。2004年にはいくつかの地方部の省の人々にとって余暇目的の団体旅行の参加が規制緩和され，2009年には日本への余暇目的の個人旅行も合法的になった。

　さらに，観光政策に加え，あまり知られていなかった観光地が国際的に有名になるためには運もまた重要である。ニセコにおけるオーストラリアからのスキー客や別府におけるインドからの訪問者，秋田における韓国からの観光客の

Tourism", such as school visiting, excursions for students and short educative programs for visitors. "Study Tourism" and "Off Shore" educational programs catering to overseas tourists have become a large market in Australia.

In Japan, excursions and study trips for schoolchildren have been a popular educational activity since the Meiji Period. International study tours arranged by Japanese schools became popular during the period of the bubble economy, and the Japanese government has been collecting statistics regarding outbound study tours by high schools and junior high schools since 1992. On the other hand, it was only recently that the Japanese government realized the importance of the inbound study tour market. To welcome school visitors from overseas, MEXT (2008: 286) initiated the "Friendship Japan Plan" (*Furendoshippu Japan Puran*) in 2005.

The tourism industry in Japan is now much diversified than it was in the 1960s and reflecting the wide-ranging changes in the tourism industry, a new tourism law called "The Tourism Nation Promotion Basic Law" (*Kankou Rikkoku Suishin Kihon Hou*) came into effect in 2007 (established in 2006). Furthermore, "The Japan Tourism Agency" was established in 2008 with a view to the ongoing promotion of tourism and creation of effective tourism.

Deregulation of international tourism is also underway in Japan. For example, China now thought to be the largest potential market for the Japanese tourism industry. According to Ryu (2008: 156-159), Chinese regulations limited outbound tourism to Japan such that only those Chinese leisure tourists that participated in group tours from some particular cities were allowed to visit Japan since 2000. However, the domicile of Chinese tourists to Japan has gradually diversified and individualized. Participation in group leisure tourism expanded to allow the residents of some regional provinces in 2004, and individual leisure tourism to Japan was finally made legal in 2009.

In addition to tourism policies, chance is also an important fact in the growth of inbound tourism because it is by chance that sometimes less popular tourist destinations become famous internationally. The popularities of Niseko among

人気は興味深い事例として挙げられる。

　オーストラリア人にとって，ヨーロッパや北アメリカと比べれば，日本はそれほど離れていない。日本とオーストラリアの季節が逆のため，オーストラリアの開発業者は北海道のニセコや長野県の白馬などの寒冷地にオーストラリアからのスキー客のためにリゾート施設を開発した。大分県の別府市は留学生を積極的に受け入れており，留学生のための住居もまた提供している。別府のある大学は日本における最大の留学生の受け入れ先の一つになり，留学生の友人や親戚もまた同市を訪問するようになった。秋田県は典型的な農村部の過疎の県である。しかし，韓国の TV 番組である IRIS にて秋田がロケ地になり，この番組が韓国で大ヒットした。韓国人観光客の間で，普通のローカルな店もまた有名な観光目的地になった。

第 7 章のおわりに

　この章では日本における観光産業と関連した政策について述べた。統一された定義は比較研究のために重要である。しかし，観光は国によって異なっており，おそらく日本の事例はユニークなケースとして挙げられるだろう。日本で社会のトレンドが変わった時，日本の観光の政策や活動，形態もまた変化した。

　1980 年代の日本人観光客は団体志向であった。しかしながら，近年の日本人観光客は個人化が進み，環境の持続可能性に対する志向を持っている。1980年代の日本の国際観光はアウトバウンド志向であった。しかし，日本政府はバブル経済の崩壊後，インバウンド観光政策の重要性を（再）認識した。観光における広い範囲での変化に対応し，観光立国推進基本法が 2007 年に施行され，2008 年には観光庁が設立されている。

Australian skiers, Beppu among Indian visitors and Akita among Korean tourists are interesting examples.

For Australian people, Japan is not a remote place, compared at least with Europe and North America. As the seasons of Japan and Australia are opposite, Australian developers are establishing resort facilities in Niseko (Hokkaido), Hakuba (Nagano) and other cold places to cater for Australian skiers. Beppu in Oita prefecture is welcoming international students and the city is offering public residences to students from overseas. A University in Beppu became one of the largest international receivers of overseas students in Japan, and friends and relatives of international students are also visiting that city. Akita is a typical rural prefecture experiencing severe depopulation. However, a Korean TV program, "IRIS", filmed on location in some places in Akita became a smash-hit in Korea. Even ordinary local stores became popular destinations among Korean tourists.

Conclusion of Chapter 7

This chapter introduced tourism industry and related policies in Japan. Unified definitions are important for comparative studies internationally. However, as tourism is different from country to country, studies exemplifying Japanese may be treated as unique cases. When social trends changed in Japan, policies, activities and forms of Japanese tourism also changed.

Japanese tourists in the 1980s were group-oriented. On the other hand, the current form of Japanese tourism is increasingly individualized and orientated towards ecological sustainability. Japan's international tourism in the 1980s was outbound-oriented. However, the Japanese government (re)realized the importance of inbound tourism policies after the burst of bubble economy. Reflecting the wide-ranging changes in the tourism industry, "The Tourism Nation Promotion Basic Law" came into effect in 2007 and "The Japan Tourism Agency" was established in 2008.

補足資料 1　2008 年の地域別国際観光客訪問数

ヨーロッパ　489.4（100 万人）
アジア太平洋　184.1
南北アメリカ　147.0
アフリカ　46.7
中東　55.1
出典：UNWTO 2009, p. 4

補足資料 2　2008 年の国際観光客訪問数上位 10 か国

フランス　79.3（100 万人）
アメリカ合衆国　58.0
スペイン　57.3
中国　53.0
イタリア　42.7
イギリス　30.2
ウクライナ　25.4
トルコ　25.0
ドイツ　24.9
メキシコ　22.6
出典：UNWTO 2009, p. 6

補足資料 3　2008 年の国際観光客訪問数（アジア太平洋）

中国　53,049（1000 人）
マレーシア　22,052
香港　17,320
タイ　14,584
マカオ　10,605
日本　8,351
シンガポール　7,778
韓国　6,891
インドネシア　6,234
オーストラリア　5,586
出典：UNWTO 2009, p. 7

参考文献

ASAMIZU, Munehiko（2008）"Some Current Affairs of International Tourism Researches Related to Japan", *Journal of Asia Pacific Tourism and Hospitality*, Vol. 3, pp. 37-45

ASAMIZU, Munehiko（2007）"Tourism in Japan", in KAWAKAMI, Ikuo *et al.* eds., *Japan's*

Appendix 1 International Tourist Arrivals in 2008 (By Region)
Europe 489.4 (Million)
Asia and the Pacific 184.1
Americas 147.0
Africa 46.7
Middle East 55.1
Source: UNWTO 2009, p. 4

Appendix 2 International Tourist Arrivals in 2008 (World Top 10)
France 79.3 (Million)
United States 58.0
Spain 57.3
China 53.0
Italy 42.7
United Kingdom 30.2
Ukraine 25.4
Turkey 25.0
Germany 24.9
Mexico 22.6
Source: UNWTO 2009, p. 6

Appendix 3 International Tourist Arrivals in 2008 (Asia and the Pacific)
China 53,049 (Thousand)
Malaysia 22,052
Hong Kong 17,320
Thailand 14,584
Macao 10,605
Japan 8,351
Singapore 7,778
Republic of Korea 6,891
Indonesia 6,234
Australia 5,586
Source: UNWTO 2009, p. 7

References

ASAMIZU, Munehiko (2008) "Some Current Affairs of International Tourism Researches Related to Japan", *Journal of Asia Pacific Tourism and Hospitality*, Vol. 3, pp. 37-45

ASAMIZU, Munehiko (2007) "Tourism in Japan", in KAWAKAMI, Ikuo *et al.* eds., *Japan's*

Globalization, Kumpul, pp. 137-154

文部科学省（2008）『文部科学白書』文部科学省

MOCK, John and METALKOVA-MARKOVA, Milena（2007）"Social and Cultural Impact of Depopulation in Central Akita", in KAWAKAMI, Ikuo *et al.* eds., *Japan's Globalization*, Kumpul, pp. 27-44

外務省（n.d.）『外国人入国者数　日本人出国者数の推移』，http://www.moj.go.jp/content/000023812.pdf，2010 年 4 月 5 日閲覧

RYU, Min（2008）"Marketing Strategy for Destination Kyushu", in ASAMIZU, Munehiko ed., *Human Mobility in Asia Pacific*, Office SAKUTA, pp. 136-185

SCHUMANN, Fred R.（2007）"Changing Trends in Japanese Overseas Travel", in KAWAKAMI, Ikuo *et al.* eds., *Japan's Globalization*, Kumpul, pp. 175-199

SUGITA, Yukiko（2007）"Development of Air Transportation in Japan and its Impetus to the Growth of Outbound Tourism from Japan", in KAWAKAMI, Ikuo *et al.* eds., *Japan's Globalization*, Kumpul, pp. 155-174

UMEDA, Hideharu（2008）"Island of Entertainment or Paradise of Healing?", in ASAMIZU, Munehiko ed., *Human Mobility in Asia Pacific*, Office SAKUTA, pp. 24-51

UNWTO（2009）*Tourism Highlights 2009 Edition*, UNWTO

Globalization, Kumpul, pp. 137–154

MEXT（2008）*Monbukagaku Hakusho*, MEXT

MOCK, John and METALKOVA-MARKOVA, Milena（2007）"Social and Cultural Impact of Depopulation in Central Akita", in KAWAKAMI, Ikuo *et al.* eds., *Japan's Globalization*, Kumpul, pp. 27–44

MOFA（n.d.）*Gaikokujin Nyukokushasuu/Nihonjin Syukkokushasuu no Suii*, http://www.moj.go.jp/content/000023812.pdf, Accessed April 5, 2010

RYU, Min（2008）"Marketing Strategy for Destination Kyushu", in ASAMIZU, Munehiko ed., *Human Mobility in Asia Pacific*, Office SAKUTA, pp. 136–185

SCHUMANN, Fred R.（2007）"Changing Trends in Japanese Overseas Travel", in KAWAKAMI, Ikuo *et al.* eds., *Japan's Globalization*, Kumpul, pp. 175–199

SUGITA, Yukiko（2007）"Development of Air Transportation in Japan and its Impetus to the Growth of Outbound Tourism from Japan", in KAWAKAMI, Ikuo *et al.* eds., *Japan's Globalization*, Kumpul, pp. 155–174

UMEDA, Hideharu（2008）"Island of Entertainment or Paradise of Healing?", in ASAMIZU, Munehiko ed., *Human Mobility in Asia Pacific*, Office SAKUTA, pp. 24–51

UNWTO（2009）*Tourism Highlights 2009 Edition*, UNWTO

第 **8** 章

インバウンド観光プロモーションのトレンド

第 8 章のはじめに

国際観光客の興味を引くために，特定の観光機関が重要な役割を演じている。STB（シンガポール政府観光局），KTO（韓国政府観光局），JNTO（日本政府観光局），TA（ツーリズム・オーストラリア），ビジット・ブリテン（UK）など，様々な国に様々な政府観光機関がある。

これらの政府観光機関に加え，地域の政府間の機関もまた国際観光客の注目を得るために重要である。ETC（ヨーロッパ観光委員会），PATA（太平洋アジア観光協会），ASEANTA（ASEAN 観光協会）など，いくつかの例がある。

これらの国家・政府間観光機関にとって，オリンピックやサッカーワールドカップ，万国博覧会などの世界的に知名度の高いイベントは大きなアドバンテージになる。しかしながら，特定の年のキャンペーンや継続的なキャンペーンもまた，一貫して観光客数を増やすために必要である。

特定の国に焦点を当てたとき，政策的な変化が歴史的に見えてくる。たとえば，ビジット・ジャパン・キャンペーンは 2003 年に日本政府によって導入された公的なインバウンド観光プロモーションである。1970 年代の後，安定した経済成長に続き，日本はアウトバウンド観光国になった。しかしながら，1990 年代初頭のバブル経済の崩壊により，日本政府は観光政策を変えた。ビジット・ジャパン・キャンペーンの導入により，日本政府はより遠くより広い

Chapter 8

Trends of Inbound Tourism Promotions

Introduction of Chapter 8

To attract the attention of international tourists, specific tourism organizations play important roles. These include the STB (Singapore Tourism Board), KTO (Korea Tourism Organization), JNTO (Japan National Tourism Organization), TA (Tourism Australia) and "VisitBritain" (UK), as well as many other national tourism organizations in various countries.

In addition to these national tourism organizations, regional intergovernmental organizations play important roles in capturing the attention of international tourists. The ETC (European Travel Commission), PATA (Pacific Asia Travel Association), ASEANTA (ASEAN Tourism Association), and a few examples.

For these national and intergovernmental tourism organizations, prestigious international events such as the Olympic Games, FIFA World Cup and EXPO (Universal Exposition) offer many advantages. However, specific year campaigns and continuous campaigns are also needed to increase tourist numbers with any consistency.

When focusing on a particular country, changes in political trends can be seen historically. For example, the "Visit Japan Campaign" is an official inbound tourism promotion launched by the Japanese government in 2003. After the 1970s, following robust economic development, Japan became an outbound tourism country. Since the bursting of the bubble economy in the early 1990s, however, the Japanese government has been changing its tourism policies. Since the initiation of the Visit Japan

範囲から国際観光客を受け入れようとしている。

　通常のプロモーション・キャンペーンに加え，国際観光客のための緊急情報もまた重要である。地震や津波，洪水などの災害避難情報は必須である。災害は予測が困難であるため，将来のリピーターのためには観光客を含んだ避難と応答の計画を保証することが必要である。災害の後，マスメディアによる衝撃的な報道が見られるが，復興が進んだ後もなかなか観光客は戻ってこない。時に，復興キャンペーンや効果的な宣伝が，以前の来客数まで回復させるために必要である。

8-1. 研究方法と先行研究

　本研究は文献の比較に依拠している。世界中の観光政策を比較するためには多くの文献が必須である。できれば複数の言語で文献研究を行った方が望ましいが，国際観光プロモーションの分野では英語が主流になりつつある。英語による観光情報に加え，政府観光局による政策レポートや統計資料もまた，多くの国から英語で出版されている。

　英語による資料は比較研究のため便利である。UNWTO や OECD，ASEAN などの国際機関によって算出された統計は複数の国々を比較する上で必須である。ビジット・ブリテンや TA，STB など，英語圏における政府観光局は年次報告書や統計，その他の観光に関する資料を英語で公開している。

　いくつかの非英語圏の国々も英語でレポートを出版している。たとえば，1964 年に改組された日本政府観光局（当時は国際観光振興機構）は多言語の観光情報に加え，観光業者向けの英語の資料も提供している。現在の韓国政府観光局である KTO（元々は 1962 年に韓国国際振興機構として設立され，英語では KNTO と呼ばれた）は時事問題やニュースを韓国語，英語，中国語，日本語で

Campaign, the Japanese government has been trying to heartily welcome international tourists from far and wide.

In addition to ordinary promotional campaigns, emergency information for international visitors is also needed. In the event of a disaster such as an earthquake, tsunami or flood, evacuation information is essential. As disasters are hard to predict, future repeat visitors need assurance that evacuation and response plans will include them. Following a disaster, sensational reports of the mass media often have the effect of greatly reducing the number of visitors even well after recovery has progressed. Sometimes, recovery campaigns and effective advertisements are needed to regain the previous number of visitors.

8-1. Research Methods and Literature Reviews

This study relies on a comparative literature approach. To compare several tourism policies used worldwide, a large volume of literature is essential. Though it would be better to study the literature of several languages, English is becoming dominant in the field of international tourism promotion. In addition to English tourist information, political reports and statistical papers published by national tourism organizations in English are also available in many countries.

Documents written in English are convenient sources for comparative studies. Statistics calculated by international organizations such as UNWTO, OECD and ASEAN are essential when comparing several countries. National tourism organizations in English speaking countries, such as VisitBritain, TA and STB, publish annual reports, statistics and other tourism documents in English.

Some non-native English speaking countries also publish reports in English. For example, the JNTO, reestablished in 1964, offers English materials to tourism providers as well as multilingual information for tourists. The KTO, formerly called the KNTO: Korea National Tourism Organization (and originally established in 1962 as the Korea International Tourism Corporation), offers current affairs and news in

提供している。

　他方，観光に関する歴史的な研究は違った話である。社会科学にて多くの文献を比較することは必要であるが，いくつかの分野では困難である。個人のインバウンド観光客が少なかった時，多くの政策レポートは現地語のみで書かれていた。本研究では，言語上の制約から，歴史的なアプローチは英語と日本語の文献から行う。

　記念出版は，広範な歴史的情報，特に様々な設立のバックグラウンドを手短にまとめるのに良い方法である。いくつかの政府間組織もまた記念のため歴史的な文献を出版している。たとえば，ETC は『共同アクション 60 周年記念 1948-2008』を 2008 年の歴史的な記念時に出版している（ETC 2008）。

　公式の記念本に加え，幾人かの観光専門家は彼らの回顧録を出版している。Picolla（1987）は PATA の歴史を要約している（Picolla：137-139）。Wong 他（2001）は特に ASEAN 諸国の国際観光協力について歴史的にケースを分析している（Wong *et al.*：367-376）。Chang（1998）は 1964 年の旧 STPB（シンガポール観光プロモーション公社）設立以降のシンガポールにおける観光政策の歴史について研究している（Chang：73-74）。Chang はまた，旧 STPB と現在の STB，世界の他の政府観光局との比較もまた行っている。

　現地の言語を使うことは，歴史的な事象や現地の文化，サブカルチャーを研究する上で利点がある。しかしながら，非英語圏における英語文献もまた比較研究のために有意義である。たとえば，Soshiroda（2005）は 1859 年から 2003 年までの日本の観光政策の歴史を要約しており（Soshiroda：1100-1120），Uzama（2009）は 2003 年のビジット・ジャパン・キャンペーン以降の日本の観光プロモーションの変遷を紹介している（Uzama：356-365）。

Korean, English, Chinese and Japanese.

On the other hand, historical research related to tourism is a different story. Wider literature comparisons are needed for social science research, though this can be difficult in some fields. At a time when there were few individual inbound tourists, many political reports were written in the local language alone. This study assumes a limitation of languages, and depends on papers in English and Japanese in its historical approach.

Anniversary publications are a good way to briefly summarize extended historical information, especially the backgrounds of various establishments. Some intergovernmental organizations have also published historical texts for their anniversary. For example, the ETC published *60 YEARS OF JOINT ACTION 1948–2008* for its historical anniversary in 2008 (ETC 2008).

In addition to official anniversary books, some tourism specialists have published their own historical retrospectives. Picolla (1987) summarized the history of PATA (Picolla: 137–139), Wong *et al.* (2011) analyzed historical cases of international tourism collaborations particularly with ASEAN nations (Wong *et al.*: 367–376), and Chang (1998) studied the history of tourism policies in Singapore following the establishment of the former STPB (Singapore Tourist Promotion Board) in 1964 (Chang: 73–74). Chang also compared the former STPB, current STB and other tourism organizations around the world.

Usage of the local language is an advantage when researching historical matters, local cultures and subcultures. However, some English literature focused on non–native English countries is also useful for comparative studies. For example, Soshiroda (2005) summarized the history of Japanese tourism policies from 1859 to 2003 (Soshiroda: 1100–1120), and Uzama (2009) introduced Japan's promotional changes after the "Visit Japan Campaign" of 2003 (Uzama: 356–365).

8-2. 国家組織による観光開発と観光プロモーション

　ある国が十分な観光の多様性を持った時，政府の支援による国家観光プロモーションは国際観光客を受け入れるのに効果がある。時に，観光資源は国際コンベンションのための重要なアトラクションになる。さらに，何人かの留学生が教育目的のため観光地を訪問することもある。観光の多様化のため，多くの観光機関やプロモーションが，たとえば「ビジット・ブリテン」（2003 年改組），「ビジット・スウェーデン」（2006 年改名），「ビジット・コリア・イヤー」（2001 年，2004 年など），「ビジット・ジャパン・キャンペーン」（2003 年から）のように「visit」という単語を用いている。

　観光産業と観光プロモーションはいつも同じように発達するわけではない。たとえば，イギリスはトーマス・クック（1808-1892）の時代から，国際観光客の送り出しの長い歴史を持っている。しかしながら，1851 年のロンドン万博から，最初の産業革命（18-19 世紀）の国として，イギリスは博覧会や技術・産業関連のイベントを行う際に優位である。他方，スイスやフランス，イタリア，その他のヨーロッパの国々と比べれば，イギリスは国家レベルでの継続したインバウンド観光プロモーションの歴史が比較的短い。

　さらに，いくつかのアジア太平洋地域の国々は国際観光政策を強化してきた。韓国は観光プロモーション法を 1961 年に施行し（KTO n.d.: web），日本は 1963 年に観光基本法を施行した。シンガポールは独立の前年の 1964 年に STPB（Singapore Tourist Promotion Board）を設立し，オーストラリアは ATC（Australia Tourist Commission）を 1967 年に設立した（朝水 2001：366）。観光プロモーションにもかかわらず，日本は 1970 年代からアウトバウンド観光国として知られており，オーストラリアも近年では同様の国として知られている。

　国家の観光機関として，1969 年観光開発法により，英国政府観光庁（BTA）

176　　第 8 章　インバウンド観光プロモーションのトレンド

8-2. Tourism Developments and Promotions by National Organizations

When a country acquires enough touristic diversity, government supported national tourism promotions can be effective in bringing in international tourists. Sometimes tourism resources are an important attraction for international conventions. In addition, some international students visit tourism destinations with an educational purpose in mind. As the meaning of tourism diversifies, there are a lot of tourism organizations and promotions that use the word "visit." VisitBritain (reformed in 2003), "Visit Sweden" (renamed in 2006), "Visit Korea Year" (2001, 2004 etc.) and the "Visit Japan Campaign" (since 2003) are examples.

The tourism industry and tourism promotions do not always develop in the same manner. For example, the UK has had a long history as an international tourist sender since the era of Thomas Cook (1808-1892). However, since the first London EXPO of 1851, as the first country to enter the industrial revolution (18th-19th centuries), the UK has had integral advantages when it comes to exhibitions and other international events related to technology and industry. On the other hand, when compared to Switzerland, France, Italy and other European countries, the UK has still had a relatively short history of continuous inbound tourism promotion policies at a national level.

In addition, some countries in the Asia Pacific region have strengthened their international tourism policies. South Korea enacted the Tourism Promotion Act of 1961 (KTO n.d.: web) and Japan enacted its Basic Law on Tourism in 1963. Singapore established the STPB (Singapore Tourist Promotion Board) in 1964, one year before independence, and Australia established the ATC (Australia Tourist Commission) in 1967 (Asamizu 2001: 366). Despite its tourism promotions, Japan has been known as an outbound tourist country since the 1970s and Australia is gaining the same reputation more recently.

As a national tourism authority, the British Tourist Authority (BTA) was

が 1969 年に設立され，イングランド，スコットランド，ウェールズの各地の観光局が協力した（VisitBritain 2008：2）。国際観光客を引き寄せ，国際プロモーションを強化するために，BTA とこれらの観光局は 2003 年にビジット・ブリテンとして再編された（VisitBritain 2009：9）。

ビジット・ブリテンの海外ネットワークは産業と戦略パートナーのための共有されたサービスとして再編された。イギリスへの訪問を促す時限的なキャンペーンは国内と海外で展開されているが，コンテンツのレビューやチャンネル，利用者が育成したコンテンツ，共有プラットフォームの機会は発展途中である。ビジット・ブリテンは 2003 年に設立された時，DCMS によって英国政府観光庁から政策を移行した。

*DCMS＝文化メディア・スポーツ省
出典：VisitBritain（2009）*VISITBRITAIN Annual Report and Accounts*, p. 9

国家観光機関が存在しているのにもかかわらず，イギリスでは地方の観光局が観光プロモーションの強い影響を持っている。この多様性がイギリスの観光の強みであるが，競合国は観光を国家プロジェクトとしてプロモートしている。イギリス政府は観光プロモーションの構造をビジット・ブリテンによる国家レベルとビジット・ロンドン，ビジット・イングランド，ビジット・スコットランド，ビジット・ウェールズの各地方機関のレベルに再構築した（VisitBritain 2009：10）。

近年，ビジット・ブリテンの海外ネットワークは，イギリスだけよりも，ビジット・イングランド，ビジット・スコットランド，ビジット・ウェールズ，ビジット・ロンドンといった戦略パートナーの明確なブランドが市場化に必要と認識している。この方向のアプローチはイギリス観光フレームワーク・レビューにて表されている。実際，これは近年参入したマーケットやイギリスを構成する各地を分かっていないマーケットは引き続きイギリスのブランドに焦点を持つことを意味する。

出典：VisitBritain（2009）*VISITBRITAIN Annual Report and Accounts*, p. 10

継続的なプロモーションに加え，オリンピックやサッカーのワールドカップ

established in 1969 under the Development of Tourism Act of 1969 and in cooperation with regional tourist boards such as the English Tourist Board, the Scottish Tourist Board and the Wales Tourist Board (VisitBritain 2008: 2). To attract international tourists, the BTA and these tourist boards were reformed as VisitBritain in 2003 to strengthen international promotions (VisitBritain 2009: 9).

VisitBritain's overseas network has been re-positioned as a shared service for industry and strategic partners. A timely value campaign is currently running both domestically and overseas to encourage visitors to explore Britain, while a review of content, channels, user-generated content and shared platform opportunities is underway. VisitBritain has also resumed its policy remit which was removed from the British Tourist Authority by DCMS when VisitBritain was created in 2003.

*DCMS = Department for Culture, Media and Sport
Source: VisitBritain (2009) *VISITBRITAIN Annual Report and Accounts*, p. 9

Despite the existence of a national tourism authority, local tourism authorities had been a strong influence on tourism promotion in the UK. Though this diversity was a strength for tourism in the UK, competitive countries were promoting tourism as national projects. The British government reorganized the tourism promotion structures both at the national level with VisitBritain and the local level with such local authorities as Visit London, Visit England Visit Scotland and Visit Wales (VisitBritain 2009: 10).

Over recent years, VisitBritain's Overseas Network has been recognising the need to market the distinct brands of its strategic partners – VisitEngland, VisitScotland, Visit Wales and Visit London, rather than just the Britain brand. This direction of this approach was confirmed in the outcomes of the British Tourism Framework Review. In practice, this means that recently entered markets and/or markets that do not understand the constituent parts of the country will continue to have a Britain brand focus.

Source: VisitBritain (2009) *VISITBRITAIN Annual Report and Accounts*, p. 10

In addition to continuous promotion, high-profile international events such as the

Chapter 8   Trends of Inbound Tourism Promotions   179

など，よく知られた国際イベントは国際観光客を引き付けるために重要な方法である（VisitBritain 2009：10）。ロンドンは1908年と1948年にオリンピックを開催したが，2012年のオリンピックも今なお重要である。2012年オリンピックとパラリンピックの観光収益を最大化することはビジット・ブリテンとビジット・ロンドンの重要な役割の1つであった（Visit Britain 2010：2）。

　ビジット・ブリテンは2012年ロンドン・オリンピックおよびパラリンピックによるすべてのイギリス訪問経済の収益の最大化のため，引き続き戦略を改善していく。2008年の北京オリンピックの経験により，オリンピック・コミュニティの貴重なコネクションが作られ，私たちは主要なステークホルダーと公的外交パートナーと共有された行動プランを開発した。ビジット・ブリテンのデリバリー・プランが中心に置くことは，オリンピックのメディアとスポンサーを結びつけ，イギリスの観光ビジネスとオリンピックから生じるビジネス機会を結びつけることである。
出典：VisitBritain（2009）*VISITBRITAIN Annual Report and Accounts*, p. 10

　国際観光客を引き付けるため，目を引くコピーを書くことは有効的である。「visit」に加え，「incredible」，「amazing」，「ultimate」などの強調する語句は強いインパクトを与える。たとえば，「インクレディブル・インディア」（2002年導入）はローカルな独自性を観光客に売り込むためのプロモーションであり，ユニークな公的観光機関である。「100% ピュア・ニュージーランド」，「マレーシア・本当にアジア」，「インドネシア・多様性の究極」，「アメージング・タイランド」のように，独特な地元の特徴や文化は国際的に観光客を引き付ける。

　インドは，特に建築的なアトラクションから，長い間文化観光の目的地として知られてきた。これに加え，インドの観光省（MOT）は無形文化も観光客に売り込もうとしている。アドベンチャー観光，ルーラル・ツーリズム，医療観光，MICE（会議，インセンティブ，コンベンション，博覧会）などもインドに国際観光客を呼び込むのに重要である。特別な関心のショッピング，特に田舎の手工芸品もまたMOTによって潜在的な優良アトラクションである。

180　　第8章　インバウンド観光プロモーションのトレンド

Olympic Games and FIFA World Cup are an important method of attracting international tourists (VisitBritain 2009: 10). Though London previously hosted the Olympic Games in 1908 and 1948, the 2012 Games are still a very important event. Maximizing the tourism legacy benefits of the 2012 Olympic Games and Paralympic Games is one of the important roles of VisitBritain and Visit London (Visit Britain 2010: 2).

> VisitBritain has continued to refine its strategy to maximise the benefits for the whole British visitor economy for the London 2012 Olympic and Paralympic Games. Building on the experience from the Beijing Games in 2008, valuable connections with the Olympic community were made and we developed shared activity plans with key stakeholders and public diplomacy partners. Central to VisitBritain's delivery plan is engagement with Games media and sponsors, and to connect British tourism businesses with the business opportunities arising from the Games.
>
> Source: VisitBritain (2009) *VISITBRITAIN Annual Report and Accounts*, p. 10

To attract international tourists, outstanding copywriting can be vital. In addition to "visit," expressive words such as "incredible," "amazing" and "ultimate" may have a strong impact. For example, "Incredible India" (launched in 2002) is a unique official tourism organization with promotional activities used to sell its local uniqueness to tourists. Like "100% Pure New Zealand," "Malaysia Truly Asia,"· "Indonesia Ultimate in Diversity" and "Amazing Thailand," unique local characteristics and cultures attract tourists internationally.

India has long been known as a cultural tourism destination, especially because of its architectural attractions. In addition to this, the Ministry of Tourism (MOT) in India is also trying to introduce its intangible cultural attractions to tourists. Adventure tourism, rural tourism, medical tourism and MICE (Meeting, Incentive, Convention, Exhibition) have all become important ways to attract international tourists to India. Special interest shopping, especially for rural handicrafts, is also targeted as a good

Chapter 8   Trends of Inbound Tourism Promotions   181

様々な観光プロダクトを効果的に売り込むため，インドの MOT はインクレ
ディブル・インディアという観光キャンペーンをブランド化し，「!ncredible
India」という統一したロゴを製作した。MOT はすでに海外プロモーション・
オフィスを運営しており，これらのオフィスを「Indiatourism」のバナーで改
名している。Indiatourism はニューヨーク，トロント，ロンドン，フランクフ
ルト，パリ，アムステルダム，ミラノ，ロサンゼルス，ドバイ，ヨハネスブル
ク，シンガポール，東京，シドニーに 13 の国際オフィスを有している（MOT
2009：52）。

　13 の国際オフィスは驚く数ではない。補助のため，MOT はオンライン・
キャンペーンやビデオ・プロモーションを行っている。2007-2008 会計年度だ
けでも，MOT は「アドベンチャー・ツーリズム」，「クルーズ・ツーリズム」，
「医療観光」，「MICE 観光」，「インドの仏教サイト」，「世界遺産サイト」など
の CD-Rom シリーズをリリースしている（MOT 2009：49）。個人観光客に直接
売り込むだけでなく，インドは UNWTO，ESCAP，ASEAN，その他の国際機
関が主催する国際会議やトラベル・フェアにも参加いている（MOT 2009：49）。

　オリンピックのように，英連邦ゲームやアジアン・ゲームもまた観光客を強
く呼び寄せる。デリーは 1951 年と 1982 年にアジアン・ゲームを主催したが，
2010 年のデリーにおける英連邦ゲームもまたインドにとって重要なイベント
であった。しかしながら，国際イベントのインパクトは両刃の剣である。1951
年のアジアン・ゲームで起こったように，英連邦ゲームでも建設が遅れ，デ
リーの国際空港からのメトロ・トレインは英連邦ゲームの開催中に営業が間に
合わなかった。

8-3. 国際観光客のための多国籍開発とプロモーション

　時に，観光キャンペーンとプロモーションは多国籍の組織によって行われる。

182　　第8章　インバウンド観光プロモーションのトレンド

potential attraction by the MOT.

To sell various tourism products effectively, India's MOT branded its tourism campaigns as Incredible India, and created a unified logo with "!ncredible India." MOT was already running international promotion offices, and renamed these offices under the Indiatourism banner. Indiatourism has 13 international offices in New York, Toronto, London, Frankfurt, Paris, Amsterdam, Milan, Los Angeles, Dubai, Johannesburg, Singapore, Tokyo and Sydney (MOT 2009: 52).

That said, 13 international offices is not exactly an incredible number. To assist, MOT has initiated online campaigns and video promotions. In the 2007-2008 financial year alone, the MOT released a CD-Rom series with the titles of "Adventure Tourism," "Cruise Tourism," "Medical Tourism," "MICE Tourism," "Buddhist Sites of India" and "World Heritage Sites" (MOT 2009: 49). Not content to sell to individual tourists directly, India joins international conferences and travel fairs organized by UNWTO, ESCAP, ASEAN and other international organizations (MOT 2009: 70).

Like the Olympic Games, the Commonwealth Games and Asian Games also provide a strong pull for tourists. Though Delhi hosted the Asian Games in 1951 and 1982, the 2010 Commonwealth Games in Delhi were still an important event for India. However, the impact of international events can be a double-edged sword. As happened with the Asian Games of 1951, construction for the Commonwealth Games fell behind, and the Metro Train from Delhi International Airport did not start running until the Commonwealth Games had come and gone.

8-3. Multinational Developments and Promotions for International Tourists

Sometimes tourism campaigns and promotions are conducted by multinational

旧ECによる「ヨーロッパ文化首都」(1985年から),「ビジットASEAN年キャンペーン」(1992年), ETCによる「ビジット・ヨーロッパ」キャンペーン(2006年再編)などが例として挙げられる(石井 2007:2)。大規模な多国籍組織に加え,地域的には数か国の協定も見られる。

　複数の国が共同で行う観光プロモーションはヨーロッパでは比較的長い歴史を持っている。1948年にETCが設立されているが,それ以前の1925年には公的観光広報機関国際連盟(IUOTPO)が設立されている。この組織は1947年に公的旅行機関国際連盟(IUOTO,現在のUNWTO)に再編されている(UNWTO n.d: web)。ヨーロッパの地域観光プロモーションを特化するために,ETCが設立された(ETC 2008:3)。

　1948年,ヨーロッパ経済共同体やヨーロッパ連合を誰も聞いたことが無かったころ,19のヨーロッパの政府観光局(NTO)はヨーロッパ観光局(ETC)を結成するために集まった。彼らの目的は？　第二次世界大戦の荒廃からヨーロッパの経済復興を行う上で重要な観光を共同でプロモートするために協力することである。アメリカ合衆国のスポンサーによるマーシャルプランの初期の援助により,ETCは戦後のヨーロッパの観光産業を復活させる重要な役割を果たした。60年後,2008年,加盟国は39か国に増加し,さらに強化しつつある。近年優先している点は,非ヨーロッパ・マーケットからヨーロッパへ観光をプロモートすることである。
出典：ETC (2008) *60 YEARS OF JOINT ACTION 1948-2008*, p. 3

　ETCはまた,ヨーロッパ文化首都のプロモーションを共同でプロモートしている。ETCはヨーロッパ文化首都になる絶対的な4つの理由を挙げている(ETC 2005:45)。

・都市は年間を通して文化首都として広報される。
・文化首都の年にその都市への訪問客が増加する。
・その都市の文化所産とインフラの弾みを与える。
・イメージとその都市への訪問者数の長期の効果がある。

184　第8章　インバウンド観光プロモーションのトレンド

organizations. "European Capitals of Culture" by the former European Community (since 1985), the "Visit ASEAN Year Campaign" (1992) and "Visit Europe" campaign (remade in 2006) of the ETC are examples (Ishii 2007: 2). In addition to large multinational organizations, the cooperative agreements of several countries can be seen regionally.

Tourism promotions involving several countries together have a relatively long history in Europe. ETC was established in 1948, and well before that, in 1934, the International Union of Official Tourist Propaganda Organizations (IUOTPO) was already established. It was reorganized as the International Union of Official Travel Organizations (IUOTO, now known as UNWTO) in 1947 (UNWTO n.d: web). To specify European regional tourism promotion, ETC was then established (ETC 2008: 3).

In 1948, before anyone had heard of the European Economic Community or the European Union, nineteen of Europe's national tourism organisations (NTOs) joined forces to form the European Travel Commission (ETC). Their aim? To work together to promote the importance of tourism in revitalising Europe's economy after the devastation of World War II. With early help from the US-sponsored Marshall Plan, ETC played a vital role in the regeneration of Europe's tourism industry after the war. Sixty years later, in 2008, it is still going strong and has seen its membership grow to 39 members. The priority these days remains focused on promoting tourism to Europe from non-European markets.

Source: ETC (2008) *60 YEARS OF JOINT ACTION 1948-2008*, p. 3

ETC is also promoting the European Capitals of Culture as a cooperative promotion. ETC cites what they consider to be the four most compelling reasons to be a European Capital of Culture (ETC 2005: 45).

· The publicity the cities obtain during the year that the city is Cultural Capital;
· The extra tourists that visit the city during the year of being Cultural Capital;
· The impulse that it gives to the cultural product and infrastructure of the city;
· The long term effects on the image and the number of visitors to the city.

Chapter 8　Trends of Inbound Tourism Promotions　185

出典：ETC（2005）*CITY TOURISM & CULTURE*, p. 45

インターネットでの広報はまた効果的である。ETC はインターネットの広報と共同し，多言語化のために 2006 年にビジット・ヨーロッパのウェブサイトをアップグレードした（ETC 2008：6）。

早くも 1990 年代中庸に，US オペレーション・グループはアメリカ・マーケット向けのシンプルなウェブサイトを www.visiteurope.com に設け，そこにはたくさんのアクティビティとキャンペーンが含まれていた。2006 年，ETC 全体で，世界中にヨーロッパをプロモートするためにデザインされた新しいインターネット・ポータルとして，この web アドレスを用いるようになった。2003 年，ヨーロッパ共同体（EC）は，行政間データ交換（IDA）プログラムの予算を含む汎ヨーロッパ観光ポータルの開発プロジェクトを実施した。EC は ETC を招待し，プロジェクト・アドバイザーとして活躍し，新たに開発されるサイトの代表として運営することを求めた。新たなウェブ・ポータルは 2006 年 3 月にウィーンで開催された EU の観光大臣会議にて実行された。

出典：ETC（2008）*60 YEARS OF JOINT ACTION 1948-2008*, p. 6

観光プロモーションに関する国際協力はアジア太平洋地域でも見られる。1951 年に設立された PATA は世界的に知られている。1950 年代の PATA の主なターゲットはアメリカ合衆国であったが，1960 年代後半にはヨーロッパに焦点がシフトし，70-80 年代にはマーケットが多様化した（Picolla 1987：137）。

広域の組織に加え，理にかなった地域の協力もまた重要である。たとえば，ASEAN は観光のプロモーションと開発の強化を行っている。1981 年に ASEANTA が設立され，1988 年に ASEAN 観光情報センターが設立され（1996 年廃止），2001 年にビジット ASEAN キャンペーンが実施された（Scott 2007：2）。スコット（2007）によると，ビジット ASEAN キャンペーンには 3 つのフェーズがある（Scott：2）。

1999 年，ビジット ASEAN キャンペーンは持続可能で現在進行のプログラムを考慮していた。最初のフェーズは 2001 年に，ビジット ASEAN キャンペーンを世

Source: ETC (2005) *CITY TOURISM & CULTURE*, p. 45

Advertising on the internet is also effective. ETC engaged in internet advertising, and upgraded the VisitEurope website in 2006 while making it multilingual (ETC 2008: 6).

As early as the mid 1990s, the US Operations Group had run a simple consumer website for the US market at www.visiteurope.com, incorporating it into many of their activities and campaigns. In 2006, the whole ETC adopted this web address for a brand new internet portal designed to promote Europe worldwide. In 2003, the European Commission (EC) launched a project to develop a pan-European tourism portal with funding from its Interchange of Data between Administrations (IDA) programme. The EC invited ETC and its members to act as project advisers and to operate the newly created site on its behalf. The new web portal was launched at a meeting of the EU's tourism ministers in Vienna in March 2006.
Source: ETC (2008) *60 YEARS OF JOINT ACTION 1948-2008*, p. 6

International cooperation related to tourism promotions can also be seen in the Asia Pacific region. PATA, established in 1951, is recognized throughout the world. Though the main target of PATA in the 1950s was the USA, it shifted its focus to Europe in the late 60s, and the market diversified during the 70s and 80s (Picolla 1987: 137).

In addition to broadly based organizations, cooperation within reasonable areas is also important. For example, ASEAN is strengthening its tourism promotions and development. The ASEANTA was established in 1981, the ASEAN Tourism Information Center was established in 1988 (though discontinued in 1996), and the Visit ASEAN Campaign was launched in 2001 (Scott 2007: 2). According to Scott (2007), there are three phases to the Visit ASEAN Campaign (Scott: 2).

In 1999 the Visit ASEAN Campaign was considered to be a sustainable and ongoing program. The first phase was launched in 2001 as an "Awareness Year" for the VAC to

Chapter 8　Trends of Inbound Tourism Promotions　187

界的な旅行トレードと民間業者の間でブランドづくりを行うための「気づきの年」
として導入された。ビジット ASEAN キャンペーンでの付帯，広報活動，広告，旅
行トレード活動などの4つの主要なマーケティング・プロモーションの要素が含ま
れていた。

*VAC＝Visit ASEAN Campaign

出典：Scott（2007）*Impact Assessment of the Visit ASEAN Campaign*, p. 2

　第2フェーズは2002年を通して行われ，ブランドづくりから，たとえば日本の
ようなターゲットとしたマーケットの消費者のための特定のプロモーション・コ
ミュニケーション活動を含んだものに拡大した。ビジット ASEAN キャンペーンの
ロゴやタグラインが ASEAN 政府観光局（NTOs）のマーケティング・プロモー
ション出版物にサブ・ブランドとして付帯された。

出典：Scott（2007）*ibid*, p. 2

　ビジット ASEAN キャンペーンの第3フェーズは ASEAN 間の観光に焦点を当て，
観光投資プロモーションや ASEAN を単一の観光目的地として広報することを含ん
だ。キャンペーンを通し，CNN 国際メディア・キャンペーンや旅行トレード・
キャンペーン，ASEAN ヒップ・ホップ・パス（AHHP）の全国導入（インドネシ
ア，シンガポール，フィリピン），AHHP の ASEAN5 か国（インドネシア，マレー
シア，フィリピン，シンガポール，タイ）プロモーションなどを，全国テレビ局や
新聞，ラジオ，SMS コンテストなどの異なったマーケティング・チャンネルを通
し，いくつかのマーケティング・プロモーションのアプローチが実施された。

出典：Scott（2007）*ibid*, p. 2

　2002年 ASEAN 観光合意書により，ビジット ASEAN キャンペーンは次第に
アップグレードし，2004年に観光セクターの統合のためのロードマップが導
入され（Wong *et al.* 2011：369），2006年にビジット ASEAN パス（vap!）が導入
された（Scott 2007：15）。魅力的なプロダクトに加え，効果的な宣伝もまた必
要である。ビジット ASEAN パスは便利であるが，2007年に8000パスしか売
れなかった（Wong *et al.* 2011：372）。

　政府間組織に加え，いくつかの国々では観光の協力に成功している。一例と
して，「シンガポール・アンリミテッド」開発計画の一環として実施された

188　　第8章　インバウンド観光プロモーションのトレンド

build the brand among the global travel trade and the private sector. It involved four key marketing and promotional elements: VAC collaterals, public relations, advertising, and travel trade activities.

*VAC = Visit ASEAN Campaign

Source: Scott (2007) *Impact Assessment of the Visit ASEAN Campaign,* p. 2

The second phase, undertaken throughout 2002, expanded the brand-building activities to include specific promotional and communications activities aimed at consumers in target markets like Japan. The VAC logo and tag line have been incorporated as a sub-brand into the collateral and marketing promotional material of the ASEAN National Tourism Organisations (NTOs).

Source: Scott (2007) *ibid,* p. 2

The VAC third phase focused on intra-ASEAN tourism and included tourism investment promotion and advertising ASEAN as a single destination. Throughout the campaign, several marketing and promotional approaches were undertaken, such as CNN international media campaign; travel trade campaign; the launching of ASEAN Hip Hop Pass (AHHP) nationally (Indonesia, Singapore and Philippines); the promotion of AHHP in five ASEAN Member Countries (Indonesia, Malaysia, Philippines, Singapore and Thailand) through different marketing channels such as national TV stations, newspaper and radio; and SMS contest.

Source: Scott (2007) *ibid,* p. 2

Under the 2002 ASEAN Tourism Agreement, the Visit ASEAN Campaign was gradually upgraded, the Roadmap for Integration of the Tourism Sector was introduced in 2004 (Wong *et al.* 2011: 369) and the Visit ASEAN Pass (vap!) was introduced in 2006 (Scott 2007: 15). In addition to attractive products, effective advertising is also needed. The Visit ASEAN Pass was convenient, but only 8000 passes were sold in 2007 (Wong *et al.* 2011: 372).

In addition to intergovernmental organizations, some individual countries have shown success with tourism cooperation. One example is "Tourism Unlimited," an

「ツーリズム・アンリミテッド」がある。リピーターの観光客を観光地に誘致するため，多様性のあるアクティビティを知らせることは重要である。シンガポール・アンリミテッドは1993年に実施された多国間の開発プランであり，単に観光プロモーションのみに限られていない。しかしながら，シンガポール・アンリミテッドに続き，ツーリズム・アンリミテッド（1994）やツーリズム21（1996）など，関連した観光開発・プロモーションが行われた。

　1990年代初頭，「清潔でグリーン」，「ガーデンシティ」，「ファイン・シティ」，「インスタント・アジア」などのフレーズを含んだプロモーションによって，シンガポールはすでに東南アジアで最も知られた観光地の一つになっていた。しかしながら，シンガポールは小さな島国であるため，観光のために開発可能な場所は限られていた。シンガポール・アンリミテッドはより広大なシンガポールの隣国との共同開発プランである。このコンセプトにより，ツーリズム・アンリミテッドやその後のプロジェクトによって，シンガポールはインドネシアのリアウ諸島やマレーシアのジョホールにてホテルやリゾート施設の開発を行った。シンガポールはこの地の航空輸送のハブであるため，シンガポールと隣国はwin-winの関係ができた。

　シンガポールは小さな国であるため，元々観光プロモーションはインバウンドに重点を置いていた。1964年から，シンガポールの独立前であるが，STPBはシンガポールを国際観光地としてプロモートしてきた（Chang 1998：72）。1960-70年代，STPBはマルチエスニックな特性を観光アトラクションとし，シンガポールを「インスタント・アジア」としてプロモートしてきた（Chang and Yeoh 1999：108）。STPBから改名したSTBは1990年代にシンガポールを「ニューアジア──西洋と東洋の文化が共生する場所」としてプロモートしてきた（Chang and Yeoh 1999：101）。

　Chang（1998）によると，ツーリズム・アンリミテッドのコンセプトは日本の借景がベースとなっており（Chang：87），これはおおざっぱに翻訳すれば風景を借りることである。このコンセプトは特に都市部で込み合っている日本庭園や建築で用いられており，周りの風景をデザインに調和させている。ツーリ

offshoot of "Singapore Unlimited" development projects. To promote tourism destinations to repeat tourists, the presentation of a wide variety of activities is important. Singapore Unlimited was a multinational development plan launched in 1993, and was not simply a tourism promotion alone. However, following Singapore Unlimited, related tourism developments and promotions such as Tourism Unlimited (1994) and "Tourism 21" (1996) were created.

In the early 1990s, Singapore was already one of the most famous tourist destinations in Southeast Asia, following its promotions that included phrases such as "clean and green," "garden city," "fine city" and "instant Asia." However, since Singapore is a small island country, the number of places that can be developed for tourism is limited. Singapore Unlimited was a cooperative development plan that involved Singapore's larger neighboring countries. Building on this concept, Singapore developed hotels and resort facilities in the Riau Islands of Indonesia and Johor in Malaysia by taking advantage of Tourism Unlimited and subsequent projects. As Singapore is an air transportation hub for the region, Singapore and its neighboring countries created a win-win situation.

As Singapore is a small country, its tourism promotion was inbound oriented originally. Since 1964, before Singapore gained independence, the STPB has promoted Singapore as an international tourist destination (Chang 1998: 72). During the 1960s and 70s, the STPB promoted Singapore as "instant Asia," to sell its multi-ethnic qualities as a tourist attraction (Chang and Yeoh 1999: 108). The STB, renamed from the STPB, also promoted Singapore as the "New Asia—Where Western and Asian Cultures Coexist" in the 1990s (Chang and Yeoh 1999: 101).

According to Chang (1998), the concept of Tourism Unlimited is based on Japanese *Shakkei* (Chang: 87), which can be loosely translated as "borrowed scenery." This concept is especially applied to Japanese gardens and architecture in crowded urban areas that incorporate the surrounding scenery into the design. With Tourism

ズム・アンリミテッドにより，シンガポール自身が観光客にとってより魅力的になるため，シンガポールは近隣諸国のアトラクションを借りることができる。

その間日本では，政府が羽田（東京国際空港）を再開発して，日本の住民にとってハブ空港であった韓国のインチョン国際空港に追いつこうとしていた。韓国資本による日本の地方開発が行われているのにもかかわらず，（すべてではないが）幾人かの日本の政治家と極右活動家はこれらの国際共同に反対している。もちろんハブはスポークよりも大きな利益をもたらすが，地域観光開発はゼロサムゲームではない。リーケージにもかかわらず，スポークには多少の利益があり，win-win の関係を生み出すことが可能である。2002 年のサッカーワールドカップのように，韓国と日本の短期的な協力はタイアップの一つのアプローチであるが，長期間の政府間の協力もまた必要である。

8-4. 日本のインバウンド観光政策のケーススタディ
8-4-1. ポスト・バブル経済とインバウンド観光

バブル経済に続き，日本政府はゆっくりとインバウンド観光政策を進めてきた。コンベンション法とウェルカムプラン 21 の 2 つがビジット・ジャパン・キャンペーン前の代表的な事例である。

かつて，東京，大阪，京都，その他の大都市が日本における代表的な国際観光客の目的地であった。これらの大都市の周りの伝統的な寺社はインバウンド観光客にとって重要な観光資源であった。しかしながら，リピーターの観光客を得るために，他にも多くの種類のアトラクションが必要である。ビジット・ジャパン・キャンペーンを実施する前，日本政府は 1994 年にコンベンション法を導入した。不景気にもかかわらず，コンベンション・センターや博覧会場施設が開発された。

コンベンション客をターゲットにするのに加え，より多くの国際観光客を日本に呼び寄せるために，1996 年にウェルカムプラン 21 が実施された。バブル

192　第 8 章　インバウンド観光プロモーションのトレンド

Unlimited, Singapore borrows the attractions of its neighboring countries to make Singapore itself more attractive to tourists.

Meanwhile, in Japan, the government is eager to redevelop Haneda (Tokyo International Airport) to catch up with Inchon International Airport in South Korea, which serves as a hub airport for residents of Japan. Despite Korean-financed resort developments in rural areas in Japan, some (though not all) Japanese politicians and right-wing extremists are still against this sort of international cooperation. Of course, though the hub will derive greater benefit than the spokes, regional tourism developments are not a zero-sum game. Despite some leakage, spokes will also see benefits, and the creation of win-win relations is certainly possible. As with the 2002 FIFA World Cup, short-term collaborations between Korea and Japan are one way to approach these tie-ups, though long-term intergovernmental collaborations are also needed.

8-4. Case Studies of Japanese Inbound Tourism Policies

8-4-1. Post Bubble Economy and Inbound Tourism

Following the bubble economy, the Japanese government created inbound tourism policies only very gradually. The Convention Law and Welcome Plan 21 are two prominent examples of the pre Visit Japan Campaign.

At one time, Tokyo, Osaka, Kyoto and other large cities were the major international tourist destinations in Japan. Traditional temples and shrines around these large cities were major tourist resources for inbound tourists. However, to attract repeat visitors, many other types of attractions are needed. Before the Visit Japan Campaign started, the Japanese government initiated the Convention Law of 1994. Despite the depression, convention centers and facilities for exhibitions were developed.

In addition to targeting convention visitors, the "Welcome Plan 21" was initiated to attract more international tourists to Japan in 1996. Some theme parks and resort

経済期に国内観光客向けにテーマパークやリゾート施設が造られたが，国際観光客を再度ターゲットとするために改修された。日本食レストランとパフォーミング・アート劇場もまた観光資源である。工業地帯や工場もまた次第に観光地として認識されるようになった。

　ビジット・ジャパン・キャンペーンにより，日本政府は観光プロモーションを強化した。2005 年，日本政府は韓国と台湾からの短期観光客をビザなしで渡航できるようにした。日本は 2000 年に中国からの団体観光客のためのビザ制度を導入し，2009 年には個人の観光客へ規制緩和した（甲斐 2010：32）。2008 年，観光政策と広報活動を強化するために，日本の観光庁（JTA）が設立された（JTA n.d.: web）。

1）日本は国家レベルでの観光立国を創り，同時に観光交流を拡大するために外国政府との効果的な交渉を結びつけた事実を広範囲に伝えた。

2）観光立国の数値目標を達成するためのリーダーシップを発揮し，関係するすべての省庁の結びつけとコーディネートを賢固にした。

3）観光目的地を創るために地方公共団体と民間セクターの努力に対する賢固な支援と同時に，「住むに良し，訪れるに良しの国づくり」のための政府としての統一された役割を広範に伝えた。

出典：JTA（n.d.）"The Birth of the Japan Tourism Agency", web

　これらの新たな観光政策にもかかわらず，日本の観光予算は比較的小さかった。2008 年の観光プロモーションのための JNTO の予算は 55 億円，同時期の TA（オーストラリア）は 106 億円，TAT（タイ観光庁）は 94 億円，BTA（英国観光庁）は 73 億円だった（加藤 2010：21）。他方，日本の 2008 年の訪問者は 835 万人，オーストラリアは 558 万人，タイは 1458 万人，イギリスは 3193 万人であった（加藤 2010：21）。これらの統計によると，観光客当たりの日本のコストパフォーマンスはイギリスよりは悪いが，タイ並みで，オーストラリアより優れている。

facilities that were developed during the bubble era for domestic tourists have been renovated and retargeted at international tourists. Japanese restaurants and performing arts theaters are also seen as tourism resources. Even some industrial areas and factories have gradually gained recognition as tourist destinations.

With the Visit Japan Campaign, the Japanese government has been strengthening tourism promotion. In 2005, the Japanese government established a non-visa immigration policy for short-term tourists from South Korea and Taiwan. Japan initiated a visa system for Chinese group tourists in 2000, and deregulated individual tourists in 2009 (Kai 2010: 32). In 2008, the Japan Tourism Agency (JTA) was established to strengthen tourism policies and promotional activities (JTA n.d.: web).

---

1) Widespread communication of the fact that Japan was engaged in creating a tourism nation on a national level, concurrent with effective negotiation with foreign governments regarding expanded tourism exchange

2) Exercise of leadership in achieving numerical goals for a tourism nation, and robust engagement and coordination of all the ministries and agencies involved

3) Widespread communication of the government's unified efforts to "build a country that is good to live in, and good to visit," concurrent with robust support for efforts of local public bodies and the private sector to build tourism destinations.

Source: JTA (n.d.) "The Birth of the Japan Tourism Agency", web

---

Despite these newer tourism policies, Japan's tourism budget was relatively small. The budget for tourism promotions by the JNTO was 5.5 billion yen in 2008. In the same period, TA (Australia) was funded with the equivalent of 10.6 billion yen, TAT (Tourism Authority of Thailand) received 9.4 billion yen and BTA (UK) received 7.3 billion yen (Kato 2010: 21). On the other hand, there were 8.35 million international visitors to Japan in 2008, 5.58 million to Australia, 14.58 million to Thailand and 31.93 million to the UK (Kato 2010: 21). According to these statistics, Japan's cost performance per international tourist is worse than the UK's, almost the same as Thailand's and better than Australia's.

Chapter 8   Trends of Inbound Tourism Promotions   195

バブル経済の終焉から，日本政府は慢性的に予算不足である。限られた予算で国際観光をプロモートするため，選択と集中が重要である。たとえば，1990年代以降，日本にとってコンベンション客の成長は比較的強い点である。これにもかかわらず，日本は多くの博覧客のための十分な施設を持っていなかった。日本政府は2010年を日本MICE年とし，日本での国際コンベンション客へのアトラクション強化と他の主要なコンベンション地と比べると比較的弱い博覧部門の強化を両方行うことを目的とした（甲斐 2010：36）。

8-4-2. 地方における観光のグローバル化

　リピーターの訪問者を引き付けるために，観光資源の多様性は有利になる。日本には日本人の国内観光客のために多くの興味深いアトラクションがあり，これらのいくつかはインバウンド観光客にも再ターゲット化できる。日本にはインバウンド観光客を引き付けるための2つのトレンドがある。1つは特別な関心を持つ人のためのツアー（SIT）で，もう一つは地理的な多様性がもたらす地方の特産である。

　日本の国際政策は，近年では設備重視からコンテンツ重視に変わってきた。「クール・ブリタニア」や「クール・コリア」のように，いくつかの国ではポピュラー文化や現代文化が国際的な販売に成功している。韓国映画，韓国のテレビ番組，K-popが日本人，特に韓流の間に人気が高まったことから，日本政府は現代文化のアトラクションの重要性を認識した。

　ハリウッド映画に見られるように，文化コンテンツはしばしば国境を容易に越える。たとえば，韓国の文化所産は日本の観光目的地を世界的に有名にした。本州北部の秋田は国際観光客だけでなく国内でもあまり知られていなかった。しかしながら，韓国のテレビドラマのIRISが秋田で撮影された後，国際観光客への知名度が急騰した。

Since the end of the bubble economy, the Japanese government has been chronically short of funds. To promote international tourism with a limited budget, selection and concentration are important. For example, the growth of convention visitors has been a relatively strong point for Japan since the 1990s. Despite this, Japan did not have sufficient facilities for many international exhibitions. The Japanese government initiated Japan MICE Year in 2010. This project aims to both strengthen the attraction for international conventions in Japan and to partly redevelop exhibitions that are relatively weak when compared with other major international convention sites (Kai 2010: 36).

8-4-2. Local Globalization on Tourism

To attract repeat visitors, a variety of tourism resources is an advantage. There are a lot of interesting attractions for Japanese domestic tourists in Japan, and some of these attractions can be retargeted at inbound tourists. There are two trends that attract inbound tourists to Japan. One is the special interest tour (SIT), which focuses on specific people. Another is geographical diversification that features local specialties.

Japanese international policies have recently been changing from a facility-based approach to a content-oriented approach. Like "Cool Britannia" and "Cool Korea," some countries find success in selling popular and contemporary cultures internationally. As Korean movies, Korean TV programs and K-pop became popular among Japanese people, especially during *hallyu* or *hanryu* (the Korean movement), the Japanese government realized the importance of contemporary cultural attractions.

As Hollywood movies have shown us, cultural contents often cross borders easily. For example, Korean cultural products have made Japanese destinations famous internationally. Akita, in the northern part of Honshu Island, was not as well known among international tourists as it was domestically. However, after a popular Korean television drama called "IRIS" was filmed in Akita, its recognition among

日本政府は「クール・ジャパン」政策の下，文化所産の商業化を試みている。クール・ジャパンは部分的に観光と関連している。一例として，東京の秋葉原があり，元々電化製品を購入する客にとって知られていたが，現在では独特な現代文化とサブカルチャーで知られている。

　インクレディブル・インディアやアメージング・タイランドのように，地方の独自性は観光客，特にリピート客を魅了する。しかしながら，言語の壁と多言語観光ガイドの不足は日本の農村部にとって重大な問題である。ビジット・ジャパン・キャンペーンの下，日本政府は国際観光客のための多言語地図や多言語標識を作成する地方自治体を援助している。グリーンツーリズムやエコツーリズムなど農村部の観光はすでに国内観光客にとって人気が高いため，ルーラル・ツーリズムは国際観光客を魅了する大きな可能性を持っている。

　かつて，日本の国家観光政策は国土交通省が開発し，運営してきた。しかしながら，近年では，他の省庁が観光の計画や開発に加わっている。バブル経済後，日本人観光客，特に忙しい都市部の出身者は，平和で静かな場所を求めている。農林水産省の支援により，グリーンツーリズム法が1995年に施行された。農村コミュニティと都市からの訪問者との関係を活性化させるため，農林水産省はオーライ・ニッポン（都市と農山漁村の共生・対流推進会議）の設立も支援した。この名前は，英語の「all right Japan」の表現を借りて作られている（Asamizu ed. 2008：114）。農林水産省はグリーンツーリズムの国際化への拡大も探っている。

　独特な自然環境もまた国際観光客誘致の成功を描ける。国立公園での自然観光は日本において常に人気が高い。環境にやさしいエコツアーは近年日本人観光客にとって人気が高い。環境省はエコツーリズムを支援し，2008年にエコツーリズム推進法を施行した。いくつかのエコツーリズムと自然観光の目的地

international tourists soared.

The Japanese government is trying to commercialize the cultural products under its "Cool Japan" policies. Cool Japan is partly related to tourism. One example is Akihabara in Tokyo. While Akihabara was originally famous among shoppers for its electrical goods, it is now known for its unique contemporary cultures and subcultures.

Like Incredible India and Amazing Thailand, local uniqueness is vital to attracting tourists, especially repeat visitors. However, language barriers and a shortage of multilingual tour guides are serious problems in rural areas in Japan. Under the Visit Japan Campaign, the Japanese government is supporting local authorities in making multilingual maps and signs for international tourists. Since tourism in rural areas, such as green tourism and ecotourism, is already popular among domestic tourists, rural tourism may also have great potential in attracting international tourists.

At one time, national tourism policies in Japan were developed and managed by MLIT (Ministry of Land, Infrastructure, Transport and Tourism). However, more recently, some other ministries have been joining in with tourism planning and development. After the bubble era, Japanese tourists especially from busy urban areas began to seek peaceful and quiet destinations. Supported by MAFF (Ministry of Agriculture, Forestry and Fisheries), the Green Tourism Law was enacted in 1995. To accelerate relations between rural communities and urban visitors, MAFF also supported the establishment of Orai Nippon (the council for the promotion of interchange and coexistence between urban and rural communities). The name is coined from the pronunciation of the borrowed English expression "all right Japan" (Asamizu ed. 2008: 114). MAFF is also seeking to expand green tourism internationally.

A unique natural environment is another successful draw for international tourists. Nature-based tourism in national parks has always been a popular activity in Japan. Environmentally friendly ecotours are also popular among Japanese tourists more recently. The Ministry of the Environment supports ecotourism, and the Law for the

は国際観光客にとっても人気が高い。たとえば，北海道のニセコは国内スキー客にとって人気が高かったが，現在ではオーストラリアからの観光客に人気がある（Asamizu and Schumann eds. 2010：15）。オーストラリアの開発業者がいくつかの自然体験アクティビティの導入とプロモーションを行ったため，ニセコは年間を通しての国際観光地になった。ニセコは典型的な遠隔地の人口減少地域であったが，現在ではオーストラリアに続き，中国の開発業者もリゾート施設の開発を行っている。

8-4-3. 災害，避難，復興

観光客にとって最も大事な情報は安全に関することである。この章が書き終わりつつあった 2011 年 3 月に，本州北部の東北地方太平洋岸で日本の歴史上最大規模の地震が起こった。仙台国際空港は津波で水没し，東北新幹線や東北東部を走る他の鉄道も被害を受けて運休になった。東北自動車道や他の主要な道路も通行止めになった。

日本は以前，本州西部の阪神地方にて 1995 年に他の巨大地震に遭遇しており，特に神戸が大きな被害を受けた。阪神淡路大震災の痛ましい教訓から，多くの地方自治体は英語による避難情報，いくつかの大都市は複数の言語による情報を準備してきた。

阪神の場合，地元のラジオ局が英語で災害情報を提供し，東北の時には英語の緊急プログラムが全国的に展開していた。1988 年に設立された CLAIR（自治体国際化協会）は阪神淡路大震災の後，災害避難のための多言語コミュニケーション・ツールを準備した。仙台は 2000 年から自然災害のためのボランティア通訳組織を作っており（Tohoku Wide-Area Tourism Guide n.d.: web），東北地方に隣接している茨城県と群馬県もまた複数言語による避難ガイドブックを準備していた。

Promotion of Ecotourism was enacted in 2008. Some ecotourism and nature-based tourism destinations have also become popular among international visitors as well. For example, Niseko in Hokkaido was famous among domestic skiers, but is popular among Australian tourists now (Asamizu and Schumann eds. 2010: 15). As Australian developers also introduced several nature-based activities and promotions, Niseko became an international year-round tourism destination. Niseko was a typical remote and depopulated area, but now even Chinese developers have joined to build resort facilities following the Australian example.

8-4-3. Disasters, Evacuations and Recoveries

The most important information for tourists might ultimately be something related to safety. As this chapter was being finished up in March 2011, the largest earthquake in Japanese history struck the Pacific Coast of the Tohoku Region, on the northern part of Honshu Island. Sendai International Airport was submerged by the tsunami, and the Tohoku Shinkansen and other trains in the eastern part of Tohoku were shut down by the damage. The Tohoku Highway and other main roads were also closed.

Japan had previously experienced another large earthquake in the Hanshin Region in the western part of Honshu Island in 1995, with the city of Kobe being especially hard-struck. Learning from the painful experience of the Hanshin-Awaji earthquake, many municipalities have been preparing evacuation information in English, and some large cities now offer the information in several languages.

In the case of Hanshin, local radio stations offered disaster information in English, while English emergency programs became nationwide by the time of Tohoku. CLAIR (the Council of Local Authorities for International Relations), established in 1988, prepared multilingual communication tools for disaster evacuation after the Hanshin-Awaji earthquake. Sendai has organized volunteer interpreters for natural disasters since 2000 (Tohoku Wide-Area Tourism Guide n.d.: web), and Ibaraki and Gunma prefectures, near the Tohoku Region, prepared emergency guidebooks in

しかしながら，避難情報は外国人住民を想定して作られており，多くの場合は観光客の必要性を踏まえていなかった。東北の地震が起こった直後，JNTOは北部日本を旅行中の外国人訪問者向けのお知らせ，東北地方の空港の運行情報，鉄道の運行状況，ウェブ通訳のアシスト，外国人観光客向けのコールサービスの電話番号などをカバーするウェブサイトを準備した。日本語による情報と比べれば少ないが，1995年の地震の時と比べれば改善された。

　すでに旅行中の個人観光客にとって，ローカルな情報は必要である。岩手県や福島県と共に大きな被害を受けた宮城県では，日本語，英語，中国語，韓国語，ポルトガル語で緊急情報を公式ウエブサイトに掲載した。

地震情報
　3月14日　15：17現在
本日15：13ごろ宮城で地震がありました。
震源地は福島県沿岸近く。
地震のマグニチュード6.3。
〈震度4〉　登米市
今のところ新たな情報はありません。
出典：Miyagi Prefecture（2011）"Emergency Information System for Foreigners in Miyagi", web

---

　しかしながら，災害は私たちの想像を絶する。福島県の公式ウエブサイトは原発事故の後の過度なアクセスによりダウンした。サーバーのダウンを防ぐため，岩手県は通常の日本語，簡易な日本語，英語，中国語で緊急情報のミラーサイトを準備した。隣接する山形県と秋田県も，あまり被害を受けなかった東北西海岸の主要駅と空港からの避難情報を複数の言語で提供した。

several languages.

However, this information was designed for international residents, and does not address the needs of tourists in many cases. As soon as the Tohoku earthquake struck, the JNTO also prepared websites covering subjects such as notices for overseas visitors traveling in northeastern Japan and surrounding areas, the operational status of airports in the Tohoku area, the operational status of railway services, web translation services assistance, and telephone numbers to call for foreign tourists. Compared with the information available in the Japanese language, the information above is limited, but it is still an improvement when compared with the 1995 earthquake.

For individual tourists who are already traveling, local information is needed. Miyagi Prefecture, one of the most heavily damaged prefectures along with Iwate and Fukushima, published emergency information in Japanese, English, Chinese, Korean and Portuguese on its official website.

Earthquake information

This information was released at 15: 17, 14, 3

At about 15: 13 today, there was an earthquake in MIYAGI.

The epicenter was near Fukushima Ken Oki (Off the Fukushima Coast).

The earthquake had a Magnitude of approximately 6.3.

〈seismic intensity 4〉 Tome Shi

Currently there is no new information.

Source: Miyagi Prefecture (2011) "Emergency Information System for Foreigners in Miyagi", web

---

However, sometimes the scope of disasters exceeds our imagination. The official website of Fukushima Prefecture was brought down due to heavy access after the nuclear power plant incidents. To protect against server downtimes, Iwate Prefecture prepared an emergency mirror website in normal Japanese, simplified Japanese, English and Chinese. Neighboring Yamagata Prefecture and Akita Prefecture also offered emergency evacuation information in several languages to the nearest major stations and airports on the west coast of Tohoku, which suffered less damage.

3月11日14：46に岩手県を大きな地震が襲い，大きな被害を受けました。現在，岩手は余震が続いています。鉄道は運休中です。全県的に電気を使えません。沿岸部の方は引き続き避難所に避難してください。火には用心してください。

出典：Iwate Prefecture（2011）"Iwate Prefecture Website（Mirror Page）", web

　災害は物理的以上に被害を及ぼす。災害による経済的なダメージもまた巨大である。東京は被害が少なく，大阪や四国，九州は被害がなかったのにもかかわらず，日本へのインバウンド観光客は地震の後減少した。東北から1000 km以上離れた九州でさえ，ツアーのキャンセルを被った。日本国外の人々にとって，日本全体が安全でないという印象があった。

　2004年にインドネシアのスマトラで大きな地震が起こった時，プーケットやスリランカなどの観光地に津波が襲い，これらの観光地が復旧しても，しばらくの間は観光客数が元に戻らなかった。津波に加え，日本では原発事故と放射能のニュースがセンセーショナルに報道された。マスメディアは災害による深刻な被害について重点的に扱うが，復興についてニュースになることはあまりない。復興のキャンペーンや広告はこの地を世界的に注目してもらうために必要である。

第8章のおわりに

　本章の前半部分では，アジア太平洋諸国のいくつかは国家的なインバウンドプロモーションの歴史が比較的長いことについて述べた。もちろん興味深い文化コンテンツやアトラクションが必要ではあるが，効果的な観光プロモーションもまた重要であり，多政府の組織もまた重要な役割を演じることがある。

　本章の後半部では日本に関するケースについて注目した。ビジット・ジャパン・キャンペーンに続き，インバウンド観光客は増加している。しかしながら，

> On March 11 at 14:46, a strong earthquake hit Iwate Prefecture, causing much damage. Currently, Iwate is still experiencing aftershocks. Rail and trains have been stopped. The whole prefecture is without electricity. Those by the coastal areas should continue taking refuge in evacuation areas. Please also take caution of fires
>
> Source: Iwate Prefecture (2011) "Iwate Prefecture Website (Mirror Page)", web

Disasters do more than inflict physical damage. The economic damage incurred by disasters can be immense. Despite relatively little damage in Tokyo and no damage at all in Osaka, Shikoku and Kyushu, the number of inbound tourists to Japan fell after the earthquake. Even Kyushu, more than 1000 km away from Tohoku, suffered from cancelled tours. The impression of people outside of Japan seems to be that all of Japan is unsafe.

When a large earthquake in Sumatra, Indonesia in 2004 triggered a tsunami that struck tourist destinations such as Phuket and Sri Lanka, these tourist destinations recovered, but the previous number of tourists did not come back anytime soon. In addition to the tsunami, Japan is suffering from sensational news reports of nuclear hazards and radioactivity. While the mass media focuses heavily on serious damage in any disaster, recovery is rarely considered to be news at all. Recovery campaigns and advertisements will be needed to make the world aware of progress in this area.

Conclusion of Chapter 8

In the first half of this chapter, we discussed how some countries in the Asia Pacific have a relatively longer history of national inbound tourism promotions. Of course, while interesting cultural content and attractions are needed, effective tourism promotions are also important, and intergovernmental organizations often play important roles in this regard.

The second half of this chapter focused on case studies related to Japan. Following the Visit Japan Campaign, the number of inbound visitors has been

日本はインバウンド観光に関してまだまだ発展途上であり，日本は特に質に関して多くのことを学ぶ必要がある。

　国際観光のプロモーションはグローバル，ローカルの両面から緊密に関連している。日本政府がベンチマークしている国々が達成しているような，さらなる観光政策が必要である。国際空港のある主要都市に国際観光客を導くのは重要な段階の一つではあるが，リピーターの訪問者を他の場所へ送り込むことは次の段階として重要である。この第二の段階を進めるため，ローカルな文化やサブカルチャーが重要である。シンガポールのように，近隣諸国と共同で開発やプロモーションを行うことは第三段階として有望であろう。日本政府は隣国経由での国際観光客をあまり強くターゲットにしていないが，このアプローチは将来的に大きなポテンシャルを持っているかもしれない。

　本章を書いていた時，日本の東北地方で大きな災害が起こった。深刻な地震と津波にもかかわらず，国際観光客のための避難情報は阪神淡路大震災の時よりもうまく働いていたように見える。しかしながら，国際観光客が減少したため，復興に関する観光キャンペーンや広告もまた将来的に必要である。

参考文献

Akita International Association（2011）"Emergency Information for the Earthquake", http://www. aiahome.or.jp/2011/03/emergency_information_for_the.html，2011 年 3 月 17 日閲覧

ASAMIZU, Munehiko（2004）*World Travel and Japanese Tourists*, Tokyo: Gakubunsha

朝水宗彦（2001）『多文化社会オーストラリアにおけるエスニック・ツーリズム形成過程に関する研究』（英語要約有）くんぷる

ASAMIZU, Munehiko ed.（2008）*Human Mobility in Asia Pacific*, Oita: Office Sakuta

ASAMIZU, Munehiko and SCHUMANN, Fred R. eds.（2010）*Global Tourism*, Tokyo: Kumpul

ASEANTA（2006）*VISIT ASEAN PASS TO PROMOTE ASEAN TOURISM*, Kuala Lumpur: ASEANTA

CHANG T. C.（1998）"Regionalism and tourism: exploring integral links in Singapore", *Asia Pacific Viewpoint*, 39（1），73-94

increasing. However, Japan still has a long way to go with regard to inbound tourism, and Japan has much to learn especially in matters of quality.

International Tourism Promotions are close related, both globally and locally. As the Japanese government achieves its benchmarks, further tourism policies will be needed. Introducing international tourists to major cities with international airports is one important step, but sending repeat visitors to other places is an important second step. To proceed to this second step, local cultures and subcultures must be promoted. Like Singapore, joint development and promotions with neighbors will be useful as a third step. The Japanese government does not yet strongly target international tourists via neighboring countries, but this approach will have great potential in the future.

While writing this chapter, a major disaster struck the Tohoku Region in North Eastern Japan. Despite the seriousness of the earthquake and tsunami, evacuation information for international visitors seems to be working well when compared to the Hanshin−Awaji earthquake. However, as the number of international visitors has fallen, tourism campaigns and advertisements related to the recovery still remain as a future need.

References

Akita International Association (2011) "Emergency Information for the Earthquake", http://www.aiahome.or.jp/2011/03/emergency_information_for_the.html, accessed March 17, 2011

ASAMIZU, Munehiko (2004) *World Travel and Japanese Tourists*, Tokyo: Gakubunsha

ASAMIZU, Munehiko (2001) *A Study of the Formation Process of Ethnic Tourism in Australia's Multicultural Society*, (in Japanese with English Summary), Tokyo: Kumpul

ASAMIZU, Munehiko ed. (2008) *Human Mobility in Asia Pacific*, Oita: Office Sakuta

ASAMIZU, Munehiko and SCHUMANN, Fred R. eds. (2010) *Global Tourism*, Tokyo: Kumpul

ASEANTA (2006) *VISIT ASEAN PASS TO PROMOTE ASEAN TOURISM*, Kuala Lumpur: ASEANTA

CHANG T. C. (1998) "Regionalism and tourism: exploring integral links in Singapore", *Asia Pacific Viewpoint*, 39(1), 73−94

CHANG T. C. and YEOH, Brenda S. A.（1999）""New Asia‐Singapore": communicating local cultures through global tourism", *Geoforum*, 30, 101-115

CLAIR（n.d.）「災害時多言語情報作成ツール」, http://www.clair.or.jp/j/culture/disaster/index.html, 2011 年 3 月 15 日閲覧

ETC（2008）*60 YEARS OF JOINT ACTION 1948-2008*, Brussels: ETC

ETC（2005）*CITY TOURISM & CULTURE*, Brussels: ETC

Fukushima Prefecture（n.d.）"homepage", http://wwwcms.pref.fukushima.jp/, 2011 年 3 月 17 日閲覧

Gunma Prefecture（2008）"In case of emergency", Gunma: Gunma Prefecture

Ibaraki International Association（n.d.）"Disaster Manual", http://www.ia-ibaraki.or.jp/kokusai/soudan/kyousei/disastermanual/english.pdf, 2011 年 3 月 15 日閲覧

石井昭夫（2007）「EU の文化観光政策」『国際観光情報』2, 1-2 頁

Iwate Prefecture（2011）"Iwate Prefecture Website（Mirror Page)", http://pref-iwate-main.cloudapp.net/index.rbz, 2011 年 3 月 17 日閲覧

Japan EXPO（n.d.）「Japan EXPO とは」, http://nihongo.japan-expo.com/, 2011 年 3 月 29 日閲覧

JNTO（n.d.）"About JNTO", http://www.jnto.go.jp/eng/about/index.html, 2011 年 3 月 14 日閲覧

JNTO（n.d.）"Notice for Overseas Visitors Traveling Northeastern Japan and the Surrounding Areas Include Tokyo", http://www.jnto.go.jp/eq/, 2011 年 3 月 15 日閲覧

JNTO（n.d.）"Operational status of airports in Tohoku Area", http://www.jnto.go.jp/eng/topics/pdf/110315_airport_0500.pdf, 2011 年 3 月 15 日閲覧

JNTO（n.d.）"Operational status of railroad", http://www.jnto.go.jp/eng/topics/pdf/110315_railway_0500.pdf, 2011 年 3 月 15 日閲覧

JNTO（n.d）"Manual for Web Translation Service", http://www.jnto.go.jp/eq/manual_eng.html, 2011 年 3 月 15 日閲覧

JNTO（n.d.）"Telephone service for foreign tourists available at the following", http://www.jnto.go.jp/eq/touristinfo.pdf, 2011 年 3 月 15 日閲覧

JTA（n.d.）"The Birth of the Japan Tourism Agency", http://www.mlit.go.jp/kankocho/en/about/setsuritsu.html, 2011 年 3 月 29 日閲覧

甲斐正彰（2010）『観光立国の実現に向けた取り組みについて』観光庁

加藤隆司（2010）「日本の観光政策の概観」, http://www.tij.or.jp/report/event/20100726_2b.pdf, 2011 年 3 月 28 日閲覧

KTO（n.d.）"Brief History of KTO", http://kto.visitkorea.or.kr/enu/ek/ek_1_1_3_1.jsp, 2011 年 3 月 14 日閲覧

Miyagi Prefecture（2011）"Emergency Information System for Foreigners in Miyagi", http://emis-

CHANG T. C. and YEOH, Brenda S. A. (1999) ""New Asia - Singapore": communicating local cultures through global tourism", *Geoforum*, 30, 101-115

CLAIR (n.d.) "Saigaiji Tagengo Jyouhou Sakusei Tool", http://www.clair.or.jp/j/culture/disaster/index.html, accessed March 15, 2011

ETC (2008) *60 YEARS OF JOINT ACTION 1948-2008*, Brussels: ETC

ETC (2005) *CITY TOURISM & CULTURE*, Brussels: ETC

Fukushima Prefecture (n.d.) "homepage", http://wwwcms.pref.fukushima.jp/, accessed March 17, 2011

Gunma Prefecture (2008) "In case of emergency", Gunma: Gunma Prefecture

Ibaraki International Association (n.d.) "Disaster Manual", http://www.ia-ibaraki.or.jp/kokusai/soudan/kyousei/disastermanual/english.pdf, accessed March 15, 2011

ISHII, Akio (2007) "EU no Bunka Kankou Seisaku", *Kokusai Kankou Jyouhou*, 2, 1-2

Iwate Prefecture (2011) "Iwate Prefecture Website (Mirror Page)", http://pref-iwate-main.cloudapp.net/index.rbz, accessed March 17, 2011

Japan EXPO (n.d.) "Japan EXPO toha", http://nihongo.japan-expo.com/, accessed March 29, 2011

JNTO (n.d.) "About JNTO", http://www.jnto.go.jp/eng/about/index.html, accessed March 14, 2011

JNTO (n.d.) "Notice for Overseas Visitors Traveling Northeastern Japan and the Surrounding Areas Include Tokyo", http://www.jnto.go.jp/eq/, accessed March 15, 2011

JNTO (n.d.) "Operational status of airports in Tohoku Area", http://www.jnto.go.jp/eng/topics/pdf/110315_airport_0500.pdf, accessed March 15, 2011

JNTO (n.d.) "Operational status of railroad", http://www.jnto.go.jp/eng/topics/pdf/110315_railway_0500.pdf, accessed March 15, 2011

JNTO (n.d) "Manual for Web Translation Service", http://www.jnto.go.jp/eq/manual_eng.html, accessed March 15, 2011

JNTO (n.d.) "Telephone service for foreign tourists available at the following", http://www.jnto.go.jp/eq/touristinfo.pdf, accessed March 15, 2011

JTA (n.d.) "The Birth of the Japan Tourism Agency", http://www.mlit.go.jp/kankocho/en/about/setsuritsu.html, accessed March 29, 2011

KAI, Masaaki (2010) *Kankou Rikkoku no Jitsugen ni muketa Torikumi ni tsuite*, Tokyo: JTA

KATO, Takashi (2010) "Nihon no Kankou Seisaku no Gaikan", http://www.tij.or.jp/report/event/20100726_2b.pdf, accessed March 28, 2011

KTO (n.d.) "Brief History of KTO", http://kto.visitkorea.or.kr/enu/ek/ek_1_1_3_1.jsp, accessed March 14, 2011

Miyagi Prefecture (2011) "Emergency Information System for Foreigners in Miyagi", http://emismiyagi.jp/index.php, 2011 年 3 月 17 日閲覧

MOT（2009）*Ministry of Tourism Annual Report*, New Delhi: MOT

PATA（n.d.）"About PATA" http://www.pata.org/About-PATA, 2011 年 3 月 14 日閲覧

PICOLLA, Gerald E.（1987）"Tourism in Asia and the Pacific", *Tourism Management*, 8（2）, 137-139

SCHOTT, Noel（2007）*Impact Assessment of the Visit ASEAN Campaign*, Queensland: UniQuest

SOSHIRODA, Akira（2005）"INBOUND TOURISM POLICIES IN JAPAN FROM 1859 TO 2003", *Annals of Tourism Research*, 32（4）, 1100-1120

Tohoku Wide-area Tourism Guide（n.d.）「平成 22 年度仙台市災害時言語ボランティア公開講習会」, http://www.tohokukanko.jp/topics/detail.php?topics_id=511, 2011 年 3 月 15 日閲覧

UNWTO（n.d.）"History", http://www2.unwto.org/content/history-0, 2017 年 9 月 1 日閲覧

UNWTO（2010）*Budgets of National Tourism Organizations, 2008-2009*, Madrid: UNWTO

UZAMA, Austin（2009）"Marketing Japan's travel and tourism industry to international tourists", *International Journal of Contemporary Hospitality Management*, 21（3）, 356-365

VisitBritain（2008）*VISITBRITAIN Annual Report and Accounts*, London: VisitBritain

VisitBritain（2009）*VISITBRITAIN Annual Report and Accounts*, London: VisitBritain

VisitBritain（2010）*VISITBRITAIN Annual Report and Accounts*, London: VisitBritain

WONG, Emma P. Y., MISTLIS, Nina and DWYER, Larry（2011）"A framework for analyzing intergovernmental collaboration – The case of ASEAN tourism", *Tourism Management*, 32（2）, 367-376

Yamagata Prefecture（2011）"Public Transportation Network among SENDAI, TOKYO, OSAKA, NIIGATA", http://www.pref.yamagata.jp/ou/somu/020054/transportation.pdf, 2011 年 3 月 17 日閲覧

miyagi.jp/index.php, accessed March 17, 2011

MOT（2009）*Ministry of Tourism Annual Report*, New Delhi: MOT

PATA（n.d.）"About PATA" http://www.pata.org/About-PATA, accessed March 14, 2011

PICOLLA, Gerald E.（1987）"Tourism in Asia and the Pacific", *Tourism Management*, 8 (2), 137-139

SCHOTT, Noel（2007）*Impact Assessment of the Visit ASEAN Campaign*, Queensland: UniQuest

SOSHIRODA, Akira（2005）"INBOUND TOURISM POLICIES IN JAPAN FROM 1859 TO 2003", *Annals of Tourism Research*, 32 (4), 1100-1120

Tohoku Wide-area Tourism Guide（n.d.）"Heisei 22 Nendo Sendai-shi Saigaiji Gengo Volunteer Koukai Koushukai", http://www. tohokukanko. jp/topics/detail. php? topics_id=511, accessed March 15, 2011

UNWTO（n.d.）"History", http://www2.unwto.org/content/history-0, accessed September 1, 2017

UNWTO（2010）*Budgets of National Tourism Organizations, 2008-2009*, Madrid: UNWTO

UZAMA, Austin（2009）"Marketing Japan's travel and tourism industry to international tourists", *International Journal of Contemporary Hospitality Management*, 21 (3), 356-365

VisitBritain（2008）*VISITBRITAIN Annual Report and Accounts*, London: VisitBritain

VisitBritain（2009）*VISITBRITAIN Annual Report and Accounts*, London: VisitBritain

VisitBritain（2010）*VISITBRITAIN Annual Report and Accounts*, London: VisitBritain

WONG, Emma P. Y., MISTLIS, Nina and DWYER, Larry（2011）"A framework for analyzing intergovernmental collaboration - The case of ASEAN tourism", *Tourism Management*, 32 (2), 367-376

Yamagata Prefecture（2011）"Public Transportation Network among SENDAI, TOKYO, OSAKA, NIIGATA", http://www.pref.yamagata.jp/ou/somu/020054/transportation.pdf, accessed March 17, 2011

あ と が き

　著者は観光客と留学生，地球規模の労働者を分けて扱っている。一般論ではあるが，観光客の主な目的は楽しむことであり，留学生は教育を求め，移民労働者は収入を求める。しかしながら，近年の国際移動は複雑である。

　たとえば，日本の場合，留学生は在学時には低賃金労働者として働いているかもしれないが，同じ留学生が卒業時には高度技能人材に結びついている。経済的に不利な留学生にとって，就学期間中に収入を得ることは必須である。経済的に恵まれた留学生にとって，学習環境やライフスタイルは重要である。

　別の人的移動の複雑な事例として，ワーキングホリデーが挙げられる。日本人のワーキングホリデー参加者は働く前にしばしば現地の語学学校で学ぶ。ワーキングホリデー・ビザは本来余暇が主であり，労働は従であった。しかしながら，日豪関係を見ると，ワーキングホリデー参加者は事実上低賃金の外国人労働者として機能している。

　日本が経済的に強かったとき，オーストラリアからのワーキングホリデー参加者は初級レベルの英語教員として働き，教員免許を持っていない場合もあった。ワーキングホリデー・ビザは元々1年間の期限であったが，オーストラリアが経済的に強くなると，遠隔地におけるビザの延長制度が作られた。元々この延長ビザは農業のために作られたが，幾人かの日本人ワーキングホリデー参加者は遠隔地における観光ホスピタリティ産業で働いている。

　本書には限界がある。観光客や留学生，国際的な労働者に関する典型的な国

Postscript

The author of this book treats tourists, international students and global workforces as separate cases. Generally speaking, tourists' major purpose in travelling is pleasure; international students seek education, and immigrant workers seek income. However, recent trends in international mobility are much more complicated.

For example, study abroad is linked to high-skilled workers when international students graduate, even though these same students sometimes work as low-waged laborers before they graduate in Japan. For economically disadvantaged international students, maintaining an income while studying is essential. For economically well-off international students, the learning environment and way of life might be very important.

Another example that demonstrates the complexity of international mobility is the working holiday scheme. Japanese working holiday-makers often learn local languages in local language schools before beginning to work. Working holiday visas were initially designed mainly for holiday and working was a supplemental activity. However, in the case of the Japan-Australia relationship, working holiday-makers are used as de facto low-waged foreign labor.

When Japan was economically stronger, working holiday-makers from Australia worked as introductory level English teachers, sometimes without a teaching license. A working holiday visa was originally valid for up to 1 year; however, as Australia became economically stronger, an extended working holiday visa for workers in remote areas was also initiated. Originally, this extended visa was designed for agriculture; however, some Japanese working holiday-makers now also work in the tourism and hospitality industries in remote areas.

This book has some limitations. There is a great deal of research about the typical

際移動の研究はたくさんある。これらの人的な移動に関する主流の研究では，古典的なプッシュープル理論で十分説明できた。本書では日本における外国人研修生やオーストラリアにおける日本人ワーキングホリデー参加者など，ニッチなケースをいくつか紹介した。しかしながら，長期滞在型の国際観光客やワークライフ・バランス目的の移民などについて十分掘り下げることができなかった。これらのミッシング・リンクを埋めるため，ジェンダーや年齢，心理的なアプローチによるさらなる研究が必要であろう。

注記

3 章は「外国人労働者に関する小史」『山口経済学論集』66(3)，2017 を部分的に翻訳したものである。

4 章の初出は "Migration Trends and Social Backgrounds of International Migrant Workers from and to Japan," *Yamaguchi Keizaigaku Ronshu*, 66(4), 2017 である。本章は山口大学経済学部「平成 29 年度部局長裁量経費」の助成を受けた。

5 章と 6 章は *the XII International Seminar on Globalization of Higher Education*, New Delhi, 2011 にて "From Study Abroad to Educational Tourism: Diversifications of English-based Programs on the Higher Education in Japan" として報告した。本研究は山口大学「平成 22 年度経済学部学術振興基金個人研究助成 B」の助成を受けた。

8 章は *the Asia Pacific Tourism Association 2011 Seoul Conference* にて "Visit, Incredible and Unlimited: Trends of Inbound Tourism Promotions in the Asia Pacific" として報告した。本研究は山口大学「平成 23 年度経済学部学術振興基金個人研究助成 B」にて実施した。

human mobility categories of tourists, international students and global workers. In many mainstream studies of human mobility, classical push-pull theory was enough to explain mobility trends. This book has tried to introduce some niche cases such as those of international trainees in Japan and Japanese working holiday-makers in Australia. However, the cases of both long-term international tourists and work life balance-based immigrants are not examined in depth. To fulfill these missing links, additional research that takes into account gender, age and psychological approaches may be required.

Note

Chapter 3 is partly translated from "Gaikokujin Roudousha ni Kansuru Shoushi (A Brief History of Immigrant Workers)," *Yamaguchi Keizaigaku Ronshu*, 66(3), 2017.

Chapter 4 is originally published as "Migration Trends and Social Backgrounds of International Migrant Workers from and to Japan," *Yamaguchi Keizaigaku Ronshu*, 66(4), 2017. This chapter is funded by the Faculty of Economics, Yamaguchi University (*Heisei 29 Nendo Bukyokuchou Sairyou Keihi*).

Chapter 5 and Chapter 6 are originally prepared for *the XII International Seminar on Globalization of Higher Education*, New Delhi, 2011, as "From Study Abroad to Educational Tourism: Diversifications of English-based Programs on the Higher Education in Japan." This study was supported by the Research Foundation of Economics (*Heisei 22 nendo Keizai Gakubu Gakujutsu Shinkou Kikin, Kojin Kenkyu Josei B*) in Yamaguchi University.

Chapter 8 is originally prepared for *the Asia Pacific Tourism Association 2011 Seoul Conference*, as "Visit, Incredible and Unlimited: Trends of Inbound Tourism Promotions in the Asia Pacific." This study was enabled by the Research Foundation of Economics (*Heisei 23 nendo Keizai Gakubu Gakujutsu Shinkou Kikin, Kojin Kenkyu Jyosei B*) in Yamaguchi University.

索　引

あ

アーリー　24
アメリカ国際教育基金（AIEF）　108

インチョン国際空港　192

ウミガメ　26,52

駅弁　150
エコツーリズム　198
エコツーリズム推進法　156
エラスムス　106

オーストラリア政府観光局（TA）　160,
　170,194

か

ガーデンシティ　190
改革開放政策　26
外務省　58,72,84,150
ガストアルバイター　48
観光基本法　152,176
観光庁（JTA）　136,162,194
観光立国基本法　162
韓流　196

技能実習　68
技能実習生　66
キャンパス・フランス　108
教育観光　110,160,162

クール・ジャパン　198
クール・ブリタニア　196
クック　34

グランド・ツアー　30
グリーンツーリズム　156,198
グリーンツーリズム法　156,198

経済産業省　146,158
研修生　66,68

国際化　130
国際交流基金（JF）　126,134
国土交通省　146,158,198
コロンブス　32,44
昆布　54
コンベンション法　158,192

さ

サンティアゴ・デ・コンポステーラ　32

シェンゲン条約　50
終身雇用制度　66
巡礼　148
シンガポール・アンリミテッド　188,
　190

政府開発援助（ODA）　116

た

第三セクター　154

中世大学　100

ツーリズム・アンリミテッド　190

帝国大学　122
テンミリオン計画　152

216

Index

A

AIEF (American International Education Foundation)　109
ASEAN　173,175,183,185,187,189
ASEANTA (ASEAN Tourism Association)　171

B

Basic Law on Tourism　177
Berlin University　37
Black Kigyou　83
Bologna Declaration　107
Bracero Program　49
bubble economy　67,155

C

Campus France　109
CLAIR (the Council of Local Authorities for International Relations)　201
Columbus　33,45
Convention Law　159,193
Cook　35
Cool Britannia　197
Cool Japan　199

E

ecotourism　199
Ecotourism Promotion Law　157
educational tourism　111,161
EJU (Examination for Japanese University Admission forInternational Students)　131
ekiben　151
EPA (Economic Partnership Agreement)　69
ERASMUS　107

ESCAP　183
ETC (European Travel Commission)　171,175,185
ETS　105

F

Friendship Japan Plan　137,163
Fulbright　105

G

garden city　191
Gastarbeiter　49
Ginou Jisshu　69
Ginou Jisshu-sei　67
Grand Tour　31
green tourism　157,199
Green Tourism Law　157,199

H

Haken　83
Haken Shain　67
Hakuba　165
hallyu　197

I

ILO　17
Imperial University　123
Inchon International Airport　193

J

Japanese inn (ryokan)　151
JASSO　131
JDS (Japanese Grant Aid for Human Resource Development Scholarship)　127
JF (The Japan Foundation)　127,135
JICA (Japan International Cooperation Agency)　127,131,135

217

東京オリンピック　150

な

ニセコ　164,200
日本語能力試験（JLPT）　126
日本政府観光局　172
日本留学試験（EJU）　130

農林水産省　146,156,198

は

白馬　164
派遣　82
派遣社員　66
バブル経済　66,154

ビジット・ジャパン・キャンペーン
　136,160,170,174,176,192,194
ビジット・ブリテン　170,176

ブラセロ・プログラム　48
ブラック企業　82
フルブライト　104
フレンドシップ・ジャパン・プラン
　136,162

ベルリン大学　36

ポイントシステム　18,52,72
ボローニア宣言　106
ボローニャ大学　30

ま

文部科学省　146

ら

リゾート法　152,154
留学生10万人受け入れ計画　116,126
留学生30万人受け入れ計画　116,130
旅館　150

わ

ワーキングホリデー　16,52,82
ワークライフバランス　78,80

欧文略語

ASEAN（東南アジア諸国連合）　172,
　174,182,184,186,188
ASEANTA（ASEAN観光協会）　170
CLAIR（自治体国際化協会）　200
EPA（Economic Partnership Agreement）
　68
ESCAP（アジア太平洋経済社会委員会）
　182
ETC（ヨーロッパ観光委員会）　170,174,
　184
ETS（教育試験サービス）　104
ILO（国際労働機関）　16
JASSO（日本学生支援機構）　130
JDSプログラム（人財育成奨学計画）
　126
JICA（国際協力機構）　126,130,134
JICE（日本国際協力センター）　126
JNTO（日本政府観光局）　170,194,202
KTO（韓国政府観光局）　170,172
MICE（会議，インセンティブ，コンベン
　ション，博覧会）　180,182,196
MOT（インド観光省）　180,182
NGO（非政府組織）　140

JICE (Japan International Cooperation Center) 127

JLPT (Japanese Language Proficiency Test) 127

JNTO (Japan National Tourism Organization) 171,173,195,203

JTA (Japan Tourism Agency)   163,195

K

Kankou Kihon Hou   153

kelp   55

Kenshu-sei   67,69

kokusaika   131

Korean movement   197

KTO (Korea Tourism Organization)   171, 173

M

MAFF (Ministry of Agriculture, Forestry and Fisheries)   149,157,199

medievaluniversities   101

METI (Ministry of Economy, Trade and Industry)   147,159

MEXT (Ministry of Education, Culture, Sports Science and Technology)   147

MICE (Meeting, Incentive, Convention, Exhibition)   181,183,197

MLIT (Ministry of Land, Infrastructure, Transport and Tourism)   147,159,199

MOFA (Ministry of Foreign Affairs)   59, 73,85,151

MOT (Ministry of Tourism)   181,183

N

NGOs (Non Governmental Organization) 141

Niseko   165,201

O

ODA (Official Development Assistance) 117

OECD   173

open-door policy   27

P

PATA (Pacific Asia Travel Association) 171,175,187

Pilgrimage   149

Plan to Accept 100,000 International Students 117

Plan to Accept 300,000 International Students 117,131

points system   19,53,73

R

Resort Law   153,155

Ryugakusei 10 Mannin Keikaku   127

Ryugakusei 30 Mannin Keikaku   131

S

Santiago de Compostela   33

Schengen agreement   51

sea turtle   27,53

Singapore Unlimited   191

SIT (Special Interest Tour/Tourism)   155, 197

station lunches   151

STB (Singapore Tourism Board)   171,175

Study Tourism   163

T

TA (Tourism Australia)   171,161,195

TAT (Tourism Authority of Thailand) 195

Ten million program   153

tenured employed system   67

thirdsector   155

Index   219

OECD（経済協力開発機構） 172
PATA（太平洋アジア観光協会） 170,
174,186
SIT（スペシャル・インタレスト・ツアー
／ツーリズム） 154,196
STB（シンガポール政府観光局） 170,
174
TA（ツーリズム・オーストラリア）
160,170,194
TAT（タイ観光庁） 194
TOEFL（外国語としての英語テスト）
104
TOEIC（国際コミュニケーション英語能力
テスト） 104
UNESCO（国際連合教育科学文化機関）
14,104,108,110
UNWTO（国際連合世界観光機関） 12,
146,182,184

TOEFL 105
TOEIC 105
Tokyo Olympic Games 151
Tourism Agency of Japan 137
Tourism Nation Promotion Basic Law 163
Tourism Unlimited 189, 191

UNESCO 17, 105, 109, 111
University of Bologna 31
UNWTO 13, 147, 183, 185
Urry 25

Visit Japan Campaign 137, 161, 171, 175, 177, 193, 195
VisitBritain 171, 177

working holiday 17, 53, 83
work-life balance 79, 81

著 者 紹 介

朝 水 宗 彦（あさみず　むねひこ）
　山口大学経済学部教授（観光地理学）。桜美林大学にて博士（学術）と修士（国際学），秋田大学にて学士（教育学）を修得。秋田県出身で，北海道（北海学園北見大学）と大分（立命館アジア太平洋大学）に勤務後，現在山口に居住。非常勤講師として，青山学院女子短期大学，東京農業大学，久留米大学，広島修道大学に勤務。

〈人的移動に関する主な著書〉
『地域・観光・文化』（徳久球雄・塚本珪一と共編，嵯峨野書院 2001），『オーストラリアの観光と食文化』（学文社 2003），*World Travel and Japanese Tourists*（Gakubunsha 2005），『開発と環境保護の国際比較』（嵯峨野書院 2007），*Global Mobility*（編著　Kumpul 2008），『アジア太平洋の人的移動』（編著　オフィス SAKUTA 2008），*Global Tourism*（Fred R. Schumann と共編，Kumpul 2010），『北アメリカ・オセアニアのエスニシティと文化』（くんぷる 2012），『持続可能な開発と日豪関係』（くんぷる 2014），『集客交流産業と国際教育旅行』（くんぷる 2016）。

About author

Munehiko Asamizu is a Professor of Tourism Geography in the Faculty of Economics, Yamaguchi University. He received Ph.D (Academics) and MA (International Studies) from J. F. Oberlin University, and BA (Education) from Akita University. He originates from Akita and lives in Yamaguchi; however, in the present, he has also lived in Hokkaido (Hokkai Gakuen University of Kitami) and Oita (Ritsumeikan Asia Pacific University). As a part time lecturer, he has also worked at Aoyama Gakuin Women's Junior College, Tokyo University of Agriculture, Kurume University, and Hiroshima Shudo University.

Many publications related to human mobility are available. Major publications are as follows: *Chiiki Kankou Bunka* (Sagano Shoin 2001 with Tamao TOKUHISA and Keiichi TSUKAMOTO eds.), *Australia no Kankou to Shokubunka* (Gakubunsha 2003), *World Travel and Japanese Tourists* (Gakubunsha 2005), *Kaihatsu to Kankyou Hogo no Kokusai Hikaku* (Sagano Shoin 2007), *Global Mobility* (Kumpul 2008 ed.), *Human Mobility in Asia Pacific* (Office SAKUTA 2008 ed.), *Global Tourism* (Kumpul 2010 with Dr. Fred R. Schumann eds.), Kita Amerika / Oceania no Ethnicity to Bunka (Kumpul 2012), Jizokukanou na Kaihatsu to Nichigou Kankei (Kumpul 2014), and *Shukyaku Kouryu Sangyou to Kokusai Kyouiku Ryokou* (Kumpul 2016).

観光客・留学生・地球規模の労働者
Tourists, International Students, and Global Workforce 〈検印省略〉

2019年9月20日　第1版第1刷発行

著　　者　　朝 水 宗 彦
　　　　　　Munehiko Asamizu

発 行 者　　前 田　　茂
　　　　　　Shigeru Maeda

発 行 所　　嵯 峨 野 書 院
　　　　　　Sagano Shoin

〒615-8045　京都市西京区牛ヶ瀬南ノ口町39　電話(075)391-7686　振替01020-8-40694

© Munehiko Asamizu, 2019　　　　　　　　　　創栄図書印刷・吉田三誠堂製本所

ISBN978-4-7823-0579-9

JCOPY〈出版者著作権管理機構 委託出版物〉
本書の無断複製は著作権法上での例外を除き禁じられ
ています。複製される場合は，そのつど事前に，出版
者著作権管理機構（電話 03-5244-5088，FAX 03-5244-
5089，e-mail: info@jcopy.or.jp）の許諾を得てください。

◎本書のコピー，スキャン，デジタル化等の無断複製
は著作権法上での例外を除き禁じられています。本書
を代行業者等の第三者に依頼してスキャンやデジタル
化することは，たとえ個人や家庭内の利用でも著作権
法違反です。